Printed in the United States of America

Library of Congress Card Number: 2001091325
ISBN: 1-57589-234-0

Massachusetts Continuing Legal Education, Inc.'s publications are offered as an aid to maintaining professional competence with the understanding that the publisher is not rendering legal, accounting or other professional advice.

The views and conclusions expressed in this book are those of the author and do not reflect a position of MCLE or of any of its committees.

To
The Memory of
ELR and EBH

Acknowledgments

Particular thanks are due, among the numerous supporters who helped on this project, to my wife Judith, who conceived it, to Ropes & Gray and my partners, who provided facilities and encouragement, and to my long-time secretary, Rose M. Senatore, who, while enduring transcription of countless drafts, made many valuable suggestions.

Table of Contents

Appendix III
Mandamus Petitions, Court Findings, Orders, Opinions, and Certain Exhibits 245

Re Chapter 1—War with Judge Wyzanski

Re Chapter 2—Undoing Sale of the Boston Marathon

Illustrations

Introduction

The five cases about to be described were chosen in part because they involve important questions of the day. Does the right of fair speech, to many a super-right, overcome rights of privacy, contract, and trademarks? Chapter 4. What can a litigant do when the judge sitting on his case does not obey the rules and there is no right of appeal? Chapters 1 and 5. Does a charitable corporation have a right to change its mission and pass on profits to another's business? Chapter 2.

Several of the cases arose out of newsworthy events of the recent past, including sale of the Boston Marathon and the Commonwealth's efforts to ban showings of Frederick Wiseman's *Titicut Follies* film of "various forms of madness" displayed by nude inmates of the Massachusetts maximum security prison and hospital, MCI Bridgewater. The middle case, *Vindication of Rufus the Ram*, is a throwback to 19th century cases about animals on the loose. It could have been a walkover for the plaintiff under a repealed 1825 statute requiring rams to be fenced during the second half of the year.

The cases other than *Rufus* all generated judicial opinions—of state and federal trial courts, the Supreme Judicial Court of the Commonwealth, the Court of Appeals for the First Circuit, and the Supreme Court of the United States. These provide disinterested commentary to leaven some inevitable author bias.

This book was written for the general public, not just for lawyers. The workings of the judicial system can seem mysterious, arcane, and sometimes irrational. American law—a distillation of common sense, morality, and social policy, tested and retested, stated and restated in countless continuing crucibles—is surely the best in the world. But its application by ordinary mortals, however highly qualified, is subject to all the flaws of the human condition. These accounts of lower court action and inaction, and the grappling of appellate courts with the resulting issues, illustrate both propositions. And they may also give the reader a better understanding of what may unfold when he or she enters the halls of justice as a litigant, attorney, witness, or juror.

Chapter 1

War with Judge Wyzanski

In the fall of 1957 I left the Boston law firm of Ropes & Gray, temporarily as it turned out, to become an Assistant U.S. Attorney for the District of Massachusetts. I served first under U.S. Attorney Anthony Julian and later under his successor, Elliot L. Richardson. Assistant U.S. attorneys represent the United States in virtually all District of Massachusetts civil and criminal cases. The U.S. Attorney's office was then located in the Federal Building at Boston's Post Office Square, which also housed the federal judiciary and its courtrooms. Federal cases were tried before one of the judges of the U.S. District Court for the District of Massachusetts. At that time the sitting judges were George C. Sweeney (Chief Judge), Bailey Aldrich, Francis J. W. Ford, William T. McCarthy, and Charles E. Wyzanski, Jr.

As each case was filed, it was assigned by lot to one of the five judges. A box filled with cards each bearing a single initial—that of one of the five judges—was in the custody of clerk Helen Tweedy. Upon the filing of an indictment or civil complaint, Miss Tweedy would draw a fateful card from the box. Her draw was often the most significant action taken in the case. Certainly this was true when the card had a *W* on it. At this point, the facts of the case became secondary.

Soon after my arrival in the U.S. Attorney's office, I was assigned a matter involving Standard Coil Products, Inc., a manufacturer of electronic weather-reporting instruments called radiosondes, which were supplied to the U.S. Army for use in the Korean War. Radiosondes were dropped from airplanes to report back weather conditions while floating down to earth by parachute. A number had failed to function properly. There was evidence that the manufacturer had falsified quality control tests. Standard Coil and several employees were indicted by a federal grand jury. When the indictment was filed with the district court, Miss Tweedy drew a *W.* Her drawing led ultimately to a battle between Judge Wyzanski and me, marking the low and one of the highs of my legal career.

Charles Wyzanski presided over courtroom number six. He was short in stature, but with piercing eyes, a brilliant mind, and a commanding voice, he dominated his courtroom. He had starred academically at Harvard College and Harvard Law School. After New Deal service as Solicitor of Labor for Labor Secretary Frances Perkins and brief stints with Ropes & Gray, Wyzanski became a judge of the U.S. District Court for the District of Massachusetts in 1942, appointed at age 35 by President Franklin D. Roosevelt.

Judge Wyzanski was the author of many judicial decisions and articles on the judging process. He was an overseer of Harvard University and a recipient of numerous honorary degrees. On good behavior, he could be, in his courtroom, fair, perceptive and incisive; outside his courtroom, witty and charming. When he died in 1986, he received many accolades. A *Boston Globe* columnist eulogized him as "an authentic giant," a "gravel-voiced legend" known "as Ivan the Terrible" only to "courtroom imposters."[1]

As his judicial career advanced, another side of Judge Wyzanski on display in his courtroom was that of supreme egotist and arrogant bully. Any case he had taken a slant against was in trouble. He was somewhat conscious of these characteristics. In his report for the 50th anniversary of his Harvard class, he wrote that he was aware that, "I often failed to heed the [ ] admonition that the worst faults of a judge are to be conceited and arbitrary. I forgot the saying attributed to Thucydides that 'Of all manifestations of power, restraint impresses men most!'" That he was mentally unstable,[2] he did not view as a handicap. His report continued: "Had I not at times been depressed, I never could have been, in Wordsworth's phrase, 'a man pleased with his own passions and volitions, and who rejoices more than other men in the spirit of life that is in him.'"

Wyzanski and the Prosecution

Judge Wyzanski's docket was short. *W* civil actions were to be settled, if humanly possible. Unless you were a favorite, a trial before Judge Wyzanski would be an unpleasant experience and, unless the issue had a liberal aspect to it, the result would be unpredictable.

Judge Wyzanski was particularly hostile to prosecutors. William Koen, a dedicated career assistant U.S. attorney and our leader on the criminal side, was persona non grata in courtroom number six. Prosecutors there faced the fact that they would have no appeal to an appellate court from adverse rulings. Defense counsel in the case would have a right of appeal, but the double jeopardy provision of the U.S. Constitution has been construed to preclude appeal by the government in criminal cases for errors once trial has begun. Thus a judge in a federal criminal trial need not fear reversal because of rulings or behavior prejudicing only the prosecution. The public is generally unaware that there is no effective deterrent to judicial error or misconduct against the prosecution. In any criminal case, this can be important. In my *Standard Coil* case, it would be decisive.

Judge Wyzanski's behavior in *Standard Coil*, however, was only the most egregious of his aberrations in federal criminal cases during my era. Shortly after I came into the U.S. Attorney's office, Vera Green and her husband Albert had been indicted for evasion of federal income taxes in six figures over a period of four years.[3] The Greens served as assistant treasurer and president, respectively, of Botwinik Brothers, a corporation with a Worcester retail store. They had enriched themselves with embezzled corporate funds and had not reported the embezzled amounts as income on their personal federal income tax returns. Also, by misdescribing embezzled amounts as business expenses on the corporate returns, they had reduced corporate taxable income.[4] The indictment charged the Greens with evading payment of their personal taxes and causing evasion by Botwinik of its corporate taxes.

Vera Green was tried first, separately from her husband. She claimed that the money she had stolen through her embezzlement was not "income" within the meaning of the Internal Revenue Code,[5] hence it did not have to be reported on her personal return. As for the corporate taxes, Green contended that her intent to steal from the corporation was inconsistent with the intent the government had to prove—intent to cause evasion of corporate taxes.[6] The defense waived trial by jury, doubtless unwilling to present such desperate arguments to a jury. Judge Wyzanski accepted both defenses and acquitted Green. The U.S. Attorney's office was stunned. The Greens escaped; honest taxpayers were mocked.

A year later, Judge Wyzanski had a similar issue before him. After paying bribe money, corporate building contractor Thomas Worcester then deducted the amount as an ordinary and necessary corporate expense. The judge made a ruling exactly opposite to the one he had made in *Green*. In his charge to the jury of the *Worcester* case, Judge Wyzanski instructed that by "well-established" rule there could be no allowance of a deduction "where a taxpayer has violated a federal or a state statute."[7] Worcester had violated Massachusetts criminal law by paying bribes, a state felony, and federal criminal law by deducting the bribe amounts under spurious labels as expenses on his federal return. He was convicted of evasion of the corporate taxes.

The embezzlement by the Greens had also been a state felony, a violation of a Massachusetts criminal statute,[8] and Vera Green had admitted the violation. If Judge Wyzanski had followed himself the "well-established" rule he charged the jury to follow in the *Worcester* case, Vera Green too would have had to have been convicted.

The acquittal of Vera Green immediately preceded my *Standard Coil* case in courtroom number six. These cases would be followed in the next few years by criminal cases involving drugs and selective service violations fueled by the Vietnam War. Judge Wyzanski developed a theory that the composition of federal grand juries in Massachusetts was flawed, and their indictments therefore defective. Raymond Andrews was indicted in 1972 for failure to report for induction into the armed services. The case was assigned to Judge Wyzanski. On a certain Friday, defense counsel moved to dismiss the indictment, alleging that paupers had been improperly excluded from the grand jury. On the following Monday, without hearing or notice to the prosecution, Judge Wyzanski allowed the motion ex parte and dismissed the case because the grand jury assertedly was unconstitutionally composed. He had proceeded, he said in his opinion, "in the manner familiar to most appellate courts and many trial courts."[9]

The Court of Appeals for the First Circuit took the government's appeal from dismissal of the indictment[10] on an expedited basis. It condemned the district court's procedure in not giving notice or a hearing to the government, ruled that Judge Wyzanski had misinterpreted and misapplied Massachusetts law, sustained as constitutional the grand jury selection process, and reinstated the indictment. Regarding the judge's procedure—dismissing the indictment on a novel ground and without even giving the government a chance to argue the indictment's validity—the court of appeals said: "The court's statement that it proceeded in a 'manner familiar to most appellate courts' does not comport with any method with which we are familiar, or would wish to be familiar. A party's day in court should not have to begin in the court of appeals. Reversed."[11]

On the drug front, as retaliation for what he regarded as undue and hypocritical attention by the U.S. Attorney's office to the prosecution of drug offenses, Judge Wyzanski in 1973 ordered all assistant U.S. attorneys to file sworn statements about whether they had smoked marijuana.[12] Judge Wyzanski had no right or jurisdiction to make such an order. His power to enforce it rested on his ability to retaliate against the government in criminal cases where the government could not appeal and in civil cases where his actions were discretionary.

Though a continuing hero to his favorites and those who did not frequent his courtroom, Judge Wyzanski's conduct did not go unnoticed by others. On April 3, 1973, the Massachusetts House of Representatives voted 111 to 65 in favor of a resolution that Judge Wyzanski step down from the bench.[13] He did not oblige. The federal court, however, directed that no further criminal cases be drawn to him. (By this time, Judge Wyzanski was a senior judge and regular sitting judges of the circuit had the power to control case assignments to him.) *Boston Herald* cartoonist Jim Dobbins celebrated Judge Wyzanski's disqualification as long overdue.

ORDER DISQUALIFYING
JUDGE WYZANSKI—ONE VIEW

James Dobbins cartoon, reprinted with permission of the *Boston Herald.*

Abortion of the Standard Coil *Trial*

United States v. Standard Coil, Inc. et al came to trial before Judge Wyzanski in September 1960. James D. St. Clair of the Boston law firm Hale and Dorr represented Standard Coil. St. Clair was prominent locally and had assisted Joseph Welch, also of Hale and Dorr, representing the U.S. Army in hearings conducted by Senator Joseph McCarthy. He would later represent President Nixon in the end stages of Watergate. St. Clair was a great favorite of Judge Wyzanski. Awarding St. Clair attorney fees in an antitrust case won in 1954 against National Cranberry Association (later Ocean Spray), Judge Wyzanski had showered him with praise; he was "a model [of trial counsel] not likely to be surpassed."[14]

Just before the impaneling of the *Standard Coil* jury, St. Clair offered to have the corporation plead nolo contendere in exchange for leniency on sentencing. Inadvisedly, as it turned out, the government refused to agree to such a plea.

So that the jury could appreciate the significance of steps taken to falsify the quality control tests of the radiosondes, I planned testimony spelling out how the radiosondes worked. In a trial brief and in my opening statement, I outlined the prosecution's plan to call a government quality control officer, Anthony Paliotto, and other witnesses to explain the product and production process. The government would then present the testimony of approximately a dozen witnesses to prove the fraud by acts of concealment and falsification.

Soon after I began direct examination of Paliotto on the characteristics of radiosondes, Judge Wyzanski took over the examination, asking broad-ranging questions, some in areas for which Paliotto was not prepared and on topics with which he was not familiar. Wyzanski quickly took a slant against the witness. His hostility increased as he continued his questioning, and this so unnerved Paliotto that his testimony became incomplete and contradictory.

Judges of course have power to question a witness themselves. Until the end of the case, however, they do not know all the facts and properly leave the questioning of witnesses largely to counsel, whose job it is to develop the facts through examination of the witnesses who do know them. Questioning by the judge has great impact, both on the jury and on the witness, and is a power to be used sparingly.

Not only did Judge Wyzanski cross-examine the witness at length, but as he elicited testimony that he disapproved, he would mimic the accent of the witness and disparage his choice of words and phraseology. As Paliotto became more and more distressed, the Judge added to his cross-examination periodic warnings of his powers to hold a witness in contempt and bring about a perjury prosecution. Paliotto was terrorized and could hardly function.

As the testimony of this first government witness drew to a close, Judge Wyzanski called me to the bench and said that I should nol-pros the case—that I should discontinue the prosecution. I refused, protesting that Paliotto was an early witness, that any deficiencies in his testimony were not fatal to the case, and that his testimony did not bear on the fraud at all. The judge ordered me to produce Elliot L. Richardson, *the* U.S. Attorney.

I was lucky in my superior. Richardson and I had been associates together for a brief period at Ropes & Gray before he had gone to Washington and I to the Boston U.S. Attorney's office. We had been reunited when Richardson had succeeded Anthony Julian as U.S. Attorney for the District of Massachusetts. Richardson was a Harvard graduate and had been president of the *Harvard Law Review*. He would shortly be elected lieutenant governor and thereafter attorney general of the Commonwealth. He would go on to hold no fewer than ten presidential appointments, including secretary of the department of health, education and welfare, secretary of defense, attorney general of the United States (resigning when directed by the President to fire special prosecutor Archibald Cox), secretary of commerce, and ambassador both to the Court of St. James and to the Law of the Sea Conference.

Richardson joined the bench conference. He was told that the case should be dismissed. He replied that it would not be dismissed, it would be proved. By so doing, he put in jeopardy every fifth case in his office—all the *W* cases.

After another witness who identified some charts and further described the workings of radiosondes, I called a government inspector of the radiosondes, Rosenholm, whose testimony would begin the government's evidence on the fraud.

During his testimony, I refused still more demands by the judge that I dismiss the case. Toward the end of the day, I intended to question the witness on what had happened at a conference attended by Standard Coil officials and, preliminarily, had asked Rosenholm for the date of the conference. Rosenholm at first did not remember. On being pressed, he testified he believed it was in February 1958 but was not sure. At about that time, the court recessed for the day.

During the evening, I met with the witness and went over the direct examination planned for the next day. One item was correction of the date of the conference, which had actually taken place in September 1957, to be followed by what was said at the conference. During the preparation, Rosenholm expressed surprise that he had testified to the later date. He had been rattled, like the rest of us, during his testimony, one consequence of the climate of hostility against the government in the courtroom.

At the resumption of Rosenholm's testimony the next day, Judge Wyzanski was grim and everyone in the courtroom was on edge. His Honor had not been pleased by the prosecution's refusals to dismiss. One of my first questions concerned the date of the conference and the witness testified that he had been mistaken the day before, the conference had been held in September 1957. I was about to get into what had taken place at the conference when Judge Wyzanski asked Rosenholm if he had talked with Mr. Caner during the period of his testimony in the case. When the witness said yes, Judge Wyzanski declared that the conduct of counsel was not "correct." On cross-

examination, the witness testified he had changed the date of the conference as a result of a meeting with me during the overnight recess.

Judge Wyzanski flew into a rage, and sent the jury out of the courtroom. Turning to me, he said, "Mr. Caner, as a matter of personal privilege, do you want to make any statement"? From a prosecutor one moment, I had been converted into a defendant the next—apparently charged with an offense akin to subornation—inducement—of perjury. It was hardly a role for which I was prepared. Reviewing a witness's proposed testimony in advance was standard procedure, particularly necessary in this case where the witness would probably soon be assailed by the judge. I had never heard of an exception for testimony continued from day to day. But the judge about to come down on me was a world-famous jurist.

Uncertain of my ground, as my statement of personal privilege I protested that I knew of no rule that I could not talk to my witness during the course of examination; that I could not understand why this conduct should be considered incorrect.

"You will very soon learn," I was told. "You know that . . . tampering with a witness is one of the most dangerous things in connection with a case, and particularly in a criminal case, that a person should be left entirely alone during the course of his testimony. You must know that elementary fact and elementary rule."

As this daunting scenario unfolded, with the berobed judge now standing, drawn up to his full five-foot height and his eyes blazing upon me, an offbeat image came into my mind. A contemporary cartoon strip Fearless Fosdick[15] by Al Capp, of Li'l Abner fame, featured an Evil-eyed Fleegle who could atomize his victims with a fearsome glance. I was about to be zapped by Evil-eyed Fleegle.

Trying to salvage the case, I pointed out that correction of the conference date could not have prejudiced the defendants—it was only a prelude to testimony not yet presented as to what happened at the conference. The evidence had not yet closed and indeed had barely begun on the fraud issue. "There are many witnesses to be heard from," I remonstrated, "many more besides this witness. We have not heard the testimony of any of the test operators. We have only heard three witnesses in a case involving many witnesses."

Counsel for the defendants moved for judgments of acquittal. Judge Wyzanski recalled the jury. Because the prosecution had committed "a violation of civil liberties," he asserted, and because he considered the government's witnesses to be unworthy of belief, he was directing the jury to return verdicts of acquittal. Judge Wyzanski turned to the defendants, "You have been acquitted by direction of the Court and by the Court. Your bail is terminated. You are free." He marched out of the courtroom.

Everyone was stunned. The defendants and their counsel could not believe their good fortune. The government side—

prosecutors, FBI investigators, U.S. Army representatives—was crushed. The dozen witnesses who were scheduled to testify about the defendants' fraud, sequestered in the witness room and waiting to testify, were bewildered. How could the case end before they had been heard from?

United States v. Wyzanski, J.

When we came out of shock, Richardson and I cast about for a remedy. We had no right of appeal. We were faced with the judge's pronouncement that the defendants had been "acquitted." The Fifth Amendment to the U.S. Constitution provides that no person shall "for the same offense . . . be twice put in jeopardy of life and limb." The court's abortion of the case before it had fairly gotten under way was without precedent. Rule 29 of the Federal Rules of Criminal Procedure stated explicitly that the power of a judge to enter an acquittal was to be invoked after the evidence had "closed," at which time the government's evidence would be known and a judgment could be made as to whether the evidence was sufficient to justify a conviction. Judge Wyzanski was a member of a judicial committee on the Rules of Criminal Procedure, had presided over hundreds of criminal trials, and knew the law on this point as well as anyone. Rule 29 provides: "The court on motion of a defendant or of its own motion shall order the entry of judgment of acquittal of one or more offenses charged in the indictment or information *after the evidence on either side is closed* if the evidence is insufficient to sustain a conviction of such offense or offenses." (emphasis mine)

In the *Standard Coil* case, the evidence had not closed; indeed, evidence on the fraud aspects of the case had just commenced. There was no basis upon which a judgment could be made that the evidence would be "insufficient to sustain a conviction."

As for the asserted misconduct of counsel, legal research and consultation with the bar convinced us that the "elementary rule" that "a person should be left entirely alone during the course of his testimony" was a rule only to Judge Wyzanski. The implication of subornation of perjury—"tampering with a witness"—was equally baseless. We considered seeking an interpretation on the ethics of my conduct from the Boston Bar Association, but the lawyers we consulted were not anxious to become involved in a trial of strength with Judge Wyzanski. They had or might have cases before Judge Wyzanski and could not afford to cross him. No one wanted to have his head on the block in courtroom number six.

Judge Wyzanski's action had gone beyond legal error. He had acted beyond his jurisdiction; he had asserted a power to abort the government's criminal prosecution that by law he did not have. He had acted illegally—directly contrary to prescribed criminal rules. It was as if he had acquitted an accused purely on the basis that he considered the defendant an honest man. Yet the government had no appeal to reinstate the indictment. In this government, supposedly "of laws, and not of men," was there no remedy?

It happens from time to time in criminal trials that a case has to be terminated short of a verdict. There may be a "hung" jury that cannot agree on a verdict, or one that has been prejudiced by outside publicity. Misconduct during trial by a lawyer or party may have irretrievably prejudiced the other side. In such cases, the court has the power to declare a mistrial. Generally speaking, unless the cause of a mistrial in a criminal case is serious misconduct by the prosecution that prejudices the defense, the double-jeopardy provision of the Constitution does not prevent a new trial from being called after a mistrial.

Richardson and I conceived that Judge Wyzanski's action should be regarded in law as a nullity, not an acquittal at all, since the judge had no power to acquit at that stage of the proceedings. We theorized that, notwithstanding his announcement of an acquittal, Judge Wyzanski's order ending the trial should be judged a declaration of a mistrial. There was authority in both civil and criminal cases that the mislabeling of a court action is not controlling, and that the substance of the action or document overrides an erroneous label.

Appellate courts have power to issue extraordinary writs, and, in rare cases, a higher court will issue a writ of mandamus to a lower court judge mandating that the judge perform some legal duty. A typical instance is one in which a judge without justification has failed or refused to render a decision in a case.[16] The Court of Appeals for the First Circuit, presided over by

Chief Judge Peter Woodbury, and Circuit Judges John Hartigan and Bailey Aldrich (who had recently been elevated to the circuit court), would have jurisdiction of a petition for mandamus against Judge Wyzanski, a subordinate judge in their circuit.

Richardson and I decided on the course of a circuit court mandamus petition arguing that the "acquittal" was in effect a declaration of a mistrial, and seeking an order that the case be retried. First, we had to exhaust any remedy theoretically available in the district court. At the risk of being struck by lightning a second time, I filed with Judge Wyzanski a motion to vacate "judgment of acquittal" and for reassignment of the case for trial (reproduced in Appendix III, 1A). The motion came back within the hour, "Denied."

I ordered a transcript of the trial and went to work searching for precedent to support our theory that the acquittal should be viewed as a mistrial. I met with the clerk of the court of appeals, Roger Stinchfield, to solicit his thoughts about mandamus procedure. There were few guides for the filing of a petition for a writ of mandamus against a sitting federal judge. At that time, there was no rule governing such a petition—no time period within which the petition might have to be filed, no prescription of whether it might be referred preliminarily to a master to make findings of fact, whether the judge as the defendant would get special treatment, or whether there would ultimately be a hearing on the petition. Stinchfield got to the heart of the matter when he asked me whether I was sure I had behaved properly myself—whether I had considered how I might fare were I to lose in the court of appeals, in which case that court's condemnation would be added to that of Judge Wyzanski. I would have to take my chances, I replied.

Before a U.S. attorney of one of the federal districts can commence action in a court of appeals, authorization must be obtained from the Department of Justice. This central control enables the Justice Department to assure a uniform approach in federal cases throughout the country and to limit appellate and other court of appeals proceedings to appropriate situations.

Justice Department officials advised Richardson and me that for the radical action of suing one of the federal judges of our district, we would have to get permission from Solicitor General J. Lee Rankin in person. We journeyed to Washington and met with the solicitor general in his cavernous office. Mr. Rankin was aware of Judge Wyzanski's treatment of the government in Massachusetts, but his focus was on the future. He had enough problems with Judge Wyzanski, he said, without suing him. He refused permission. Richardson and I returned to Boston disconsolate. Our only hope had been snuffed out.

On arrival back in Boston, however, Sally Morrissey, Richardson's secretary, said that the solicitor general had telephoned and we were to call him back. Rankin told us that when he had informed his staff of his decision, they had protested and insisted that the Massachusetts office should be permitted to defend itself. He had reconsidered, he said, and we could go ahead!

I threw myself into preparing a petition for issuance of a writ of mandamus against Judge Wyzanski and a memorandum of law arguing our theory that the acquittal was in reality a declaration of a mistrial, so there could be a retrial. The petition was filed soon thereafter (see Appendix III, 1B). Its heart was the allegation:

> At the time the "Judgment of Acquittal" was entered, the government's case had not closed, nor had its evidence been concluded on any aspect of the case. As the Court had been advised, other witnesses were to testify to the date of the Rosenholm-Teichman conversation . . . , to the explanatory material . . . , and, particularly, to the fraud . . . . When the "Judgment of Acquittal" was entered, the government had under subpoena, and planned to call in its direct case fourteen additional witnesses, including the test operators and the co-conspirators (in addition to Rosenholm) named in the Indictment. It could not therefore have been determined, at the time the government's presentation was cut off, whether the government's evidence would or would not be sufficient to sustain a conviction of the offenses charged.[17]

The *Standard Coil* record, filed with the petition, contained all the testimony, bench conference colloquy, and pronouncements in the case. The Court of Appeals issued an order that Judge Wyzanski "show cause," by answer, "why a writ of mandamus should not issue."[18] The defendants in the criminal case intervened, and St. Clair filed an answer for Judge Wyzanski.

Court of Appeals Rulings on Prosecutor, Wyzanski, and Double Jeopardy

The court of appeals spent three months digesting the record of the trial and then ruled that "mandamus will issue directing that the judgment of acquittal . . . be vacated and ordering that the . . . case be reassigned . . . for trial before another judge." Chief Judge Woodbury rendered the opinion of the court, and Judge Aldrich gave a concurring opinion on the double jeopardy issue.[19] From the government standpoint, the decision had only one shortcoming: the court captioned the case "*In re United States*" and refrained from identifying the dramatis personae anywhere in its opinion. A reader had to go outside the opinion to learn that the judge involved was Wyzanski.

The court of appeals ruled that the person guilty of misconduct was the judge and not the assistant U.S. attorney. It adopted the Richardson-Caner theory that the acquittal was a nullity because the judge had no power to acquit at that early stage in the trial, when the government had only just begun its case.

The Woodbury opinion began with a description of the judge's questioning of the first government witness:

> An examination of the record shows that while this witness was on direct examination he was asked fully as many questions by the judge as by the Assistant United States Attorney. Moreover, the judge on several occasions, both during direct and cross-examination, ridiculed the witness with respect to his use of words, repeatedly corrected his grammar, and many times admonished him to remember that he should be careful in his statements since he was testifying in a criminal case.

Conceding that a judge can call on a witness to explain words he has used, the court continued:

> It is hardly necessary, however, to do so with ridicule or caustic criticism, or repeatedly to check a witness's use of words in reasonably common use by reference to the Oxford English Dictionary, or to require strict adherence to the rules of grammar. The bench is not an appropriate rostrum from which to teach the niceties of English grammar and usage.

(The written record would not, of course, reveal the judge's even more invidious tactic of further denigrating the witness by mimicking his accent.)

It was not the judge's "function or duty," the court said, "to take the conduct of a case away from counsel. . . . [W]hen the trial judge assumes the role of counsel the adversary system breaks down into confusion worse confounded as the record in this case clearly shows. This record provides a prime example of the consequences of overzealous participation in the examination of witnesses by the trial judge."

The court concluded that deficiencies in the witnesses were caused in large part by the judge himself. It acknowledged that the testimony of two witnesses "was certainly confused and conflicting" but declared:

> [I]t is clear from the record before us that the confusion and conflicts in these witnesses' testimony was due in no minor part to the trial judge's persistent, sharp and sometimes caustic cross-examination throughout their direct examination . . . [T]he judge's . . . questioning and caustic remarks first made the witnesses wary and overcautious and then confused them into inconsistencies, and in addition disrupted the orderly presentation of the Government's case according to the plan outlined to the jury by the Assistant United States Attorney by taking its witnesses into matters they were not offered to cover in their testimony. Running cross-examination from the bench, particularly during a witness's direct examination, is an innovation in trial practice which definitely does not have the approval of this court.

Judge Wyzanski's own writings showed that he knew very well he was misconducting the trial. In a dissertation entitled "The Essential Qualities of a Judge," authored just a few years earlier, Judge Wyzanski had warned: "[T]he judge should hesitate to fill [a] gap [in evidence] by becoming himself a participant in the interrogation and should not indicate his view of the evidence. For the criminal trial is as much a ceremony as an investigation. Dignity and forbearance are almost the chief desiderata."[20] Four months after Judge Wyzanski had battered the government's witnesses with hostile interrogation in *Standard Coil*, he delivered an erudite dissertation about the importance of judicial forbearance. In a digression in a *Worcester* case probation proceeding, Judge Wyzanski praised the British tradition that the judge during a trial should be aloof, neutral, and silent, saying:

> In adversary proceedings, and especially in a criminal trial, much is to be said for a judge maintaining an attitude of aloofness. Glanville Williams, *The Proof of Guilt*, (2nd ed., 1953) p. 4. Not less than others, I deserve to be reminded of "the classic advice to a . . . judge . . . that he should take a sup of holy water in his mouth at the beginning of a case, and not swallow it until the evidence on both sides has been heard." Ibid, p. 26. In their celebrated *History of English Law* (2nd ed.), vol. II, p. 671, Pollock and Maitland taught us that from its earliest days our law has looked upon the judge as, in many aspects, (but not all, see Hughes, C.J.'s description

> of the trial judge as the "governor of the trial," *Quercia v. U.S.*, 289 U.S. 466, 469) a neutral like an umpire in a cricket match who asks only "How's that?". Lord Hewart phrased the judge's role more owlishly: "the business of a judge is to hold his tongue until the last possible moment, and to try to be as wise as he is paid to look." G. Williams, *op. cit.*, p. 26.[21]

The court of appeals addressed the Wyzanski "elementary rule" that "a person should be left entirely alone during the course of his testimony." There was no such rule, the court declared:

> We are not aware of any rule of law, "elementary" or otherwise, or any canon of professional conduct forbidding the practice. Of course, as a matter of trial tactics, counsel ordinarily avoid talking with a witness during a recess called while the witness is on the stand so as not to provide opposing counsel with a point to argue to the jury. But tactics are one thing and rules of law and canons of ethics are quite another. There is nothing wrong that we know of in talking with a witness during intervals in his examination in court. Indeed in *Frazer v. United States*, 9 Cir., 1956, 233 F.2d 1, 2, counsel for the Government was commended for privately reminding a witness of a false statement in her testimony thereby causing her to

> change her testimony to conform to the truth.

In his concurring opinion, Judge Aldrich commented on counsel's ignorance of the court's "elementary rule": "An understandable ignorance, since twice before during the trial the court had expressly invited a government witness to confer with counsel during recess about his testimony, and in one instance to 'rehearse it with counsel.'" Even if there had been a rule against counsel's talking with his witness, Judge Aldrich went on, its violation had in no way prejudiced the defense so that the acquittal was a gross overreaction: "The date was a preliminary matter. Nothing about the conference had been admitted in evidence. The present effect of this new testimony upon the trial was nil. Its future effect was entirely in the control of the court . . . . Prejudice to the defendants was entirely nonexistent."

The court found that "[t]he Assistant United States Attorney was not guilty of any misconduct or impropriety." With this finding, the court confronted the question of what could be done about Judge Wyzanski's precipitous acquittal, in view of the fact that "the United States obviously cannot appeal nor may it resort to mandamus as a substitute for appeal." The court answered that the writ was available "to correct judicial action which is not mere error but usurpation of power." The judge had asserted a power that he did not have. The acquittal power was not triggered, the court of appeals said, by anything that had occurred in the case, "for the judge abruptly terminated the Government's case long before the Government had an opportunity to show whether or not it had a case; and moreover, he did so in ignorance of either the exact nature or the cogency of the specific evidence of guilt which Government's counsel said he had available and was ready to present." It follows, the court ruled, "from our conclusion that the trial judge had no power, that is to say no jurisdiction, to enter judgment of acquittal . . . that the judgment is void—a nullity—and hence affords no basis for the defense of double jeopardy."

In his concurring opinion, Judge Aldrich elaborated:

> I think there must be some limit to naked, arbitrary power. . . . [T]here is the interest of the public in the prosecution and conviction of criminals. I am unwilling to think that such a totally arbitrary act in the course of trial with no semblance of justification behind it should deprive the government of its day in court. This may be an exceptional ruling, but this is an exceptional case.

The court of appeals concluded with a welcome direction that the retrial should be before a different trial judge:

> The United States in its application for mandamus has not specifically asked us to order that the case be reassigned for trial before another judge. Nevertheless we shall do so, for we do not see how a judge who has unnecessarily taken it upon himself to cross-examine witnesses not only extensively but also sharply can either lis-

> ten to their testimony reflectively or weigh their testimony dispassionately.

Supreme Court Double Jeopardy Decision

The ruling that the *Standard Coil* defendants should be retried was short-lived. As intervenors in the mandamus case, the defendants petitioned for certiorari—a procedure in which a party seeks review by the United States Supreme Court. The Supreme Court took the case, rejected the mistrial theory, and held that Judge Wyzanski's entry of a judgment of acquittal put the case beyond redemption: "The Court of Appeals thought, not without reason, that the acquittal was based upon an egregiously erroneous foundation. Nevertheless, '[t]he verdict of acquittal was final, and could not be reviewed . . . without putting [the petitioners] twice in jeopardy, and thereby violating the constitution.' *United States v. Ball*, 163 U.S. 662, 671 . . . ."[22]

Justice Clark dissented:

> It is fundamental in our criminal jurisprudence that the public has a right to have a person who stands legally indicted by a grand jury publicly tried on the charge. No judge has the power before hearing the testimony proffered by the Government or at least canvassing the same to enter a judgment of acquittal and thus frustrate the Government in the performance of its duty to prosecute those who violate its law.[23]

Justice Clark was, however, but one voice. The damage was done; the crime would go unpunished. The case was over, but not at least a career.

Chapter 2

Undoing Sale of the Boston Marathon

Will McDonough Sounds the Alarm

The *Boston Globe* on February 26, 1982, carried a stunning announcement from premier sports reporter Will McDonough:

> The Boston Marathon is for sale. It is being sold secretly and curiously by a Boston lawyer named Marshall Medoff, who signed on as an agent for the Boston Athletic Association (BAA) the same way, secretly and curiously.
>
> The *Globe* has been told that the Boston Marathon, one of the great running events in the world—and a happening that has been wrapped in a blanket of pure amateurism for 86 years—is being hustled . . . .
>
> [BAA president] Cloney says that he, on behalf of the BAA board, made a deal with Medoff last year, to have Medoff raise

> money for this year's Marathon and beyond. Reportedly, [Medoff] will get to keep everything he raises beyond a certain figure. In other words, if he raised $500,000 and the BAA told him he could keep anything over $200,000, then Medoff could walk away with $300,000 from an event that has never paid anyone . . . .[24]

WILL McDONOUGH

Photo courtesy of the subject.

I read the McDonough article incredulously. How could someone *sell* a marathon? How could one sell the Harvard-Yale football game, the Head of the Charles regatta, hockey's Stanley Cup, or the World Series? How could the BAA permit such a thing—authorize the type of "deal" described? Could profits from a Notre Dame football game or receipts from patents owned by MIT be legally assigned to a private business? As it turned out, the questions I was asking myself as a sporting buff, I would soon be answering as a lawyer.

To the Rescue

Later press accounts reported that the Boston Marathon race had been commercialized and in effect taken over by Medoff. Surely, this was wrong, but it was not my problem. By chance, it became my problem a few months later. In early August 1982, my partner, Edward B. Hanify, invited me to join him in a meeting with attorney William Tyler, a BAA governor, and his partner, Joseph Serafini, both of the Boston law firm Rackemann, Sawyer & Brewster.

Hanify was head of the Ropes & Gray trial department, regarded in our circle, and by many outside it, as the best trial lawyer in Boston. He had the Irish gift of extemporaneous speech, honed by concentration in Greek, Latin, Oratory, and Rhetoric at the College of the Holy Cross. Tyler and Serafini gave Hanify and me a mission—restore the Boston Marathon to the BAA.

As it turned out, recovery of the Boston Marathon would be the first of many projects over six years in which I would represent the BAA. Ed Hanify stayed largely in the background, leaving tactics and execution to me and my able assistant Thomas Hannigan, but participating in strategic decisions and being always on hand to offer wise advice.

Undoing the sale of the marathon would call for a suit in the Suffolk County Superior Court to invalidate the agreement of sale between the BAA and Medoff's company, International

Marathons, Inc. (IMI). Alongside the superior court case would be hearings within the Massachusetts Attorney General's office on the theory of the director of the Division of Public Charities that the agreement violated the then Massachusetts limitation of 15 percent on fees payable to professional charitable solicitors. Eventually, there would be a superior court summary judgment on the validity of the agreement under corporate law and an appeal to the Supreme Judicial Court. A trial by jury would be held to determine the value to the BAA of IMI action in raising money from sponsors for the 1982 race. And finally, there would be a nonjury trial on the BAA's claim that Medoff was liable to the BAA for appropriating sponsorship revenues personally and rendering IMI insolvent. In the course of these proceedings, I became educated in the interesting history of the Boston Athletic Association.

The Boston Athletic Association and Marathon History

The BAA was formed as a nonprofit corporation in 1887 by special act of the Massachusetts legislature. The act provided that various prominent Boston figures, including Henry Parkman, Maurice H. Richardson, Richard D. Sears, and their associates and successors, "are made a corporation by the name of the Boston Athletic Association, for the purpose of maintaining a clubhouse for social purposes and for the encouragement of athletic exercises, and maintaining a reading room." The BAA's directors were called "governors." It had members, but no stock or stockholders.

Organized by Boston's elite, the BAA was an instant success. It had soon attracted over 1,000 members and constructed with borrowed funds a palatial clubhouse at the corner of Boylston and Exeter Streets in Boston's Back Bay. Its clubhouse housed tennis and racquet courts, a swimming pool, an indoor running track, Turkish baths, a barbershop, bowling alleys, lounging and dining rooms, a bicycling room, and a boxing ring where exhibition bouts were held.

BOSTON ATHLETIC ASSOCIATION CLUBHOUSE

The BAA Clubhouse at 80 Exeter St., Boston was built in 1888 and torn down in 1961. Photo courtesy of the BAA.

In the lobby of the clubhouse was a bronze unicorn head containing a gas flame from which the members lit their cigars.

The head of a unicorn, standing for purity and strength, served as the BAA's symbol.

BAA CLUBHOUSE LOBBY

Photo courtesy of the BAA.

The BAA had a golf course, the Unicorn Golf Club, in Stoneham, and shooting ranges for riflemen and traps. It also had a boathouse on the Charles River, by Riverside, Newton. For outdoor track and field events, the BAA used property called the Irvington Oval, a vacant lot on the south side of Huntington Avenue, just beyond where Exeter Street then ended. The BAA conducted an annual indoor track meet—the "Indoor Games," first at the Boston Arena (now Boston University's Walter A. Brown Memorial Skating Pavilion) on Babcock

Street, and later at the Boston Garden (replaced in 1995 by the FleetCenter). In its time, the BAA was one of the foremost athletic clubs in the country.

The BAA played a major role in the first modern Olympic Games. In 1892 the French nobleman Baron Pierre de Coubertin had proposed to the International Athletic Congress in Paris "the splendid and beneficent task of reviving the Olympic games." The classical games, first held at Olympia, Greece, in 776 B.C., had continued at intervals thereafter until the fourth century A.D. The baron's proposal led to the resumption of the Olympics in 1896, fittingly at Athens. The BAA assembled the team for the United States and stocked it largely with Harvard

UNITED STATES OLYMPIC TEAM, 1896

Photo courtesy of the BAA.

and Greater Boston athletes. Members of the team had to pay their own way to Athens. Of the 31 events at the 1896 Olympics, the United States team won 13! BAA member Thomas E. Burke was the outstanding performer, winning both the 100-meter and 400-meter races. Tom Derderian, in his Boston Marathon history, says that "in 1896 Boston was Olympic track and field in America, and the BAA team was the most powerful on earth."[25]

The climax of the 1896 Olympics was a long-distance race to commemorate the storied run by Pheidippides in 490 B.C. from Marathon to Athens, about 25 miles away. The Athenian army under General Militades, without the support of the Spartans who were busy observing a religious festival, opposed a Persian force that had been landed by the Persian navy on the plain of Marathon. Though outnumbered by at least two to one, with their longer spears and bronze armor the Greeks defeated the Persians and thus saved Athens and probably the other Greek city-states from destruction. Legend has it that Pheidippides ran all the way from Marathon, delivered the wonderful news in the Athens marketplace with a great shout, "Rejoice, we conquer," and then dropped to the ground, dead. Modern historians question that our hero perished at the end of his epic run, but it makes a good story. The Greeks employed swift runners to carry messages from one point to another, and it may be that the momentous news of the Marathon victory sustained the messenger in a nonstop run.

In 1896 the Greeks had no particular skill in "athletics," which at that time meant the shorter-distance track and field events that had been developed by the British. Host country athletes therefore concentrated on training for the new "marathon" event and were rewarded when Greeks finished one and two in the race. The winner, Spiridon Loues, ran the distance in 2:58:50, circling the Athens Olympic stadium at the end. The marathon has ever since served as the climax of the summer Olympics.

Although their team had but one entry in the marathon, the BAA's representatives must have been impressed by the event, for the club resolved to organize a marathon of its own at home. Members of the New York Knickerbocker Athletic Club were similarly inspired. They stole a march on the BAA by inaugurating a 25-mile marathon from Stamford, Connecticut, to a point in Manhattan on September 19, 1896. (This New York race soon died out; the present New York Marathon, organized by the late Fred Lebow, was first run in 1970.) The BAA chose Patriot's Day, commemorating the first Revolutionary War battles of Lexington and Concord, as its race day, and a finish which passed the BAA clubhouse and ended after circling the track at the Irvington Oval. Since a route from Concord to Boston afforded only half the necessary distance and would require the runners to battle their way through Cambridge, the BAA decided to strike out due west from its Boston headquarters. Bicycling more or less alongside the Boston and Albany railroad tracks, which ran past the then end of Exeter Street, close to the BAA clubhouse, BAA organizers stopped at a point in Ashland when their bicycle odometers recorded 25 miles and marked the spot by chiseling into a nearby stone railroad marker the number 25. The first two marathons began by this marker.

The marathon's starting point had to be moved two years later. The new beginning, still in Ashland, reflected a revised calculation by the authorities of the distance from Marathon to Athens—24.8 miles—and a decision to have the marathon finish by the BAA clubhouse instead of in the Irvington Oval. The revised marathon distance again became obsolete 10 years later. The Olympic Committee for the 1908 Games held in London changed the Olympic marathon distance to the present 26 miles, 385 yards—the distance between the start of the 1908 race at Windsor Castle and the finish at the London Royal Box. The BAA conformed its route to this changed distance in 1924 when the Boston Marathon was named as an Olympic qualifying race. Adoption of the 1908 Olympic distance backed up the Boston Marathon start to Hopkinton,

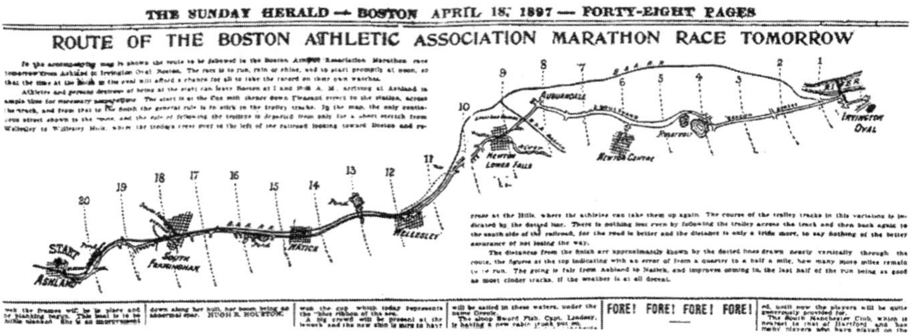

BOSTON MARATHON ROUTE, 1897

Reprinted from an article in the *Sunday Herald*, April 18, 1897.

where it remains to this day. Although there have also been modest revisions in the finish line of the race to reflect Prudential and Hancock sponsor changes, and corresponding beginning line revisions in Hopkinton, the course has stayed substantially the same since its inception.

The first Boston Athletic Association Marathon, Saturday April 19, 1897, was front-page news in Boston. Of the 15 starters, nine finished. John J. McDermott, winner of the Knickerbocker marathon the year before, won the BAA Marathon with a time of 2:55:10. Sunday's *Boston Morning Journal* gave an enthusiastic report:

> Yesterday, under the auspices of the Boston Athletic Association a road race after the style and plan of the Marathon run was held from Ashland to Boston, the finish being once around the track at the Irvington Oval, just as Loues circled the track at the Stadium. With the memory of Loues' splendid performance still green, it was eminently fitting that the BAA, whose athletes completed and helped make successful the Olympic Games in which was this big run and on which was centered the interest and enthusiasm of Greece, should conduct a race of similar character.
>
> The race excited great interest and all along the route hundreds were congregated. A small army of bicycle riders accompanied the runners, most of these

> bicyclists acting as a bodyguard or escort to those in the lead.
>
> At the [finish] there was an enormous assemblage. McDermott was cheered as only strong-limbed athletes can applaud.[26] Then to the Oval he trotted, and as he entered the gate and down into the field, where was congregated 3000 persons, there arose a great shout of welcome. Around the track once and the worsted was breasted by the blue Brazilian cross of the Pastime A.C. and McDermott, a New York boy of short stature, lithe, almost peaked in the face, but with undying courage and grit, was a winner and a record breaker.[27]

The race took place before the day of the automobile and none of the roads were paved until the runners reached Boston. With a platoon of bicyclists riding in front (including nine "ambulance corpsmen"), the runners were in for a dusty run, but at least they did not have to cope with gasoline exhaust from present-day motor vehicles.

The BAA fell on hard times during the Depression. To finance construction of its clubhouse in 1888, the BAA had sold 30-year bonds in the amount of $154,000, secured by a first mortgage on the premises. When the bonds matured in 1918 during World War I, the BAA was unable to pay them, and the payment date was extended to November 1, 1932. The bonds thus became due a second time during the depths of the Depression. As a result of the 1918 experience, the BAA had established

m the start to the
nott running well
ung along in pairs
were more than 50

shland station was
t it formed a line
use, the sleepy old
heers of her lusty
ed he received a
r passing the sta-
down to work in
re to South Fra-
was almost un-
McDermott went
imself. Hamilton
were running side
de, as they passed
ne of spectators
Ashland to South
uses all along the
people, and many
ood wishes were
tiful April day as
et, kept on.
Framingham was
er than the one at
ay and Dick Grant
lly here, and they
all along the lane
J. J. Kiernan and
ogether about 30
the Lowell young-
merrily about 300
the second men;
ason came along
nd him; Enright,
passed in the or
of the field was
file for perhaps a

Framingham cy-
about the leaders,
d suddenly opened
arriages, wagons,
fact every con-
conveyance was
d by the time the
runners had left
hardly room to

At Auburndale McDermott had a lead of nearly a mile over the field, which was strung out in single file, the last man being about five miles in the rear. Gray had been passed by Kiernan, and though he tried hard to hold his place he was too much gone.

AMBULANCE CORPS MEN HELPING AN EXHAUSTED RUNNER.

The main part of the crowd now centered about McDermott, and the attendants had hard work to keep the road clear. He was running like clockwork. His legs seemed to rise and fall like a phantom Greek, and his lithe body was bent just the least bit forward, his arms were at full length at his side, and his face was set with determination. As

ception, and like
exception of a
feet, was in as g
ho started. Of c
that they were ti
but had it been
run five miles n
done it.
A Boston man
was E. P. Rhell
the race marks h
is practically his
distances Ham
York crack, got
ing in a table of
o'clock last evenin

J J McDermott, Past
J J Kiernan, St Bart
E P Rhell, Jamaica
Hamilton Gray, St G
H D Eggleston, Past
J Mason, Star A C
W Ryan, South Bost
Brignolt, Bradford b
H Franklin (Harry 1
A T Howe, Lowell Y

John J. McDe
race, at the B.
said: "Yes, I fe
legs. My body is
are pretty sore, o
blistered and the
the bottom of my
"I weighed just
started in the r
pounds by the ru
for this race is th
It is just uneven
teresting. It is a
the New York cou
last fall. In fact,
with the race was
better. The bicyc
Nobody interfered
any stage of the r
"After I had g
took the lead from
man Grant is the
beat. He held me

FIRST AID, 1897 MARATHON

Reprinted from an article in the *Sunday Herald,* April 18, 1897.

a sinking fund to act as a reserve for paying off the bonds. Based on memory of records since lost, it is believed that the money that had built up in this sinking fund was embezzled by a BAA employee in the early 1930s. The Depression had made it impossible to restore the reserve, and the BAA defaulted on its bonds. Also because of the depression, clubhouse activities ran at a deficit, and by 1935 the BAA was unable to pay real estate taxes or cover current expenses. Efforts to refinance failed. The BAA filed for bankruptcy, and its assets were liquidated by a bankruptcy referee. Opulent clubhouse furnishings were sold at a fraction of their value. The bondholders foreclosed on the real estate, and it was sold to Boston University. The clubhouse would be torn down in 1961.

In the midst of these vicissitudes, a group within the BAA, headed by the association's president William F. Garcelon, petitioned the bankruptcy court to have transferred to the group the names "Boston Athletic Association" and "B.A.A." in order "to perpetuate the name and as much of the activities of the Boston Athletic Association as is possible."[28] The bankruptcy court authorized the sale of the names to Garcelon for $5 (see Appendix III, 2A). The Garcelon group and other BAA members continued the annual BAA Indoor Games and Marathon on a budget of about $4,000 a year. A reorganized BAA rented a floor at the Hotel Lenox, adjoining the BAA former clubhouse, and carried on the Indoor Games and Boston Marathon from there.

After World War II, the BAA and its events came under the wing of Walter A. Brown. His father, George V. Brown, of Hopkinton, had been a member of the BAA, its athletic director, general manager of the old Boston Arena, and finally manager of the Boston Garden. Walter had assisted his father as general manager of the Boston Garden and, when his father died in 1937, succeeded him. In 1940 Walter became president of the BAA and took over responsibility for the marathon and the games. By the 1950s he had also become owner and president of the Boston Garden. Soon afterward he added the Boston

WALTER A. BROWN

President, Boston Athletic Association, Boston Garden, Boston Celtics, and Boston Bruins. Photo courtesy of the BAA.

Celtics and the Boston Bruins to his portfolio, so that, until his untimely death in 1964, he was simultaneously president of the Boston Athletic Association, the Boston Garden, the Boston Celtics, and the Boston Bruins. He moved the Indoor Games, which yielded a modest profit, from the Arena to the Garden. In his Garden capacity, he made a deal with the BAA, represented by Garden employee and BAA Treasurer R. H. Kingsley Brown (no relation to Walter), who had taken over from his father as BAA Treasurer. The Garden would keep revenue realized from the Indoor Games. In exchange, the Garden would pay the BAA $1,200 annually and assume Boston Marathon deficits.

Under the Walter Brown regime, the BAA gave its address as 150 Causeway Street, the address of the Boston Garden. Day-to-day administration of the marathon was handled by Garden employees Jock Semple, runner and athletic trainer, and Tony Notogicoma. Duties of policing the marathon and cleaning up afterwards were borne by the State Police, the National Guard, the Metropolitan District Commission, and local police of the eight cities and towns through which the marathon passed.

With the end of World War II, Walter Brown hired William T. Cloney to run the BAA's activities. Before the war, Cloney had been a newspaper reporter for the *Boston Herald* and *Boston Post* and after the war he served as a Keystone Mutual Fund public relations vice president. Although his annual stipend of $1,500 a year for managing the Boston Marathon and the Indoor Games ended with Walter Brown's death in 1964, Cloney received a consolation prize—he became Walter's successor as president of the BAA. But by this time the BAA organization was dissolving. Meetings of the BAA's governors and members died away and the organization came to consist of only its president—Cloney—and its treasurer—R. H. Kingsley Brown.

In 1965, a year after Walter Brown's death, a second BAA angel providentially appeared. The race at the time still finished at Exeter Street, by the Lenox Hotel, but facilities at the Lenox were inadequate to cope with hundreds of marathon runners arriving at the finish line in various stages of collapse. The Prudential Tower, the first major construction in Boston since the Depression, had just been completed. As part of a three-day celebration of the opening of its tower, the Prudential Insurance Company offered to host the finish of the Boston Marathon. It was agreed that the race would finish abreast the Prudential Tower on Boylston Street, and in exchange the BAA would be provided with an office in the tower and administrative assistance. This arrangement continued until 1986, when the John Hancock Insurance Company replaced the Prudential as lead sponsor of the marathon.

By law Massachusetts corporations must file reports known as certificates of condition annually at the State House. After the death of Walter Brown, the BAA ceased making its required filings, and on petition of the attorney general in 1972 the organization was dissolved as a corporation. Despite its demise *de jure*, the BAA went on as before *de facto*. Cloney and Kingsley Brown continued to act as BAA representatives and, with the assistance of the Prudential, to put on the Boston Marathon. The Indoor Games were discontinued.

In 1978 attorney William B. Tyler, a friend of Kingsley Brown, headed up the restoration of the BAA to formal corporate status. Under his guidance, the corporation was legally "revived," a BAA membership of approximately 60 members was assembled, bylaws were adopted, and a board of governors was elected. The governors consisted of Cloney, Kingsley Brown, Tyler, Ellery Koch (provider of Boston Marathon prizes), and Walter Brown's brothers, George V. Brown, Jr., and Thomas Brown. Cloney was president, Tom Brown vice-president, Kingsley Brown treasurer, and Tyler secretary. The new bylaws changed the nature of the BAA. Whereas the BAA of 1887 was a nonprofit private *club*, the BAA of 1978 was constituted a nonprofit charitable organization. The BAA's legal status as a public charity would be significant in the coming litigation with Medoff and IMI.

Entering the 1980s, the BAA had thus resumed a conventional existence with corporate board, officers, and membership. It still had little money. Its annual budget was about $15,000. It had no facilities or headquarters other than the Prudential office it was allowed to use. But it did have its race, the Boston Athletic Association Marathon, a name often shortened in use to "B.A.A. Marathon," or "Boston Marathon," and, by aficionados, to "the Marathon," or simply "Boston." With the great increase in road-running fervor following the 1972 Olympic marathon triumph of an American, Frank Shorter, the number of Boston Marathon entrants had exploded. Thousands would run, millions would watch—along the route, at the finish, or on TV. The BAA's marathon had become a giant, if slumbering, asset, and also a target for exploitation.

The Agreement of Sale

At our August 1982 meeting, Tyler told Hanify and me that McDonough's report of a sale of the marathon was essentially correct. A deal had been struck ostensibly between the BAA and Medoff's company, International Marathons, Inc.—IMI. It was spelled out in a 13-page agreement dated September 23, 1981, signed by Medoff and Cloney, first shown to the other governors by Cloney after the 1982 race. The BAA was to continue to manage the running of the race, but all commercial rights were transferred to IMI. IMI was empowered to grant sponsor companies the right to associate their names with the marathon—for example, to authorize a marathon "sponsor" to advertise its product as the "official" car, beer, running shoe, or whatever, of the Boston Marathon. Out of the sponsor revenues, all of which would initially go to IMI, $400,000 would be paid over annually to the BAA. IMI would keep all proceeds over $400,000. The agreement and its division of rights between the BAA and IMI would continue as long as IMI paid the annual sponsorship fee of $400,000 to the BAA. The agreement gave the BAA no power of termination.

We were told that there had been a vote of the BAA board of governors on April 27, 1981, giving Cloney wide latitude to engage sponsors, but that the governors thought Cloney would secure the sponsors himself; that they never intended to authorize a deal such as the one made with Medoff. Now that the facts were known, the board was appalled at what had been done—that the BAA should have largely lost control over its own race. Cloney had resigned under fire. There had been much criticism from the running community, local politicians, and the press. The Prudential had given notice that it was discontinuing its role as sponsor of the marathon—the BAA faced no longer having Prudential facilities to help it cope with runners in varying degrees of distress who by then numbered in order of 10,000. As details of the agreement of September 23 became general knowledge, the situation could only get worse. Once it was fully understood that the Boston Marathon had become the commercial venture of an unknown private entrepreneur, it seemed likely that the race would lose backing and stature as a premier event. It might not continue at all. Could the BAA be extricated from the deal?

We were told that the attorney general of the Commonwealth, Francis X. Bellotti, had gotten into the act; the Division of Public Charities in his office was questioning the agreement. At that time, under Chapter 68 of the Massachusetts General Laws, fees paid professional solicitors seeking contributions to nonexempt charitable corporations were limited to 15 percent of the money raised by the solicitors. Contracts between the solicitors and nonexempt client charities had to be submitted to the director of the Public Charities Division for a determination that they were within the legal limit. The director had come up with a theory that IMI, when pursuing Boston Marathon sponsors, was engaged in soliciting charitable contributions, and since IMI would wind up in the first year with about 45 percent of the sponsor payments, the agreement exceeded the Chapter 68 limit.

Tyler and Serafini did not think Chapter 68 applied. But, for the time being, the attorney general's office was a potential ally.

IMI was represented by my adversary in other cases, James D. St. Clair of Hale and Dorr. Tyler told us that St. Clair had sent a check for $400,000 to the BAA on behalf of IMI. In St. Clair's cover letter, and over the endorsement line of the back of the check, there was the entry:

> Tendered in full payment of the obligations for 1982 of International Marathons, Inc. under Agreement of September 23, 1981, as amended, which Agreement is ratified by the acceptance of the . . . check.

The BAA had not cashed the check, and a decision had to be made on what to do about it. Settlement negotiations between the parties had gone nowhere. Medoff was insisting that the agreement stay in place for a period of years and that IMI would relinquish its rights thereafter only upon a seven-figure buyout. The BAA feared that litigation might destroy the race, particularly if IMI remained in control of sponsorships during the litigation. Apart from the $400,000 that was conditionally available from IMI, the BAA had no money to meet legal expenses. Asked our view, Hanify and I thought invalidation of the agreement by the courts was the only way to save the race. We advised a lawsuit. Ropes & Gray would wait for payment of legal fees.

If the agreement was found to be invalid, the BAA would have a claim to the over $700,000 in sponsor and TV fees IMI had collected, and the $400,000 IMI payment could be viewed, arguably, as a partial payment against what IMI already owed the BAA. A $400,000 kitty would be welcome to finance the litigation. But we did not want to start the case by giving IMI an argument that cashing the check was a ratification of the agreement, so our first move was to return IMI's $400,000 check. Once the check was returned, IMI had a problem. Because IMI's tender of the $400,000 had been conditional, arguably IMI had not made the required payment and the agreement could be terminated. Discussions ensued with St. Clair, and it was agreed that the $400,000 would be deposited in a Fidelity money market fund, in escrow, until the issues between the parties were resolved. (The escrowed amount grew to $550,000 by the time the litigation ended and the fund was distributed.)

Tyler sent us the BAA-IMI agreement of September 23, 1981 (see Appendix III, 2B), and nine other contracts with "sponsor" companies. The BAA-IMI agreement appointed IMI exclusive promoter of the Boston Marathon. It provided that IMI was entitled to represent to the public that the marathon was "presented by" IMI or its assignee. IMI was empowered to enter into agreements with Boston Marathon sponsors allowing them to identify with the marathon, and to collect from them sponsorship proceeds. Signage identifying the "presenting" and "official" sponsors was to be permitted at the start, finish, and along the route of the race.

The agreement assigned to IMI all rights in the BAA's names "Boston Marathon" and "BAA Marathon," except those "not inconsistent with this agreement" (whatever they might be—perhaps use by the BAA of its names in its conduct of the race). The BAA was to continue to "produce" the marathon, in the "same format, as in prior years," and was required to pay all expenses of the race. Except for the Japanese market, the agreement granted to IMI exclusive television, movie, and radio rights to the Boston Marathon. After any existing agreements had expired, sponsor names appearing on runners' bibs would

86th BOSTON MARATHON POSTER, 1982—"PRESENTED BY SEIKO"

Poster used at 1982 Marathon pursuant to the sale agreement of September 23, 1981 giving International Marathons, Inc. the right to designate a presenting or title sponsor of the Marathon.

be determined by IMI. IMI was given all rights of marketing and advertising relating to the event. The BAA was to cooperate fully with IMI's efforts to negotiate with sponsors, and do all things necessary to make the negotiations a success.

In consideration of assigning the commercial rights in its race to IMI, the BAA would receive from IMI an annual sponsorship fee of $400,000 a year, adjusted every five years to reflect changes in the consumer price index. After the $400,000 had been paid, IMI would keep all other revenue—sponsor, television, radio, and other payments. The agreement would "renew itself automatically and . . . continue year to year so long as the annual sponsorship fee to the BAA hereunder is paid." Except for the first year (by an amendment to the agreement), there was no requirement that IMI make a sponsorship fee payment in a given year, but upon a default in payment the agreement would terminate. So long as IMI paid the BAA the annual $400,000 fee, however, the agreement continued in force.

The agreement thus converted the Boston Marathon into a moneymaking enterprise where the nonprofit corporation conducting the event was in effect partnered with a for-profit promoter that was to receive the open-end revenues. IMI's owner and sole officer, Marshall Medoff, was a Boston lawyer who had never promoted a marathon and whose information about marathons derived from talks with Cloney and from reading materials such as articles in *Runners World*. Conceding that $400,000 was a large sum, the prestige of the Boston

Marathon virtually assured sponsorship revenues of that amount and more; the only real uncertainty was the extent to which annual revenues would exceed $400,000. In these circumstances, everyone contributing their services to the race—BAA officials, volunteers along the course, and state and municipal agencies—could be regarded as working for the benefit of IMI.

"Title" and "Official" Sponsor Contracts

After entering into the agreement, Medoff had hired a New York sports marketing firm, West Nally, Inc., as a professional finder to seek out sponsors for the Boston Marathon. West Nally produced nine companies that signed sponsor contracts drawn up by Medoff. The contracts involved three parties—the sponsor, IMI, and the BAA. Each contract stated that IMI had acquired from the BAA exclusive Boston Marathon rights, and that, for a fee, each sponsor was granted the right to identify its product with the marathon as official licensed merchandise. The "title" contract with watchmaker Seiko Corporation of America named Seiko the "presenting" sponsor of the marathon. Under the eight other contracts, "official" product status was given to Asics Tiger, Chrysler, Bristol-Meyers, Sunfield, Coca-Cola, Eastman Kodak, Belmont Springs, and Anheuser Busch. Cloney signed each of the sponsor contracts on behalf of the BAA.

The title sponsor contract with Seiko, alone, gave IMI the full amount it needed to pay the BAA for 1982. The Seiko contract was for a term of three years and called for annual sponsor payments of $400,000 (1982), $425,000 (1983), and $450,000 (1984). The other eight sponsorship contracts were for more modest amounts and ranged from one to three year terms. The nine sponsors paid a total of $690,000, which Medoff deposited in a Fidelity money market fund account, on which he had the sole power to draw, under the name of International Marathons Inc., BAA/IMI special account. IMI was later paid $22,425 for 1982 television rights. Payments received for the 1982 marathon thus totaled $712,425, all to IMI. With storm clouds gathering on the horizon after the Will

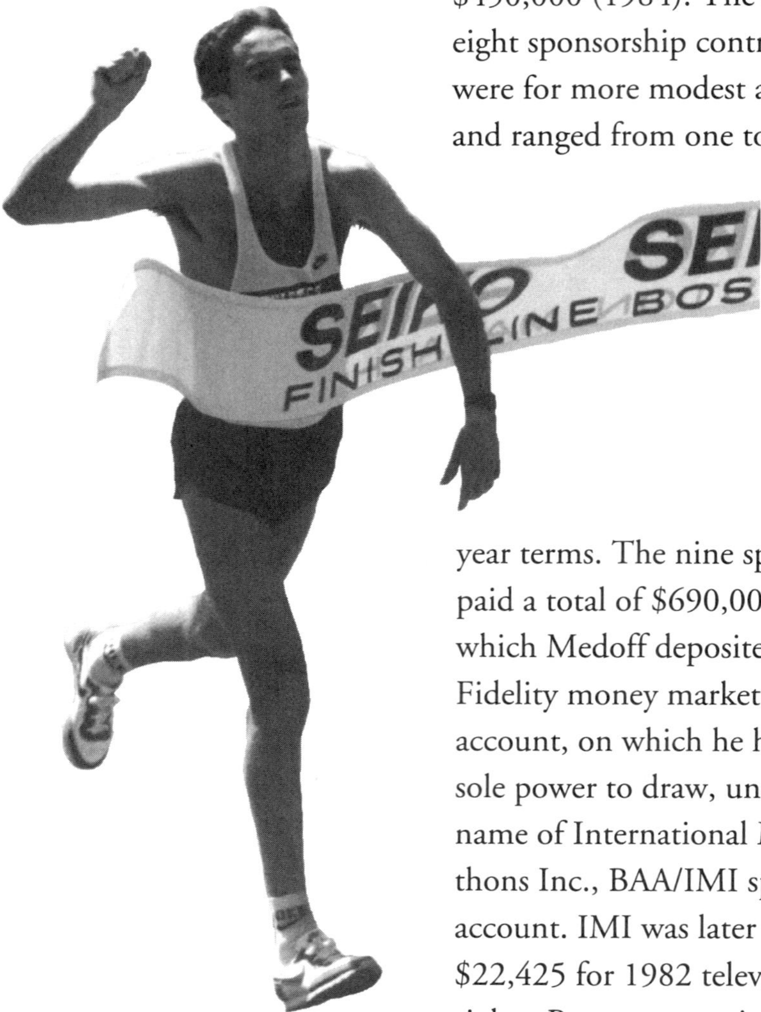

ALBERTO SALAZAR BREAKS THE SEIKO FINISH LINE TAPE, 1982

Courtesy of the *Boston Herald* and the BAA.

McDonough article, starting in March 1982 Medoff drew off for his own use all IMI funds over $400,000, supposedly for expenses and salary as an IMI officer and fees for professional and consulting services. With interest, Medoff realized $344,000.

What position should the BAA take on the performance of these tripartite sponsor contracts by the BAA in 1983 and subsequent years? What position would the sponsors take? Could the BAA accept a given sponsorship—for example, that Coca-Cola was the official drink of the marathon—but call for invalidation by the court of the provision for payment to IMI and a transfer of the payment obligation to the BAA? Was it inconsistent for the BAA to accept the benefit of sponsor contracts generated by IMI under the agreement and at the same time maintain the invalidity of the agreement?

Our primary goal, of course, was to knock out the BAA-IMI agreement. If we accomplished this, even at the cost of losing the sponsor contracts, our mission would be successful. But in the new running world the BAA was entering, sponsor revenue would be needed. Ruling track and field bodies had just authorized arrangements whereby an amateur competitor could be awarded money prizes paid to so-called competitor "trust funds" that could be accessed by the competitor upon retirement but would not until then affect the competitor's amateur status. The Boston Marathon, along with other prominent track and field events, would soon be driven to offer prize money to attract top-notch competitors. Financing of prizes would probably have to come from sponsors like Coca-Cola.

Apart from the provisions that all payments were to be made to IMI and, in the Seiko contract, that the race was to be advertised as "Presented by Seiko," the sponsor contracts were the type of arrangement the BAA board of governors had in mind in passing the vote of April 27, 1981. The vote had authorized Cloney to execute "such agreements as he deems in the best interest of the Association for the . . . sponsorship . . . of the Boston A.A. Marathon." Cloney plainly had been authorized to commit the BAA to conventional sponsor contracts, although not to agree that the sponsorship revenues be paid to a third party. Except for the as- presented-by-Seiko and payments-to-IMI provisions, we decided to recognize the contracts on condition that sponsor payments be made to the BAA. We would offer to indemnify sponsors for any consequences stemming from payment of fees to the BAA rather than to IMI, seek a court declaration that IMI had no rights under the contracts, and try to negotiate a new deal with any sponsor that wanted to continue its Boston Marathon relationship.

Theories on Invalidity of the Agreement

Ropes & Gray addressed itself to the legality of the agreement. The first avenue of attack would be that in its April 27 vote the BAA board had not authorized an agreement such as the one that Cloney had entered into. The BAA bylaws required that all contracts made on behalf of the association be authorized by the board of governors. A corporate board normally authorizes a contract either by voting on a specific proposed contract or by giving an officer authority to commit the corporation to a contract containing specified terms. The vote of April 27, 1981 did neither. No contract was then before the governors and the authority given Cloney did not specify any terms. The wording of the vote had been:

> *Voted*: That William T. Cloney, as President of the Association, be and hereby is authorized and directed to negotiate and to execute in the name of and in behalf of this Association such agreements as he deems in the best interest of the Association for the perpetuation, sponsorship, or underwriting of the Boston A. A. Marathon.

The agreements that Cloney could make if he deemed them in the "best interests" of the association included agreements not only for the "sponsorship" of the marathon, but also for its "perpetuation" and "underwriting." No limits were imposed; the language of the vote covered a lot of ground.

The terms of a vote, however, must be interpreted in the light of the circumstances surrounding the vote. Thus the April 27 vote had to be read in the light of the discussion at the meeting on the vote and the circumstances known to the governors at the time. It had been evident to all concerned that the time was coming when the marathon would have to offer prize money and that major sponsorship revenues would be needed. Although there had been discussions some months before between Cloney, Tyler, Kingsley Brown, and Medoff about a long-term Medoff promoter relationship with the Boston

Marathon, Tyler had objected, and Tyler and Brown had heard nothing further on the subject. There had been no discussion or suggestion at the April 27 meeting, or at any other governors' meeting, about hiring Medoff or any other promoter. While the governors meant to escalate the effort to secure sponsor income, they had assumed that Cloney would pursue sponsors himself, as he had done in the past.

Cloney's conduct following the vote was suggestive. A meeting of the governors was held on December 21, after the agreement of September 23 had been in place for three months. West Nally had reported to IMI on December 7 that a Japanese company was considering "title sponsorship at a figure of $400,000." Cloney had been informed. At the December 21 governor's meeting, however, Cloney never mentioned the involvement of Medoff or the existence of the September 23 agreement. He never mentioned West Nally or its report that a "Japanese company" was interested in a $400,000 sponsorship. He did report that seven companies, including Seiko, had expressed interest in sponsorship. The meeting minutes recited that "Mr. Cloney believes that the aggregate payments from these companies for the privilege of serving as participant sponsors of the marathon could amount to as much as $300,000 to $400,000." The other governors assumed that Cloney was negotiating directly with the potential sponsors. Cloney would later admit that he did not reveal the existence of the agreement to any of the other governors until February 1982, four months after it had been signed. Cloney's conduct was consistent with a recognition that he had gone beyond the intendment of the

April 27 vote, and that when his actions were known, there would be trouble.

Whether a court would ultimately find that the agreement was authorized by the April 27, 1981, vote was anybody's guess. Read broadly and literally, the vote authorized Cloney to do almost anything. If the trial court considered the vote ambiguous, evidence bearing on the intention of the parties would be admissible. Witness testimony might be allowed from which it could be argued that none of the voters save Cloney intended to authorize an agreement of the character, magnitude, or permanence of the IMI agreement. Whether the testimony would be accepted as limiting the literal language of the vote and Cloney's powers would be a close call.

There were, however, other theories as to why the agreement should be deemed invalid that did not rely on witness testimony of the intendment of the vote. To pursue them, no proof would be required beyond the agreement itself and the BAA charter and bylaws. A fundamental principle of corporate law is that important business judgments are to be made not by the corporation's officers acting individually but by its board of directors (or equivalent body) acting collectively. Consistent with this rule, the BAA's bylaws provided that, subject to limitations of law, "the property and affairs of the association shall be under the direction, control, and management of the Board of Governors, which shall have and may exercise . . . all of the powers of the Association." Courts have generally construed similar provisions in state statutes and corporate charters to require boards of directors to pass on all extraordinary corporate matters themselves. Examples of the application of this rule were Massachusetts cases holding that any sale by a corporation of a major asset has to be spelled out to the board of directors and expressly approved by the board.

A corollary of the rule that a board of directors must itself address all corporate issues of major importance is that power to decide such issues cannot be delegated to a single person or other body. The Massachusetts Supreme Judicial Court had put the rule this way:

> The directors could not delegate to [the corporation's president] the entire control of the defendant [corporation]. . . . Directors of a corporation are regarded as fiduciaries and are required to exercise their own independent judgment for the highest welfare of the corporation and its stockholders. "The functions of directors may not be abdicated."[29]

Were a court to conclude that the April 27 vote was intended to be read literally and thus to grant Cloney powers so broad that it embraced the actions taken in the September 23 agreement, such a construction would bring the vote up against the no-abdication rule. If the vote was an invalid delegation of power to Cloney, the agreement Cloney had signed based on the vote would be equally invalid. The agreement actually carried the delegation of power by the vote several steps further. After being given, arguably, carte blanche by the board vote,

Cloney had made a further delegation in the agreement by giving IMI the power to select future Boston Marathon sponsors and sign Boston Marathon contracts with TV and radio; by a combination of the vote and the agreement, the right to enter into these important subsidiary contracts was passed down from the board to Cloney and then from Cloney to IMI. And since IMI's sole officer was Medoff, he ended up as the ultimate possessor of the power to contract for the Boston Marathon. We had before us the quintessential delegation of corporate power.

Apart from its delegation of power to Medoff, other features of the agreement led us to conclude that if it had been presented to the board, the board would not have had the power to approve it. By statute in Massachusetts and elsewhere, sale of substantially all the assets of a corporation has to be approved by the corporation's stockholders, or, in the case of a corporation with members, by the membership. Board action alone is not enough to authorize such a sale. The agreement could be likened to an installment sale of all the commercial rights in the marathon. Since the race was the BAA's only asset, selling off all commercial rights, leaving the BAA only the right to conduct the race, could be said to be a sale of substantially all the assets of the corporation. If a court accepted this argument, the transaction would have to be found invalid because the membership had not approved it.

The agreement was also vulnerable because it converted a public charity into a vehicle to channel race revenues to a private enterprise organized for profit. The BAA had always been a nonprofit corporation. It had been revived in 1978 not only as a nonprofit corporation but also as a charitable corporation.[30] Profit could only be an incidental BAA objective, and the organization's activities had to benefit the general public. In legal terms, the agreement was arguably *ultra vires.*

By contrast to its nonprofit and charitable status, so long as the agreement with IMI was in force—potentially forever, since the agreement endured so long as IMI proffered the annual $400,000 payment—the BAA could be regarded as a conduit for the enrichment of a private business. Could a nonprofit charitable corporation legally perform such a function? Could Harvard College, for example, turn management of its endowment over to a business corporation upon an agreement that the manager could collect the endowment revenues, and, so long as Harvard was paid a certain agreed-upon annual fee, the manager could keep the balance? Could profits from the investment of the endowment be thus transferred from educational purposes to the profit of a private business? Was the BAA's transfer to IMI of profits from sponsorships any different?

Our research turned up a Georgia case closely on point. Georgia Association of Petroleum Retailers, Inc., a nonprofit corporation organized to promote the petroleum industry, had entered into a contract potentially for 90 years with a company organized by its executive secretary, one Allen. Allen's company agreed to publish a monthly magazine on industry developments for the Georgia Association. The association agreed that the Allen company would have the exclusive right to solicit members for the association and would be paid a major slice of the membership dues that Allen brought in. The association could neither lower nor raise the dues beyond specified amounts. It was to cooperate with the efforts of Allen's company to maximize revenues. The contract was to run for 30 years, subject to an option in the Allen company to renew for two additional 30-year terms.

The bylaws of the Georgia Association recited that the executive secretary was "to act under the direction of the president and the board of directors." The Association's board had approved the agreement with Allen and the parties had lived by it for 20 years. Then they had a falling out, and the Association sued to have the contract declared void. The Association charged that the contract was illegal "because it utilizes for private gain the rights and franchises granted to a non-profit corporation, and because it results in disposition of the association's franchise." The Georgia Supreme Court agreed. The contract was declared void because it divested the directors "of the power to determine in their discretion from time to time what is for the best interest of the Association and its members in the vital areas of membership and dues, and contracts away the greater portion of the Association's funds."[31] The contract surrendered to Allen's company powers of the Georgia Association's board of directors that were necessary to the carrying out of the Association's corporate purposes. "Rather than discharging its responsibilities as to membership," the court declared, "the Association, by this contract, seeks to invest Allen and his transferee with them. . . . Because of this divestment of the directors' authority, and its abrogation to others, the contract is void as against public policy."[32]

The assignment by the Georgia Association for potentially 90 years of rights to solicit members and realize dues was analogous, we felt, to the assignment Cloney had made of the BAA's commercial rights in the Boston Marathon to IMI. In both cases, the powers of directors charged by law with the duty to govern a nonprofit corporation had been turned over to a third party whose objective was to make a profit for itself. In the Georgia case, significant decisions would no longer be made by the association's board, and profits realized above costs would go to the Allen company and not to the association. The reasoning of the Georgia court that this arrangement violated corporate law matched our thinking about the BAA case. Although Georgia was not exactly a sister jurisdiction, the *Allen* case gave us confidence we were on the right track.

Hanify and I reported to the BAA Board of Governors our conclusion that the agreement was a violation of corporate law. At a meeting of September 9, 1982, the board formally declared that the agreement of September 23, 1981, went beyond the authorization of the board, that the agreement was invalid, and that it was disaffirmed. I notified the sponsors of this position, that IMI was considered to have no status as an owner or agent, and that all future dealings were to be directly with the BAA. We would be seeking confirmation from the Superior Court that the agreement was invalid.

The BAA Sues and Is Told Its Case Is Not Persuasive

While I prepared a complaint, Hanify discussed settlement with St. Clair. In exchange for mutual cancellation of the agreement, the BAA offered to give IMI a 15 percent royalty on all Boston Marathon income stemming from sponsors originally secured by IMI, not only from sponsorship income in 1982 but on all income from the same sponsors in future years, whenever it might be received. The lawyers on both sides thought that agreement had been reached on this basis. I prepared a memorandum of settlement and shipped it over to St. Clair. Medoff promptly rejected it. The die was cast; the BAA would go to court.

On September 27, 1982, I filed in the Suffolk Superior Court a petition for a declaratory judgment that the agreement of September 23 be declared unenforceable. The petition alleged:

> The terms and undertakings of said agreement were beyond the authority conferred on the President by the vote of April 27, 1981 and . . . were so fundamental to the purposes and operations of the Association and the Boston Marathon that their adoption could not have been delegated by the Board to anyone, and would have exceeded the powers of the Board to enter into.

The position of the attorney general that the agreement violated the law limiting the compensation of professional solicitors for charitable corporations was referred to as an additional basis for invalidating the agreement. The petition sought a preliminary injunction requiring IMI to preserve intact all sponsorship revenues until final determination of the case.

The injunction application resulted in an immediate hearing before the then motion session judge, Paul G. Garrity. St. Clair appeared for IMI in opposition. I summarized the allegations of the complaint and argued that the court should require sponsorship revenue in the possession of IMI to be preserved so that the money would be there if the BAA prevailed and was found to be entitled to it. To blunt our claim that the agreement was invalid under corporate law, St. Clair offered the imaginative argument that the perpetual nature of the agreement should not render it invalid because the court, assertedly, could "reform" its term and limit its duration to a "reasonable" period. The judge took the application under advisement without permitting rebuttal.

The next day Judge Garrity issued the preliminary injunction, accompanied by a memorandum of decision.[33] The injunction was rested on a supposed presumption of correctness for the theory of the Division of Public Charities that the agreement violated the 15 percent fee limit for professional charitable solicitations established in Chapter 68.[34] The injunction was issued, Judge Garrity said, "on that basis alone." He went on to disparage our claim that the agreement was invalid under corporate law:

> However, the plaintiff's claims both [that] the Agreement was beyond the power of its then President to enter into and that the defendant International Marathons, Inc. has breached the terms and conditions of the Agreement on the facts are not all that persuasive. First, the plaintiff concedes that on April 27, 1981 its Board of Governors made a broad-ranging grant of authority to its then President . . . as follows:
>
> > "That William T. Cloney, as President of the Association, be and hereby is authorized and directed to negotiate and to execute in the name of and in behalf of this Association such agreements *as he deems* in the best interests of the Association for perpetuation, sponsorship or underwriting of the Boston AA Marathon." (emphasis added [by the judge]).
>
> The agreement is not as one-sided as the plaintiff has characterized it although it is heavily weighted to the interests of the defendant International Marathons, Inc. as so many agreements are very often weighted to one side or the other side. Although the Agreement pursuant to its §8 apparently extends in perpetuity a

> court could reform that provision of the Agreement and mandate that it remain in existence a reasonable time. See *Beaton v. Land Court*, 367 Mass. 385, 392 (1975).

The court thus appeared to accept the literal language of the vote as authorizing the agreement, and to rule out a more restrictive construction. The no-abdication rule was not considered. The case was misconceived as involving breach of contract. As an answer to argument based on the radical nature of the agreement, Judge Garrity's acceptance of St. Clair's offering that the agreement could be rendered valid by judicial reformation that "it remain in existence [only for] a reasonable time" misstated the law. Neither the *Beaton* case, which the judge had cited, nor any other case supported his assertion that the perpetual term of the agreement could be dealt with by judicial reformation. A court's power of "reformation" is limited to insertion of a term that inferentially is intended by the parties, although unexpressed. It is elementary that an invalid contract cannot be saved by judicial reformation.

We thus came out of the hearing before Judge Garrity with an injunction, accompanied, however, by a gratuitous comment that we had an unpersuasive case on what was important—our claim that the agreement was illegal under corporate law. Since the Chapter 68 ruling decided the preliminary injunction application, the court's not-all-that-persuasive remark was as unnecessary as it was wrong. We could not seek judicial review of the adverse comment because the relief we had sought—the injunction—had been granted. We had won a

Pyrrhic victory. It reinforced Medoff's decision not to settle, and became an obstacle to convincing sponsors that they had to deal with the BAA rather than IMI.

Renegotiation of Seiko Title Sponsor Contract

While the litigation proceeded, preparations had to be made for the upcoming 1983 marathon. Most of the sponsor contracts had two or three years to run. The most important contract gave Seiko the right for two more years to "signage indicating that the race is 'Presented by Seiko.'" Seiko had paid the 1982 sponsorship fee of $400,000 but had hardly received the *quid pro quo* it had contracted for. Personnel along the route, offended at the notion that the Boston Marathon was assertedly presented by the Japanese company Seiko, had torn down Seiko indicia along the course. About the only Seiko signage that had survived was the Seiko finish line clock.

Seiko certainly had a claim against the BAA and it had asked for a meeting. I prepared for it with apprehension. Some or all of the now escrowed $400,000 that we expected would go to the BAA whether the case against IMI was won or lost might have to be returned to Seiko. Moreover, we would not be entitled to a presentation sponsorship fee in future years; we planned to tell Seiko that only the BAA could "present" the Boston Marathon. And if we lost Seiko as a sponsor, or worse, were sued by Seiko, other sponsors might follow Seiko's lead.

Three Japanese appeared, escorted by their New York representative, David Strousse. Instead of complaining about breach of contract and demanding return of their $400,000, the Seiko representatives commiserated with the BAA over its troubles with Medoff. They accepted discontinuance of the role of "presenting sponsor," but wanted to continue as "official timer" of the marathon. No request was made for return of the $400,000. With great relief, we negotiated a new deal. Seiko could position its multifaced clock at the finish line and other Seiko clocks at additional locations along the race course. For recognition as official timer over four years, Seiko would pay the BAA $130,000 in the first year (1983), and in each subsequent year, an amount $15,000 larger than the year before. The BAA would hold Seiko harmless as to any claims IMI might make against it. Similar negotiations followed with other sponsors, most of which continued as official product sponsors for varying periods and amounts. Although the Seiko numbers were one-third of the fees payable under the original "title sponsorship" contract, they were enough, together with fees from the other sponsors, to put the BAA on a sound footing.

The Superior Court Rules on the Validity of the Agreement

Meanwhile, the litigation with IMI had gone forward on a number of fronts. An administrative hearing lasting several weeks was held on the Chapter 68 claim of the Division of Public Charities. In the course of the hearing, it was revealed that Medoff, aware of BAA claims that the agreement was invalid and gave IMI no rights, had paid over to himself all IMI revenues over $400,000. The BAA's superior court action was therefore amended to target Medoff personally as recipient and constructive trustee of sponsorship funds belonging to the BAA. St. Clair withdrew from representation of the defendants, citing an unforeseen conflict of interest between the defendants and the Prudential Insurance Company, another Hale and Dorr client. Edward Barshak, a former president of the Boston Bar Association, replaced St. Clair. All the BAA governors gave affidavits on the circumstances surrounding the April 27 vote. Based on these affidavits, the BAA bylaws and charter, and the agreement itself, I filed a motion for a summary judgment that the agreement was invalid. Barshak moved for a summary judgment of validity, submitting with his motion an affidavit from Will Cloney.

We felt that the Cloney affidavit supported *our* case. The affidavits of the other governors had averred that there had been no discussion of hiring Medoff or any other promoter for the Boston Marathon at the governor's meeting of April 21, 1981, during which the vote supposedly authorizing the agreement was passed. These affidavits also stated that at the governor's meeting of December 21, 1981, Cloney had made no mention of the agreement, executed four months earlier; that until Cloney had revealed the existence of the agreement to one of the governors on February 25, 1982, and McDonough had publicized it in his article the next day, the governors knew nothing about it; and that none of them had even seen the agreement until after the 1982 race. None of these facts were denied in the Cloney affidavit.

I filed a "brief" of over 100 pages and argued the summary judgment motions to Superior Court Judge Robert L. Steadman for two days in June 1983. On August 29, 1983, we were rewarded by a decision that closely followed the BAA arguments, allowed our motion for summary judgment, and adjudged "that the agreement of September 23, 1981 is void, *ab initio*, and unenforceable" (Appendix III, 2C).

The decision began by noting that the BAA was a nonprofit corporation whose principal activity was conducting the Boston Marathon. The agreement, the court said, "indicates a sale of intangible personal property—the name and logo of the Boston Marathon—by the BAA to IMI." The agreement reserved to the BAA rights to its name only in the conduct of the race. "The most striking feature" of the financial provisions of the agreement, the court declared, "is that they assign a static commercial value to the name and logo of the marathon for *all time*, so long as IMI remits this unchanging 'fee.' See § 8. These arrangements also create at least the possibility that the name and logo of a non-profit corporation (the BAA) will be utilized to create a potentially enormous profit for IMI."

Regarding duration, the court noted, "the agreement provides no mechanism by which the BAA may effect a termination. The agreement is therefore potentially perpetual, largely at the option of IMI."

The court addressed the governors' vote of April 27, 1981, authorizing Cloney to negotiate "such agreements as he deems in the best interest of the Association for the perpetuation, sponsorship or underwriting of the Boston A.A. Marathon." "Assuming, arguendo," the court said, "that the Board intended by its vote of April 27, 1981 to confer sufficient authority on Cloney to enter the Agreement . . . such an attempted delegation was illegal and without effect." Because the agreement "contemplates the sale of the major interest in the BAA's most valuable asset—its name," because "the Agreement further contemplates its extension in perpetuity," and because "the combined effect of these two features is to assign a fixed value to the name and goodwill of the Marathon for all time," if the vote were construed to authorize the agreement then "such vote constituted an illegal delegation of the Board's fiduciary duties . . . . Compare *Milton Frank Allen Pub. v. Georgia Ass'n of Pet. Ret. . . .*"

Having found the agreement invalid under corporate law, the court considered it unnecessary to decide the attorney general's claim that the agreement was also invalid under Chapter 68 because it accorded IMI excessive fees, and ruled that issue moot.

Appellate Review

IMI appealed the judgment to the Supreme Judicial Court. The attorney general appealed the ruling that the Chapter 68 claim was moot. The court's opinion, written by Justice Neil Lynch, affirmed the invalidity of the agreement.[35] The vote could not authorize the undertakings of the agreement. "It is clear," the court declared,

> that if the delegation to Cloney was so broad as to enable him to commit the BAA to an extraordinary contract which encumbered substantially all its assets, the board would have delegated away control of the very essence of the BAA's corporate existence . . . . It is the obligation of the board of governors to oversee the presentation of the Marathon, not to surrender virtually complete control of the event to another organization. The fact that the agreement is automatically renewable and thus potentially perpetual demonstrates the pervasive nature of the limitation on the main purpose of the BAA. Authority to make such a contract was beyond the power of the board to delegate to Cloney.[36]

The agreement was all the more offensive because of the public charity status of the BAA—in a sense, the Boston Marathon was held in trust for the public. "Those entrusted with the management of funds dedicated to charitable purposes and donated out of a sense of social or moral responsibility," the court said, "owe an especially high degree of accountability to the individual donors as well as to the community."[37]

The court agreed with our position that the agreement even exceeded the powers of the board and of the association itself. Had the agreement been submitted to the board and the BAA members, and approved by a vote of each, even such approvals would not have sufficed:

> Furthermore, the contract between IMI and the BAA is especially vulnerable because it is antithetical to the BAA's nature as a nonprofit corporation inasmuch as this agreement turns the solicitation of sponsors from a way to support the Marathon to a way for IMI to make a profit. It is entirely inconsistent with the nonprofit nature of the organization to permit such a substantial segment of the revenue earning capacity of the Marathon to be used as a vehicle for personal gain. See *Milton Frank Allen Publications, Inc. v. Georgia Ass'n of Petroleum Retailers, Inc.*, 224 Ga. 518, 526-528 (1968) . . . .[38]

This was the end of the road for Medoff and IMI so far as rights under the agreement were concerned. The BAA had regained control of its marathon.

The Supreme Judicial Court did side with Medoff on the Chapter 68 issue—the claim of the Division of Public Charities that the IMI fees violated the charitable solicitation limitation. The Court ruled first that the Chapter 68 issue was not moot and second that no charitable solicitation was involved. The sponsors had no charitable intent; they expected a *quid pro quo* from their sponsor payment. "This is a commercial transaction," the court said, "It is not a gift."[39] The ruling that the 15 percent limitation was inapplicable did not affect us. With the agreement dead under corporate law, it did not need to be killed again.

Medoff Gets to Keep Revenues Scooped from IMI

The case now entered another stage. It had always been recognized that IMI had a claim for a benefit bestowed on the BAA in bringing about the 1982 sponsorship revenues. IMI had collected from sponsors and in TV payments over $712,000. Though the $400,000 placed in escrow with Fidelity would be surrendered to the BAA, with interest and gains, Medoff had paid himself the rest, justified only if IMI was entitled to a fee for its contribution of everything over the $400,000. IMI pressed for a trial by jury on the "fair value" issue, claiming it was entitled not only to the proceeds above $400,000 that Medoff had appropriated, but even more. By this time attorney Laurence Johnson had replaced Barshak as trial counsel for IMI and Medoff.

I tried the "fair value" case with my partner Thomas Hannigan against Johnson before a jury. The jury's verdict was that IMI was entitled to $178,000 for its activities, an amount higher than what we had argued for but much less than what IMI had sought. IMI and Medoff by then had realized in sponsorship fees and interest thereon $344,000 over and above the escrowed $400,000. With the jury verdict that IMI was entitled only to $178,000, IMI owed a balance of $166,000 to the BAA. But the claim against IMI was not much of an asset. Medoff had cleaned out IMI's bank accounts, and IMI was judgment-proof.

A bench trial before Judge Steadman sitting without a jury was held on the BAA's claim that Medoff was personally liable for the obligation he had caused IMI to be unable to meet by paying its assets to himself. Medoff defended on the ground that the rights of the BAA were limited to the liability of the corporation.

Judge Steadman found as facts that Medoff was the sole incorporator, employee, officer, director, and shareholder of IMI and that all acts of IMI were done by or under the authority of Medoff. IMI never prepared corporate balance sheets or financial statements; never filed certificates of condition; never kept normal accounting records such as cash receipts, cash disbursement books, payroll records, accounts receivable or accounts payable books; and made no payments under the Social Security or unemployment compensation laws. It filed no corporate tax returns. It had nominal capitalization and assets, did not pay dividends, and, from its formation to September 1982, had no separate bank accounts or credit accounts in its own name. As storm clouds had gathered on the horizon, Medoff withdrew from the IMI accounts, and deposited in personal checking accounts, all sponsorship revenues, with interest, over $400,000. Medoff throughout had used personal checking and credit accounts to pay bills rendered to IMI. By the time of the bench trial, IMI's assets were down to $300 in a bank account and an automobile.[40]

Notwithstanding the evidence that IMI as a corporation was a sham, and that Medoff had appropriated the sponsor revenues knowing of the BAA's claim to them, the Court ruled that "the facts and justice do not warrant the extreme measure of piercing the corporate veil and holding Marshall Medoff personally liable."[41] This decision limited the BAA to its worthless claim against Medoff's alter ego, IMI, and robbed the BAA of its win in the jury trial. The court had assured that Medoff would not suffer unduly from invalidation of his agreement.

We considered the decision outrageous and believed that on appeal the judgment for Medoff would be reversed. We were by this time, however, into the spring of 1986, and in the midst of another litigation—a trademark action against "Boston Marathon" T-shirt counterfeiters and infringers. The Boston Athletic Association was not a professional litigator and legal wars on two fronts were too many. The BAA was driven to settle with Medoff on the basis of the status quo; Medoff kept what he had and the BAA did not pursue him further.

The battle over sale of the Marathon thus finished with an inventory of two BAA wins and one disappointing loss. A hazard of litigation, however, is that you will lose some battles you should win, just as sometimes you will win battles you should lose. Statistically, our record against IMI and Medoff was only fair, but we had won the big one.

Chapter 3

Vindication of Rufus the Ram

The telephone rang. "My neighbor, Frank Friendly,"[42] the caller said, "has a farm. Friendly allows people to bring children to the farm to see the animals and workings of the farm. A visitor who had a group of children in tow now claims that she was butted by the farmer's ram, suffered a ruptured disk, and had to have two operations. She has sued Friendly and his wife for more than the worth of their farm, and they have no insurance. Will you represent them?" Thus began for me the saga of Rufus the Ram.

RUFUS AND FRIENDS

Photo courtesy of Farmer Friendly.

The Friendly farm covered the whole range of farming activities, and its livestock included sheep, goats, pigs, cows, and chickens. The sheep would normally be fenced at night but would be allowed to wander loose during the day. Usually they stayed in grassy areas, out of the way. Most of the sheep were ewes but there were several rams, or male sheep. According to Friendly, Rufus was the most pacific of animals, a view shared by some but not all of the farm personnel.

Mrs. Brown, the woman who had filed suit, was a Cub Scout den mother. One fall day, she and her friend Mrs. Hale had escorted a group of scouts, boys eight to nine years old, to the farm. Friendly welcomed them and told them he would be back shortly to take them around; it was milking time.

The sheep were grazing on a grassy area nearby. Several broke off and came down a path, and one of them, Rufus, rammed into a child, knocking him down. The boy got up laughing. The other children, except for Billy Terry, were also laughing. The ram seemed to sense Billy's fear, ran at him, and knocked him down, causing the others more merriment. Neither boy was hurt. Friendly then appeared and shooed the sheep away. He was told about the butting of the two boys and commiserated with the group. "Some children that were here earlier must have gotten Rufus riled up," Friendly offered. "Rufus has never caused trouble before."

No mention was made to Friendly that Mrs. Brown, also, had been butted by the ram. Friendly showed the group the sights of the farm and they departed.

A week later, Mrs. Brown complained to Mrs. Hale that her back was causing her too much pain for her to attend Cub Scout meetings any more, and said that she had gone to a doctor the day after being butted by the ram at the Friendly farm. This complaint began a history that would develop into asserted acute and continuous back pain for four years; incapacity to work or perform household functions; attempts at treatment by a multitude of physicians, including orthopedists, internists, and psychiatrists; visits to several hospitals; a back operation to remove a slightly bulging disk; another operation to remove scar tissue left by the first operation; and a suit against the Friendlys seeking a jury trial and six-figure damages. The suit illustrated a maxim familiar to litigator cynics: *No good deed goes unpunished.*

I visited the farm and planned the defense with the Friendlys. The law was that if you kept a dangerous animal such as a lion or tiger and the animal got loose and injured someone, you would be absolutely liable no matter how carefully you had attempted to keep the animal confined. In other cases involving animals not considered inherently dangerous but that had caused injury, the question generally was whether allowing the animal to be on the loose was negligence, and in what degree. Once upon a time Massachusetts had a statute premised on the assumption that rams were inherently dangerous between July 1 and December 25 of each year: "If the owner of a ram or he-goat suffers it to go at large out of his enclosure between July first and December twenty-fifth, he shall, if prosecuted within thirty days next after such ram or he-goat is found going at large, be punished by a fine of five dollars."[43]

The statute, however, had been repealed. There was nothing in the books that told why. I identified the proposer of the repeal legislation and questioned him. "Why did you sponsor repeal of the statute on rams and he-goats going at large? Had you some new information on their peaceful qualities?"

"No," said the legislator. "It just seemed that the statute was obsolete. I had made it a project to get repealed as many old and unnecessary statutes as possible, and this seemed like a good candidate." He offered to appear as a witness. I declined the offer.

All that was legally relevant was that the statute had at one time existed and that it had been repealed. There was no longer any dictate implying that rams in the second half of the year were inherently dangerous. The owner of a ram had to fulfill his duty of care but was not obliged to keep the animal within an enclosure the second half of the year.

Our position was that any butting of Mrs. Brown had been either nonexistent or trivial. Mrs. Brown claimed that the point of impact was the small of her back, which, when she was standing, was about three feet above the ground. In a butting position, Rufus's head was at most half that distance above the ground. We interviewed Mrs. Hale. She recalled that Mrs. Brown had made some complaint at the time, but the only butting she had seen was of the child. The children proved too young to be reliable witnesses and were not called at trial.

The case took forever to work its way through the county jury list. A year or so after the alleged butting episode, Friendly told me that the time had come when Rufus should be butchered and go to his reward. I protested that we would be charged with destroying evidence and, besides, that Rufus could make a great exhibit for the defense, providing that he behaved himself when called to appear in court. Friendly relented and Rufus was spared. I spent some time contemplating my proviso and wondering if I dared present Rufus in person to the jury and what he might do if let loose in the courtroom.

As it turned out, my quandary was resolved. Early one morning the telephone rang. "George," said Friendly, "something terrible has happened."

"My goodness," I responded, "what is it, Frank? What on earth has happened?"

"Rufus," he said, "has died!"

After recovering from the shock, I arranged with Friendly to preserve Rufus for the time being in the farm's refrigeration locker. I called opposing counsel. "Rufus," I reported to her, "has passed on. I thought you ought to know."

"*Why* did he die," she exclaimed, her tone implying that the nefarious defendants were doubtless responsible. "Have you had an autopsy?"

"No," I said, "he died of natural causes, and if you want an autopsy you can have one done yourself." Ultimately plaintiff's counsel was treated to a view of the deceased Rufus spread out on the grass at the Friendly farm. Photographs were introduced at the trial, but, alas, no Rufus in the flesh.

The case reached trial about four years after it had been entered. By this time, through depositions, examination of hospital records, and independent investigations, Ropes & Gray had assembled quite a file on Mrs. Brown. She was the first witness at the trial. She testified that she had been butted severely in the small of her back by a vicious ram. She had hoped to shake it off, but by the next morning she was in agony and had to go to a doctor. For the next four years her life had been a procession of visits to doctors and hospitals. She had been unable to work or perform household functions. She had experienced back pain every day. Her sex life had grievously suffered. Details were shared with the jury and embellished by Mr. Brown, who was also suing the Friendlys—for loss of consortium. The medical profession had done little for Mrs. Brown. With difficulty, she had prevailed on a surgeon to remove a bulging disk suspected as a possible cause of her symptoms. Scar tissue from this operation had to be removed in a second operation. Some of the doctors had added insult to injury by sending her to psychiatrists for treatment of her physical problems.

I cross-examined Mrs. Brown. She admitted that during the period of incapacity she had taken tap dancing classes, had climbed Mt. Katahdin, the highest mountain in Maine, and had engaged in other behaviors not especially consistent with an intractable back problem. It was suggested that any injury to her back had occurred in her own bedroom. The history given in medical records of a twisting fall she had sustained somewhat before the farm visit was introduced:

> As she describes it, there was some amorous play in the bedroom [resulting in her falling and being] twisted like a pretzel . . . . "My husband looked so appealing in bed that I decided to attack him, and I slipped off the edge of bed backwards and he grabbed me around the waist and bent me double." This brought on the present complaint with a present picture of recurrent back pain and sciatic pain.

On further cross-examination, Mrs. Brown reaffirmed her position that Rufus had struck her in the small of her back. With the witness standing, the distance to the ground from this part of her anatomy was measured, and then contrasted with photographs and measurements of Rufus. The contradiction was accentuated by a defense expert witness who testified that she was knowledgeable on the subject of rams, that rams lower their heads in butting, that there was no way Rufus could have reached Mrs. Brown's back without jumping into the air, and that ram-butting repertoire does not include jumping.

Mrs. Brown's attorney called a physician who had acted as a consultant but had not been 100 percent behind the party line on the cause of the back injury. In the midst of hospital records three inches deep, I had uncovered a handwritten note by the witness in which he had described the disk bulge that was later to be attacked by the surgeon as a "mild defect," and had suggested, in doctor-speak, that the patient's difficulty was that she suffered from "numerous supra-tentorial problems." As I had been informed by my doctor brother-in-law, the *tentorium* is a fibrous membrane supporting the cerebral hemisphere of the brain. On cross-examination, I asked the doctor, "Doesn't this note mean that her problem was mostly in her mind."

"Yes," he conceded.

The jury was out for five minutes and came in with a verdict for the Friendlys.

I still have a woolly hat made for me by Mrs. Friendly from Rufus' coat. One hopes that he sleeps soundly, with his reputation intact.

Chapter 4

Titicut Travesty

On Friday, September 29, 1967, the eyes of Massachusetts were fixed on the Boston Red Sox. It was an off day. Though the team had ranked ninth in the American League in 1966, the Sox were now one game out of first place with two games left to play—at home against the league-leading Minnesota Twins. The Detroit Tigers, also one game behind, were tied with the Sox but had four games left to play. The Red Sox would win the pennant if they could sweep the Twins on Saturday and Sunday, and if the California Angels could split with Detroit in the two Detroit-California double-headers also scheduled for the weekend. Red Sox Nation was beside itself with anticipation.

The New York Debut of Titicut Follies

Secondary news of the day included the New York City debut of a movie called *Titicut Follies*. A *Boston Herald Traveler* article said the film was a documentary featuring prisoners and inmates of the part of Massachusetts Correctional Institution, Bridgewater, commonly known as the hospital for the criminally insane.[44] The Commonwealth had brought an action against New York's Lincoln Center for the Performing Arts in the New York state courts to block showing of the film. New York Judge Francis T. Murphy had denied a preliminary injunction. The action had been brought, the *Herald Traveler* article said, by direction of Massachusetts Attorney General Elliot Richardson. After moving from the sports section that morning, I happened on the *Titicut Follies* article and took note of Richardson's mission. As U.S. Attorney for the District of Massachusetts years earlier, Richardson had been my partner in a legal war with federal Judge Charles E. Wyzanski (see Chapter 1).

I could relate to the difficulties Richardson had to be facing. He was evidently seeking what had come to be labeled, invidiously, a "prior restraint" of speech. Examples of such restraints are injunctions against publication of material in a newspaper or exhibition of a film. Courts rarely impose such restraints. The newspaper article quoted attorney Ephraim London, counsel for the exhibitor Lincoln Center and the producer, Frederick Wiseman, as claiming that Massachusetts was interested not in protecting the privacy of Bridgewater's prison inmates but in suppressing revelations about shortcomings in a state institution. Had the New York court been influenced by this ad hominem argument? What was the objection to the film that had led to the suit? Did Richardson have a bear by the tail?

Massachusetts Reaction

By Monday, the *Titicut Follies* story had moved up to the *Herald Traveler*'s editorial page. It was a distant second to exultation over the weekend's glorious Red Sox victories over the Twins. Coupled with two defeats of Detroit at the hands of California, the sweep had given the Sox their first pennant in 23 years. The paper's lead editorial was thus a celebration of Boston's "No. 1," fulfiller of the "Impossible Dream." But its next headline, "Blunder at Bridgewater,"[45] brought me back to *Titicut Follies.* The newspaper remonstrated against the showing of "inmates of the Bridgewater institution running around nude" and called upon Attorney General Richardson "to exhaust all legal remedies to right the wrong." The editorial cited a ruling by Richardson's predecessor, Attorney General Edward Brooke, that competent inmates could be filmed *if* they gave releases to the filmmaker. "In practice," the editorial went on,

> the film maker was permitted to photograph any inmate on the oral understanding that the officials would be given final authority to approve it before release. But the producer did not submit the final film for review and he now claims that this was not part of the agreement. There is also some question about whether he has releases from the inmates at all.
>
> Even if he has the releases, it is doubtful that they are valid. A legal document signed by a person who is not mentally competent

> is not binding. If a person is committed to a hospital for the criminally insane, he is not likely to be mentally competent. If he is mentally competent, he should not be there. Further, a person who signs a release permitting photographs must know what types of pictures are to [be] used and the consequences. It is doubtful that a mental patient who allows himself to be photographed nude is aware of these subtleties.

Frederick Wiseman, the director-producer of the film and a Cambridge attorney, claimed that he had assigned film distribution and exhibition rights to Grove Press, a New York publisher of sexually explicit books and films with a reputation for combativeness and success in beating back obscenity bans. Grove had secured reversals in the U.S. Supreme Court and in the Supreme Judicial Court of Massachusetts of lower court rulings enjoining distribution as obscene of the books *Tropic of Cancer*, *Tropic of Capricorn*, *Naked Lunch*, *Lady Chatterley's Lover*, and *Memoirs of a Woman of Pleasure*, a.k.a *Fanny Hill.*[46] It would champion in the year to come the cause of the most salacious film yet to be commercially shown—*I Am Curious-Yellow.*

The Commonwealth added Grove Press as a defendant to its New York suit and sought an injunction a second time, but again came up empty. Grove placed the film in movie theaters on New York City's Seventh Avenue and it began commercial runs. On October 4 the *Herald Traveler* reported that *Titicut Follies* brought to the screen "an emotionally shattering—often nauseating—snake pit of semi-existence . . . at Bridgewater." It "takes viewers through a jungle of human degradation—of taunting guards, unfeeling doctors, unnecessarily painful treatment, humiliating forced nudity, and empty living at the prison hospital in Bridgewater, Mass."[47] A *Herald Traveler* columnist, Thomas Gallagher, condemned the film:

> The objection to the film, of course, is that it shows obviously demented patients confined to a state institution for the criminally insane in a variety of naked and otherwise embarrassing situations without any effort to hide their identities.
>
> These unfortunates are now to be placed on exhibition across the country, like monkeys in a zoo, in the most flagrant invasion of privacy imaginable.[48]

Gallagher suggested that those responsible might "benefit from a change of scenery." He added that "correspondence in the bizarre case indicates they may have been misled by Wiseman."

Enlisted

My partner Edward Hanify, who would figure in invalidation of Will Cloney's agreement selling the Boston Marathon (Chapter 2), was also a former Richardson partner. On Tuesday, October 10, Hanify and I received a call from Richardson. Were we aware of the *Titicut Follies* controversy? Answer, yes—we had read that the New York courts had twice denied an injunction. The Commonwealth had first sued Wiseman and his Bridgewater Film Company, Richardson said, in the Suffolk Superior Court,[49] which had issued a preliminary injunction. But Wiseman claimed that the ongoing exhibition of the film in New York City was arranged by the New York publisher and film distributor Grove Press, that he was not responsible for the showing, and that he had no power to stop it; hence, the need for the Massachusetts authorities to resort to the New York courts. Could we accept appointment as special assistant attorneys general to represent the Commonwealth in its efforts to enforce its agreement with Wiseman and protect the rights of the prison inmates?

If we took *Titicut Follies* on, Richardson warned, we would probably have to drop everything else. We would have to somehow reverse or get around the adverse New York rulings. To secure a lasting ban, we would not only have to get an effective preliminary injunction against Grove Press, but we would have to try on the merits either the Suffolk County or the New York action and get a permanent injunction that courts of other states would be obliged to recognize. Since a preliminary injunction against Wiseman was in place in the Massachusetts case, arguably restricting rights of free speech, that case would have to be speedily tried—possibly within weeks.

Besides the judicial proceedings, Richardson continued, we would want to monitor hearings about to be conducted by the Special Legislative Commission on Mental Health. The commission wished to see the film and would be questioning Commissioner of Corrections John Gavin, Bridgewater Superintendent Gaughan, Wiseman, and others, all of whom would be potential trial witnesses. We would have to interview witnesses promptly, assemble the evidence of the contract between the State and Wiseman, and prepare to fight off the constitutional defense that free speech took precedence over rights of privacy and contract.

Richardson's call ushered in a period of furious activity at Ropes & Gray. All litigation involving the Commonwealth of Massachusetts in which Ed and I, and others at Ropes & Gray appeared, had to be measured against conflict of interest statutes. The ultimate conclusion was that Hanify could serve as a special assistant attorney general for 60 nonconsecutive days, and I could serve for an indefinite period. On Thursday, October 12, we became special assistant attorneys general; pay: $25 an hour. Others at Ropes & Gray took over our cases. We flew to New York, bought tickets for *Titicut Follies* at Cinema 57 Rendezvous, and spent the afternoon appraising our target.

The Film

The Titicut Indians once occupied the area where Massachusetts Correctional Institution, Bridgewater was located, and every year prisoners and correction officers at the institution put on a variety show they called *Titicut Follies.* The moviemaker had taken the name of the show for his film. His *Titicut Follies* began with a raucous take from the MCI Bridgewater show being rehearsed for that year. It moved from there into a conglomeration of scenes filmed mostly at the hospital for the insane, created by cobbling together shots taken at different times. The "actors"—inmates and staff, all male—seemed largely oblivious to their being filmed. Inmates were shown displaying the mental aberrations that had put them in the hospital. There was no effort to mask identities or the considerable nudity of the inmates.

Staff members were often portrayed in postures of callousness, indifference, and questionable competence. The reality of the sequences filmed was compromised by their reordering and recombination in the editing process. There was no background narrative or other explanation of the scenes that had been constructed. Viewers were left to speculate about what they had seen and what conclusions they should draw.

One scene showed prisoners milling about in the nude and featured a seemingly paranoid inmate hallucinating and using obscene, vulgar, and sacrilegious language. No explanation was offered as to what was going on. We learned later that we had been watching episodes in a "skin search" for contraband thought to have been just smuggled into the hospital.

In another episode an inmate was led out of his room fully nude, shaved, and returned to his room. Aroused by the taunting of the guards, heard in the background, he is shown stamping on the floor of his room, walking in circles, and looking toward the door—apparently conscious that he was being filmed—trying to hide his private parts with his hands. The noise of his stamping is accentuated in the film. Questioned, he gives a home address in a Massachusetts city and says he had been a high school teacher there. We learned afterward that this particular inmate was one of the most extreme cases at the hospital. He had been in the nude because he made a practice of tearing off his clothes, mixing them with his feces, and smearing the product on the walls. The taunting had probably taken place at the behest of the film crew.

Another sequence showed an emaciated nude inmate being asked by the doctor whether he will drink some soup; otherwise he will have to be fed with a tube. The inmate does not respond. He is put on his back on a table while the doctor greases a tube to be run through the man's nose and down into his stomach. An attendant belatedly puts a towel over his private parts, and tube feeding begins with the soup being poured into a funnel leading to the tube. The doctor is smoking a cigarette with a developing ash, and the viewer is fearful that the ash may fall into the funnel. The film switches back and forth a half dozen times between this scene of insensitivity and another scene, in the mortuary area, of the preparation of the corpse of the same inmate for burial. The mortician is shown putting cotton into the eyes of the corpse and carefully pulling the eyelids down with tweezers. The message here at least is clear—that the patient was treated with more care and respect in death than in life.

An inmate is shown in a bathroom, kissing the sink and the mirror, being bathed in the tub, and drinking his bathwater. A spastic paraplegic is shown gesturing in a contorted way with his fingers and delivering an infantile smile to the camera.[50] Doctors are shown interviewing patients and discussing their mental symptoms.[51] There is an apparent act of masturbation. A dying but still conscious man is filmed while being given last rites of the Roman Catholic Church. A prisoner sentenced to Bridgewater for raping an 11-year-old girl is pictured being interviewed by a doctor. In answer to the doctor's questioning, the inmate admits to committing a similar crime for which he was not caught—the rape of his daughter.

If Hanify and I needed incentive for our assignment, the film provided it. I wondered how the New York judges would have ruled if New York inmates had been Wiseman's impressed actors.

New York Good-bye

We faced two immediate problems. First, what should we do about the New York litigation? We probably had a window of several days within which we could unilaterally dismiss the Commonwealth's New York case without prejudice and abandon efforts to secure an injunction in New York courts. Once any defendant in the case filed an answer, the Commonwealth, as plaintiff, could no longer dismiss without prejudice; the defendants could hold us to trying the case in New York. If we lost such a trial, we were finished; the film could be shown anywhere. Answers from the defendants were due in a week but could be served at any time.

Did we want the New York courts to make the final decision? We recognized that those courts were not entirely to blame for the results to date. Attorney General Richardson had learned only in mid-September of the *Titicut Follies* exhibition scheduled for September 28 at New York's Lincoln Center. His team faced severe time constraints in putting together a compelling case before the scheduled showing—in assembling proof of the contract between the Commonwealth and Wiseman; drafting a complaint, affidavits, and a legal memorandum; engaging New York counsel; determining the legal entity responsible; filing and serving papers; and securing a prompt hearing. Richardson's team had offered affidavits at the hearing from Commissioner Gavin and Superintendent Gaughan of the release, competency, and approval conditions established for the filming, but had not been able to develop proof of all the circumstances in the time at hand.

The Commonwealth had filed its preliminary injunction application on September 26, and the hearing concluded only hours before the scheduled September 28 showing. The defense had countered the Commonwealth's Gavin-Gaughan affidavits by a contrary Wiseman affidavit that there never was any agreement to submit the final film for approval of any official. Wiseman also claimed that there had been only one condition of filming—obtaining consent of the subjects—and that it had been met. In addition to opposing factual scenarios, questions of law were raised as to whether the courts of Massachusetts, where the film was made, would recognize any right of privacy in Massachusetts; whether the Commonwealth had standing to sue on behalf of its prisoners and inmates; and whether the governing law was properly that of New York or Massachusetts. Judge Murphy would be blamed by the Lincoln Center audience for blocking the showing at the last minute. Collateral issues thus surrounded the court's primary mission of addressing the film's parade of outrages. In the imperfect world of litigation, it was not surprising that Judge Murphy denied a preliminary injunction.

After the first adverse decision, the Commonwealth had amended its complaint by adding as plaintiffs two inmates who were grotesquely displayed in the film, and, as a defendant, Grove Press. The Commonwealth then moved a second time to enjoin the film. The theory of the Commonwealth was that if the standing of the plaintiffs to complain was clearer, there might be a different result. This proved not to be the case; the second application, heard by New York Judge Saul S. Strait on October 2, met with the same fate as the earlier effort. Judge Strait ruled that he would not consider the issue of Wiseman's agreement with the Commonwealth at that time, and implied that any rights of privacy of the inmates could somehow be vindicated by money damages:

> The question as to whether there was an oral agreement is not for the Court to decide at this juncture on this motion. The question as to whether or not the patients have any claims or rights remains. They are wards of the Commonwealth of Massachusetts. The Commonwealth could not surrender their vested rights, whatever they

> may be; they survive the showing of this film.[52]

The principal "vested right" that the Commonwealth was asserting had been, of course, the right of prisoners of the Commonwealth to have their privacy protected—to have involuntary display of the inmates, nude and hallucinating, enjoined. The court seems not to have recognized the issue—and to have decided it by ignoring it. Each permitted showing of the film was in effect a repudiation both of contract and privacy rights. Any remaining right of damages the court may have had in mind was secondary and problematic. The reservation as to the inmates' "rights, whatever they may be" was also not promising—a greater invasion of their privacy could hardly be imagined.

Judge Strait had indicated that he might assign the case promptly for trial. Having to try our case in New York City, 200 miles from home, would not have been an appealing prospect even if the Commonwealth did not already have two strikes against it. Our witnesses, expected to number about 20, were Massachusetts residents who would have to travel to New York and be subject to an uncertain schedule. The environment surrounding the trial certainly would be unfavorable. The national media, centered in New York, could be counted on to stridently support Grove Press and local exhibitors. That the film was "banned in Boston" could well be a red flag in the New York courts. Because the case was "in equity"—seeking primarily an injunction—it would be tried before a judge and not before a jury. It was likely that the New York trial judge would follow the lead of Judges Murphy and Strait.

There was an alternative. Our target was primarily Grove Press, as the distributor of *Titicut Follies*. The Massachusetts Superior Court would have jurisdiction over Grove if the company could be shown to do business in the Commonwealth. Since Grove was a national publisher, it seemed possible that once we got a look at the company's records, we could prove sufficient business in Massachusetts to establish jurisdiction. Grove's national publisher status would probably suffice for a preliminary injunction. We could discontinue the lawsuit in New York, add Grove Press to the roster of defendants in the Suffolk Superior Court action, apply for a nationwide injunction in that court against Grove, and hope that Grove would either bow to a Massachusetts injunction or could be forced to obey it.

Assuming we got an injunction, Grove would still have as an option contending that any Massachusetts injunction against it was void for want of court jurisdiction, ignoring the injunction, continuing to show the film, and defying the order. We could deal with showings in Massachusetts by bringing contempt proceedings against the exhibitors. For showings outside of Massachusetts, we would have to get the cooperation of the out-of-state courts, verify the jurisdiction of the superior court to issue the injunction, and seek a contempt adjudication against Grove. Although enforcement litigation in other states would present a raft of problems, our chances in those arenas seemed better than winning the pending New York injunction case. Moreover, we might never have to face out-of-state litigation. Grove might be deterred by the possibility of contempt sanctions.

On our flight back from viewing the film in New York, Hanify and I decided to discontinue the New York case; we would proceed against Grove Press in Massachusetts and hope for the best. I instructed New York counsel to file a discontinuance immediately. This was done; it preceded any answers and was therefore effective. The New York case was behind us. Saturday was devoted to preparing an amendment to the Commonwealth's superior court "Bill in Equity." The amendment alleged that Grove, as Wiseman's assignee, was bound by Wiseman's contractual undertakings, that its showings of the film were both a breach of the contract and a continuing tortious invasion of inmate rights, and that the existing preliminary injunction should be extended to Grove. I would present the amendment and application for a further injunction to the superior court on Monday.

Exhibition to the General Court

A second immediate problem before us was a demand of the "General Court"—the Massachusetts House of Representatives and Senate—to be shown *Titicut Follies*. A few legislators had traveled to New York to see the film, but for most legislators their information about the film was secondhand. *The Herald Traveler* and *Record American* were demanding action to stop the showing of the film. The *Boston Globe* was ambivalent. Movie folk claimed the film was art.[53] Anti-establishment figures applauded the exposure of an imperfect state institution. Traditionalists considered involuntary display of naked and hallucinating prisoners of the state in a commercial film repellent. The general court wanted to see the film and judge for itself.

Arranging for a showing before the general court presented a dilemma. How could we justify showing the film to 300 legislators and at the same time press for a nationwide ban against exhibition to the general public? I stayed up all Saturday night at Richardson's Brookline home debating with Richardson and Frederick Greenman, the assistant attorney general who had commenced the Massachusetts action against Wiseman, how to resolve the inconsistency. We would be in court Monday on our application to extend the injunction to Grove Press. We could work in at the same time the subject of making a special exception for the general court. It could be argued that the legislators had a special interest in the subject matter—the House had before it at the time a report of the Special Legislative Commission for Mental Health on MCI Bridgewater and various bills to improve conditions there. But Grove would doubtless seize on such an argument and claim that if the legislators had a "right to know," so did their constituents. If the Commonwealth deliberately carved out an exception for the whole general court, the injunction application might be weakened. The idea finally came to us that we might refrain from taking any position ourselves and submit to the superior court the question of a special legislative showing without recommendation. There was not much doubt as to what the superior court would do.

The Wiseman side had all along been claiming that it wanted to engender reform by publicizing adverse conditions. It jumped at the chance to show the film to the general court. The showing was arranged for Tuesday, October 17, conditional on court approval.

We were blessed that on Monday everything went according to plan. I moved to amend and to extend the injunction. The Massachusetts court was no more impressed by the New York court's denials of a New York injunction against Grove Press than the New York court had been by the still earlier granting (against Wiseman) of a Massachusetts injunction. A preliminary injunction was issued against Grove. I raised whether an exception should be made for a showing to the general court and governor. The superior court ordered the exception. We had eaten our cake, but we had it too.

October 17 was a big day for *Titicut Follies.* As its first order of business, the Special Legislative Commission for Mental Health prepared to exhibit the film to the general court and governor in the Gardener Auditorium of the State House. The windows were covered with blinds or cardboard. Capitol police were at the door. Senate Counsel Charles Innes passed on who could be admitted. Following the language of our amended bill in equity, the superior court in its order excepted from the injunction—only—"the members of the general court and the Governor of the Commonwealth"; I had not thought to suggest inclusion of general court invitees. Governor John A. Volpe and sitting members of the state legislature were admitted. Innes ruled that representatives-elect of the House who had not yet been seated must be excluded. He made the same ruling for members of the Governor's Council, the secretary to the commission, members of the State House Press Association, and dozens of reporters, photographers and radio and TV people who were clamoring for admission. They were told to address their complaints to the court; I kept a low profile.

The *Boston Herald Traveler* the next morning headlined *Titicut Follies*:

BOSTON HERALD TRAVELER

THE WEATHER — SHOWERS LIKELY, (PAGE 2) WEDNESDAY, OCTOBER 18 1967 HA 6-3000 TEN CENTS

SOVIET PACKAGE LANDS ON VENUS, SENDS SIGNALS
—See Story Below

Follies Film Shocks Legislators

"Shouldn't be shown to the public."—Sen. Donahue

"Just a grade A exhibit of bad taste" —Sen. Cohen

By PETER LUCAS

Correction Commr. John A. Gavin testified Tuesday that he initially forbade the filming of the Bridgewater State Hospital shocker, "The Titicut Follies", but changed his decision after "contacts" from the lieutenant governor, then Elliot L. Richardson, and from Rep. Katherine D. Kane, D-Boston.

This was one of the features of Gavin's testimony before a legislative investigating committee as the film controversy blazed to [illegible] proportions.

Gavin appeared before the committee shortly before the members of the Legislature watched the film in a special showing in Gardner Auditorium.

Gavin testified:

• He denied permission to Atty. Frederick Wiseman to make the film in a letter to Wiseman dated Sept. 27, 1965. Wiseman had asked this permission, and had stated the conditions he would adhere to, in a letter dated Aug. 19, 1965. Following his refusal of permission he received "contacts" from Richardson and Rep. Kane.

• He then gave his authorization, something he said he might not have done had he not received a telephone call from Richardson. That authorization was based on the conditions that Wiseman had outlined in the Aug. 19 request.

• He did not see the film until Sept. 21, but learned Richardson and Bridgewater Supt. Charles W. Gaughan had seen it in June. His first view of the film was the same day—Sept. 21—he was called to a meeting with Richardson, Wiseman and legal counsel for the latter.

(Continued on Page Thirty-three)

Titicut Viewers Angry

By TIM TAYLOR

Sen. Francis X. McCann of Cambridge stood in one corner of the crowded, smoke-filled lobby of Gardner Auditorium and kicked at the tile floor.

His eyes were red-rimmed. He had just watched nearly an hour of the "Titicut Follies." And he was mad.

"Where the hell are the liberals and the advocates of civil rights? Where the hell are they now?" he demanded.

"It's just profoundly incredible that the commonwealth could [illegible] anyone expose those poor creatures at Bridgewater for the sake of a $2.50 movie house ticket," he said.

(Continued on Page Twenty-four)

Federal Film Ban Sought

The House of Representatives suspended rules Tuesday to adopt a resolution urging the attorney general to petition federal agencies to block the showing of "The Titicut Follies."

TITICUT FOLLIES PRESS, OCTOBER 18, 1967

Reprinted with permission of the *Boston Herald.*

After seeing the film, the Massachusetts House passed a resolution that "the Attorney General seek immediately a cease and desist order in the federal courts" and petition the Federal Trade Commission and the Federal Communications Commission for action to block showings of the film. The *Herald Traveler* reported individual comments on the film by the legislators.[54] Representative Katherine Kane, a Wiseman supporter who had invested in his first film, *The Cool World*, was quoted describing *Titicut Follies* as "wonderful . . . extremely educational . . . should be shown to the public . . . absolutely not sensational . . . I'm not shocked, I'm sad."

Other legislators were not so enthusiastic: House Speaker John Davoren, "A commercial enterprise that is nothing more than a sordid documentation of human misery to make money . . ."; Senate President Maurice Donahue, "Crass commercialism . . . shouldn't be shown to the public . . . [but] indicates we are still using some 17th Century methods of treatment"; Representative Robert Cawley, vice chairman of the Special Legislative Commission, "It makes you sick"; Representative Edward Flanagan, "Very depressing . . . repugnant that it is being used for commercial purposes"; Senator Francis McCann, "To commercialize on [the inmates'] misfortune . . . is criminal"; Senator Beryl Cohen, "Just a Grade A exhibit of bad taste"; David Flynn, representative from Bridgewater, "A distorted view of Bridgewater . . ."; Representative Aaron Shinberg, "We've been conned into having the state allow a commercial piece of voyeurism to be made using the poor patients as unwilling and unaware actors."

The public was not inhibited from commenting by not having seen the film. Most conservatives appeared to be behind the Commonwealth. Our action was an affront to First Amendment zealots who brooked no exception to freedoms of speech. Other liberals who gave equal value to rights of privacy were with us.

Boston attorney Gerald A. Berlin was chairman of the quintessentially liberal Civil Liberties Union of Massachusetts (CLUM). Wiseman, a member both of CLUM and the national American Civil Liberties Union, had engaged Berlin to represent him at the legislative hearings and in the superior court action. Berlin thus took up the Wiseman cause before a position had been taken by his CLUM, which might (and ultimately did) side with the Commonwealth. A *Herald Traveler* cartoon (opposite page) neatly captured the conflict.

Berlin withdrew from the case the day the cartoon was published. He was replaced by my old adversary James St. Clair, and his Hale and Dorr partner, Blair Perry.

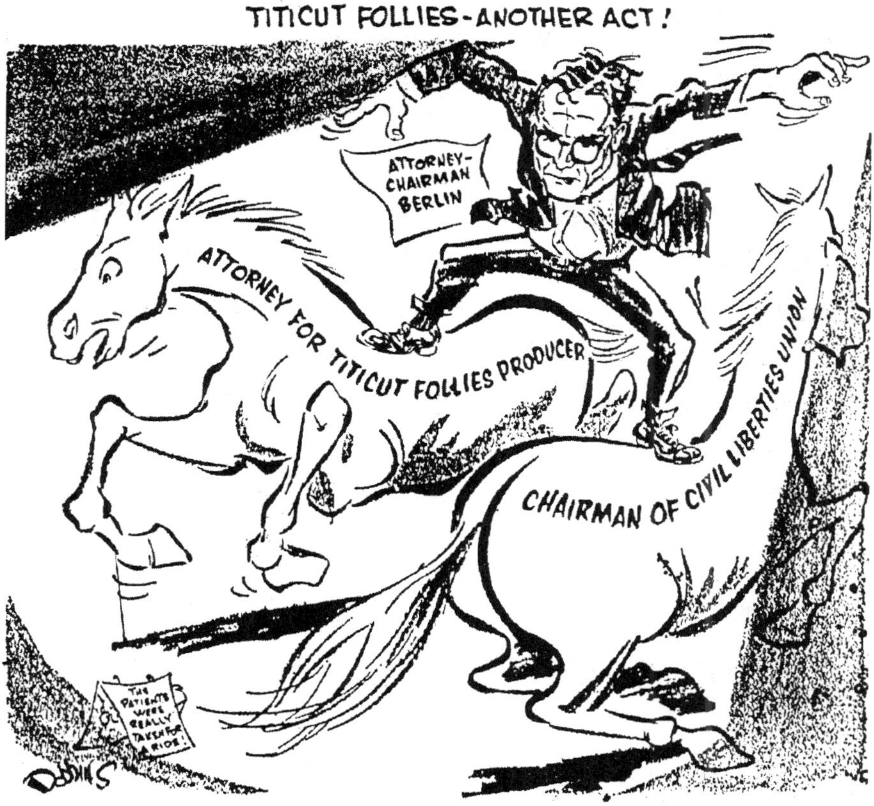

A TWO-WAY RIDE FOR CLUM'S GERRY BERLIN

Reprinted from the *Boston Herald Traveler,* October 18, 1967, p. 18, with permission from the *Boston Herald.*

On how the film was viewed by the medical community, the *Herald Traveler* had reported the judgment of an unidentified clinical psychiatrist who had seen the film in New York: "This stands on its own merits as a work of tremendous sensitivity, a work of art."[55] The director of Massachusetts General Hospital, Dr. John H. Knowles, who had attended a private showing, had an opposite reaction. He declared the film "an incredible violation of the rights of these patients . . . . I was horrified when I saw this," another *Herald Traveler* article reported.[56] Knowles had been told, the article went on, that releases had been obtained from either the patients or members of their families. He had questioned any permission given by mental patients and had stated that no such pictures would be taken in his hospital "with or without permission of the immediate family." Comparing *Titicut* to a filming of his private life at home, he protested that "what happened at Bridgewater is worse because these are sick people who are defenseless. . . . Apparently, absolutely nothing is sacred anymore."

Special Legislative Commission Hearings

Commissioner of Corrections John Gavin and Bridgewater Superintendent Charles Gaughan were the first witnesses at the Special Legislative Commission on Mental Health hearings. The commission members wanted to know how Wiseman came to be granted permission to film anything that caught his fancy at the Commonwealth's Bridgewater maximum security prison and hospital for its most intractable mental cases. The corrections officials testified that the conditions of the permission, oral and written, were that the rights of the inmates were to be fully protected, that only photographs of competent inmates were to be used in the film, that consent to the filming by the persons filmed was to be evidenced by signed releases, and that the commissioner and superintendent were to have a right of final approval and to have objectionable scenes deleted. Wiseman in his testimony denied any violation of rights, claimed everyone photographed had consented, denied the conditions of permission described by the officials, and particularly denied that he had agreed to give the officials a right of approval. Besides, he maintained, "in Bridgewater the public right to know supersedes the privacy of the inmates . . . . I believe the public has a right to know what the conditions are there."[57]

Attorney General Richardson told the commission that in 1965, when he was lieutenant governor, he had met with Wiseman at the urging of Representative Kane and had read Wiseman's film proposal. Afterwards, Richardson said, he had called Commissioner Gavin and had endorsed the idea of a documentary and educational film on Bridgewater. He had no part in the arrangements for filming. When he had seen the film in June he had questioned the nudity, the filming of incompetents, and the apparent invasion of rights of the inmates. He had told Wiseman that the film was "impressive in many ways, certainly powerful in impact," but he had hardly termed it "superb," as Wiseman had claimed. Wiseman represented that he had releases from everyone shown in the film. Richardson considered that Wiseman had double-crossed the Commonwealth both by not observing the conditions of the permission to film and, during exploration of possible compromises, by arranging behind the Commonwealth's back for showings of the film at film festivals and its commercial distribution by Grove Press.[58]

Eight days of legislative hearings provided a forum for debate over the conduct of the state officials who had granted permission to film and of Wiseman, who had run with it. The commission, however, had no power to adjudicate, and while the hearings were going on *Commonwealth v. Wiseman* was scheduled by the superior court as the first case out for trial on November 20. The hearings concluded without action, leaving the field to the courts.

Grove Press

Attorney General Richardson referred to Hanify and me the House resolution for petitions to the federal agencies and suit in the federal court. We sent the resolution on to the agencies, both of which, not unexpectedly, declined to act. The Federal Communications Commission pointed out that it was prohibited by federal law from censoring broadcast material.

In calling on the attorney general to seek a cease and desist order in the federal courts, the House presumably had in mind an action against Grove Press in the U.S. District Court for the District of Massachusetts, sitting in Boston. The resolution was not law—it had not been passed by the state Senate or signed by the governor. But it was a recommendation that we had to consider.

The only way to get into the federal court was to invoke its "diversity of citizenship" jurisdiction—its availability to resolve issues between citizens of different states. (By law, the Commonwealth was deemed a citizen of Massachusetts and Grove Press, a New York corporation, a citizen of New York.) The Commonwealth could sue Grove, singly, in the federal court in Boston. To include Wiseman as a defendant would destroy diversity since he was a Massachusetts resident. We would then have to juggle two suits at the same time—one against Wiseman and Grove in the state court and the other against Grove in the federal court. Upon filing against Grove in the federal court, we would be subject to the luck of the draw. There was one chance in five that the case would be drawn to Judge Wyzanski, who would then be in a position to decide our fate. Assuming we dodged this bullet, there was still no reason to suppose we would fare better with the other federal district court judges than we would in the Superior Court of the Commonwealth.

We had to reject the federal court program of the Massachusetts House and continue with the course we had chosen. Our judgment that we should stay where we were was soon confirmed by a Grove Press effort to remove our superior court action to the federal court on supposed "federal question" grounds. We were fortunate that the removal was drawn by Judge Frank Ford, the best of judges. I moved to remand the action, Judge Ford allowed the motion, and Grove was quickly back in the Suffolk Superior Court.

Now that we had all our eggs in the superior court basket, everything turned on whether Grove Press would obey the preliminary injunction that the court had entered October 16 against exhibition of the film. Before the preliminary injunction had been issued, Grove Press had placed *Titicut Follies* at New York City's Cinema 57 Rendezvous for a run until November 3. Arguably, Grove had no legal right to stop showings before that date. If it distributed the film to another theater *after* November 3, however, it would clearly violate the injunction. If the superior court had jurisdiction to issue the injunction, Grove would be in trouble. Although a New York court might not be enthusiastic about enforcing a Massachusetts ban that had been previously refused in New York, it would be under pressure to stick up for the system. Conduct in defiance of injunctions is not good for promoting the rule of law. For Grove to stake everything on proving that the Massachusetts injunction was void for lack of jurisdiction would be a gutsy move.

As it turned out, when the Cinema 57 engagement expired, Grove Press flinched. It decided against ignoring the Massachusetts injunction and risking failure to prove that the court had lacked jurisdiction. It entered a plea in abatement in the superior court asserting that the court lacked jurisdiction and asked the superior court to rule on the issue. Pending a decision, however, it discontinued showing of *Titicut Follies.* Since jurisdiction depended on the extent of Grove's business in Massachusetts, I scheduled depositions of Grove's officers, filed interrogatories, and demanded that Grove produce records on its Massachusetts activities—agents, advertising, sales, and other jurisdictional facts.

By its plea in abatement, Grove Press had committed itself to litigate the issue of jurisdiction in Massachusetts. But when it was hit with our discovery moves, Grove refused to comply with the rules. It ignored all the Commonwealth's requests for information, disobeyed superior court orders that it comply with discovery requirements, and was eventually defaulted on all issues. So that the dealings with Grove would not delay trial on the merits, I had the Grove side of the case temporarily severed from the Wiseman side. Grove continued to observe the injunction, however, which was what mattered to us. In effect, Grove retired for the time being from the field, leaving it to Wiseman to contest the ban and defend the action alone. Grove would lie low until the dust had settled.

The victory over Grove Press may not have been entirely due to the calls of its adversaries. At about this time, Grove had taken on another, potentially more lucrative, cause—that of the allegedly pornographic film, *I Am Curious-Yellow*. By promoting this film, Grove involved itself in defending criminal prosecutions and civil suits to enjoin the film everywhere that the film was offered for exhibition.[59] A member of the team that oversaw Grove's litigation strategy reports that Grove would arrange with the civil liberties lawyers that their fees would be paid out of box-office proceeds from the film once they had succeeded in freeing up the film for showing. This source also tells us that before Grove finally lost a squeaker in the Supreme Court, *I Am Curious-Yellow* had grossed more than $8 million.[60] Grove probably chose to concentrate its resources on the film likely to yield the highest return and to avoid litigating simultaneously on two film fronts.

Grove Press did make a parting contribution to the Wiseman side by beating back an independent effort to enjoin the film. Unbeknownst to Hanify and me, four Bridgewater corrections officers had hired counsel to attack *Titicut Follies* themselves. Just as the Commonwealth was exiting from the New York state courts licking its wounds, the guards were applying in a New York federal court—the U.S. District Court for the Southern District of New York—for a preliminary injunction against showings of the film. Their case, *Cullen v. Grove Press*, relied on a 1903 New York statute that prohibited use "for the purposes of trade" of the picture of a living person "without having first obtained the written consent of such person."[61] The guards' action seemed to fit with the literal language of the New York statute, the nation's first statute announcing a right of privacy.

There was much more behind the New York statute, however, than met the eye. Because its broad language would have prevented a picture of someone who was newsworthy, it was unconstitutional as written and the New York courts had been obliged to narrow it by judicial interpretation in order to save it. Among other things, they had ruled that truth was a complete defense to actions under the statute based on reports of newsworthy people or events.

The U.S. Supreme Court in 1966 had reviewed an award under the New York statute for portraying a New York family in a false light. James Hill and his family had been held hostage in their home by three escaped convicts. A family held hostage by convicts had later been the subject of a book and finally of a play, and the story as retold took on features not present in the Hill episode, including a beating and sexual misbehavior. Reporting on the play, *Life* magazine had published an article saying that the play was a reenactment of the experience of the Hills. The Hills had sued under the New York statute, claiming that they had been portrayed by the article in a false light—that they had not been beaten or mistreated—and they recovered modest damages. It was not clear that the Hill jury had found the falsity in the *Life* article deliberate. The Supreme Court vacated the award on the ground that the Hills could recover damages only by proving that statements in the magazine's article were false and had been made with knowledge of their falsity or in reckless disregard of the truth.[62] This decision would become a rock against which many libel actions brought against the nation's newspapers and magazines have since crashed.

The complaint in *Cullen v. Grove Press* alleged that *Titicut Follies* portrayed the guards in a false light and that the nudity of the inmates was out of order. The contention of the guards according to the federal court was

> that the display of inmates' nudity in the film was unnecessary to any public interest involved, and that the film does not give a true and balanced impression of conditions at Bridgewater but distorts conditions thereby emphasizing the bizarre and

> failing to show other aspects that would explain the scenes that are portrayed and thus put them in proper context.[63]

The guards had no standing, however, to assert the rights of *inmates*. The guards could complain only of how *they themselves* had been portrayed, and, on this score, they had fared no worse than the Hills. When they offered no proof of knowing or reckless falsity or of distortion adversely affecting them, the court denied an injunction. The plaintiffs "fail to anticipate or meet the teachings of *Time, Inc. v. Hill*," it observed. First Amendment rights governed. "The conditions in public institutions such as Bridgewater for the care of the criminally insane . . . are matters which are of great interest to the public generally."[64]

Cullen v. Grove Press would be cited against us in every stage of our litigation. Wiseman forces would argue for an interpretation of *Cullen* that the only basis for enjoining *Titicut Follies* was evidence that the scenes depicted were knowingly false. Recognizing the possibility of such a misreading, the *Cullen* court, however, had concluded its opinion by saying that its decision "does not, of course, constitute an adjudication of rights of non-parties, such as individual inmates claiming violation of their own personal rights or state officials suing for breach of contract, if any, with respect to conditions for exhibition of the film."[65] This reservation took most of the bite out of the court's opinion, but *Cullen* still added to the number of wins chalked up by promoters of *Titicut Follies*.

Wiseman Defenses

Since October 23, when *Commonwealth v. Wiseman* had been assigned a November trial date, every waking moment of the Hanify-Caner team had been devoted to getting ready. The "Answer of the Respondents Wiseman and Bridgewater Film Company" to the Commonwealth's bill in equity came in from Hale and Dorr, spelling out the positions of the Wiseman side. It was no surprise that Wiseman was denying the Commonwealth's right of approval. "At no time," the answer alleged, "was there any agreement that the finished film could not be shown without the prior approval of the petitioner Gavin, the petitioner Gaughan, or any other representative of the Commonwealth."[66] It was further claimed that there had been only one condition of filming:

> The respondents say that the only condition imposed by the petitioner Gaughan was that a member of the staff of the M.C.I. Bridgewater was to accompany the photographers at all times and that no patient or inmate would be photographed unless a member of the staff of the M.C.I. gave permission for such photographing, any decision as to the competency of such patient or inmate to consent to such photographing being left entirely to the discretion of a member of the M.C.I. staff.[67]

A gloss on this defense at the trial would be that guard noninterference implied state permission both to film the scene and to include it in the ultimate product.

On the subject of releases, Wiseman alleged that he had "obtained written releases from many, but not all of the persons shown in the film." His actions, however, were claimed to have been purely voluntary: "And further answering . . . the respondents say that such releases were obtained on the initiative of the respondent Wiseman, without any obligation on his part to obtain written releases from anyone."[68]

To the Commonwealth's allegation that "the film clearly and identifiably shows mentally incompetent inmates," the response was that "the respondents have no knowledge as to the truth of the allegations . . . and call upon the petitioners to prove the same to the extent material."[69]

The Commonwealth's allegation that the film "was an unwarranted intrusion upon the right to privacy of the individual inmates" was answered by the assertion: "The respondents . . . say that no inmate of the M.C.I. Bridgewater has any privacy or any right of privacy, by reason of the conditions and circumstances under which the inmates exist, and as a matter of law."[70] The inmates were apparently fair game.

The Wiseman side repeated its charge that the real motive behind the suit was the suppression of information on conditions at Bridgewater:

> The respondents further say . . . that the petitioners desire to prevent the disclosure of conditions at the M.C.I. Bridgewater to prevent embarrassment to the petitioners, and not in the interests of the inmates; and that the primary concern of the petitioners in this case is to preclude the public from being informed as to the conditions which the petitioners have caused or permitted to exist at the institution . . . .[71]

(The "petitioners" were the Commonwealth of Massachusetts, Commissioner John A. Gavin, and Charles W. Gaughan. Gaughan sued as superintendent of MCI Bridgewater and also as court-appointed guardian of an inmate who was featured nude and raving in the film.)

Wiseman's answer set up his last-ditch defense that any right of prior approval he had agreed to was unenforceable because in derogation of the constitutional right of freedom of speech:

> If there ever was any agreement pursuant to which the respondent Wiseman was to secure the approval of the . . . Commonwealth of Massachusetts before the showing of the film . . . such agreement was and is void and unenforceable as being contrary to public policy, contrary to the interests of the public in being informed of the conditions shown in the film, and in derogation of the constitutional rights of

> freedom of speech and freedom of the press.[72]

The battle over the facts would be won or lost in the next few weeks of trial; the battle over constitutional law would have to be fought anew in each court as the parties mounted the judicial ladder.

Judge Kalus

Superior Court Justice Harry Kalus, who had been assigned to try the case, had been a state representative, legislative counsel to former Governor Maurice J. Tobin, and a state district court judge before being appointed by Governor Volpe to the superior court. He was a solid, no-nonsense judge. Because the Commonwealth was seeking an injunction "in equity" rather than money damages, the trial would be to him alone; there would be no jury. After the trial was over, Judge Kalus would have the job of making written findings of fact and conclusions of law. His findings of fact would stand unless they could be shown to be "clearly erroneous." There would be no presumption on appeal as to the correctness of his legal conclusions, but their reception by higher courts would be affected by the strength of the underlying factual foundation.

The trial began on November 20, 1967. I had the great pleasure of trying the case in company with Ed Hanify, a skilled trial lawyer and a wise and considerate partner. Judge Kalus viewed the film, Hanify opened for the Commonwealth, I called

Commissioner Gavin as our first witness, and we were on our way. We would follow with Superintendent Gaughan; Edward Pacheco, Wiseman's principal escort at Bridgewater; David Eames, Wiseman's associate producer; a dozen Bridgewater corrections officers (guards); Attorney General Richardson; and two Bridgewater psychiatrists. The defense would rely on testimony of Wiseman, expert witness opinions on the film's claimed sociological and artistic value, and the First Amendment. There would be 18 days of testimony and two days of closing argument. Documents would include correspondence between Wiseman and state officials, the Brooke opinion, and inmate medical records. The evidence we presented at the trial, underlying the court's ultimate findings,[73] told the following story.

Permission

Wiseman requested permission to make a film at Bridgewater and met with Commissioner Gavin and Superintendent Gaughan on August 11, 1965. By statute and standing rules, visits to MCI Bridgewater and the photographing of prison inmates had always been strictly controlled.[74] The commissioner expressed concern about the competency of patient-inmates at the hospital and their rights to privacy.[75] He told Wiseman that the Department of Corrections would have to have full rights of censorship over the finished product; Wiseman agreed.[76] The commissioner said that he would consider the proposal if Wiseman put it in writing.[77] Wiseman did so in an August 19, 1965, letter addressed to the commissioner (see Appendix III, 4A) in which he began by saying that he was enclosing a statement of the proposed film.[78] Wiseman's letter promised

> No people will be photographed who do not have the competency to give a release. The question of competency would in all cases be determined by the Superintendent and his staff and we would completely defer to their judgment.

The letter further stated that "[t]he film would be made for showing on National Educational Television," with which "I am negotiating for financing."

The statement accompanying the letter represented that "[t]he story of the film would be that of three people"—a life inmate, a youthful offender committed for observation, and a corrections officer. "In showing the day to day activities of these three people, it will be possible to illustrate the various services performed." Several sociology professors and Superintendent Gaughan were listed in the statement as "consultants" on the film. The statement noted that "Bridgewater is a prison for (1) the criminally insane, (2) defective delinquents, (3) alcoholics, (4) narcotics addicts, (5) sexual deviates, (6) juvenile offenders,"[79] but did not suggest that the film would concentrate on the insane. The undertaking not to photograph incompetents implied the contrary.

The commissioner sent the materials on to deputies in his office with a cover memo:

> I am sending each of you a copy of the proposed film that they want to make of Bridgewater. It is understood that this will be financed by some Foundation and be used as an educational film.
>
> It is also understood that nothing will be filmed or included that is not approved by the Dept. of Correction."[80]

The commissioner acknowledged Wiseman's letter and advised that he was exploring "possible civil rights violations and constitutional rights."[81] He ultimately decided against the project and wrote Wiseman that because of "several complications which may arise," he could not permit the filming.[82]

Wiseman did not give up. He contacted his supporter, State Representative Katherine Kane. She arranged a meeting for Wiseman with then Lieutenant Governor Richardson, who thereafter advised the commissioner that he thought a film on Bridgewater could be helpful.[83] The commissioner reconsidered and met again with Wiseman and Superintendent Gaughan.

At this second meeting, on January 28, 1966, the commissioner told Wiseman that if the attorney general (then Edward Brooke) ruled it was within his authority as commissioner, he would allow the filming. The commissioner stipulated that every person who appeared in the film would have to sign a release. A determination of competency of every individual shown in the film would have to be made, and the Department of Correction, represented by the commissioner and superintendent, would have to have full censorship rights after the film was completed. Legal questions such as the validity of releases and the criteria for judging competency would be submitted to the attorney general for decision. The superintendent added that since filming would take several months, decisions on competency would have to be made at the time the film was put together; a corrections officer would accompany the film crew, but he would exercise no censorship function. Wiseman said he agreed to the terms.[84]

The January 28 meeting was not memorialized in writing, but the next step was a letter from the commissioner, cosigned by the superintendent, to Attorney General Brooke requesting his opinion on the authority of the officials to permit the filming[85] and a reply to the commissioner by the attorney general.[86] In his letter to the attorney general, the commissioner described Wiseman's assurances as to releases and competency:

> I have been asked by Frederick Wiseman of Cambridge for permission to make an educational film about M.C.I. Bridgewater. Mr. Wiseman is an attorney and an experienced film-maker. I have told him that I would give him permission to make the film. Provided, however, that the rights of the inmates and patients at Bridgewater are fully protected. Mr. Wiseman has assured me that he will only use the photographs of inmates and patients

> who are legally competent to sign releases and that he will obtain a written release from each inmate and patient whose photograph is used in the film.

The attorney general's reply of March 21 (Appendix III, 4B) quoted verbatim this passage from the commissioner's letter regarding Wiseman's assurances. It continued, "In light of the above you have asked whether you may legally grant Mr. Wiseman permission to make such a film." The attorney general's answer was yes. "There does not appear to be any [law] that a consenting inmate may not be photographed (assuming that such inmate is mentally competent to give his consent)."

At a meeting between Wiseman and Superintendent Gaughan on March 28, the superintendent gave Wiseman a copy of the Brooke opinion and went over it with him.[87] Wiseman read the opinion and noted its recital of his release and competency assurances.[88] He said he was happy with the opinion and could live within it.[89] He never advised the commissioner or the superintendent that he had not given the recited assurances.[90] Wiseman later showed the opinion to his associate producer, David Eames, and told him, "This means we can go ahead with the Bridgewater film."[91] Wiseman retained the opinion, and it was produced from Bridgewater Film Company files at the trial.[92]

Superintendent Gaughan and a group of his key personnel met with Wiseman at Bridgewater on April 6. The superintendent told his staff that Wiseman was going to make an educational television documentary, that he (Gaughan) and the commissioner would have a final right of approval over the use of all material, and that they would exercise their oversight at the cutting-room level because it was impossible for him, as superintendent, to be present throughout the filming process. Wiseman would have to obtain a release from each inmate filmed, and the attorney general would rule on any legal questions. All personnel were to cooperate fully. The superintendent introduced Wiseman who outlined his background in filmmaking and legal medicine and expressed his agreement with the conditions of filming.[93]

Filming

During the spring of 1966, Wiseman shot approximately 80,000 feet of film all over MCI Bridgewater. His cameraman, John Marshall, had telephoto and zoom lenses and could take pictures in any light. Wiseman had a directional microphone, which screened out sounds emanating from directions other than that in which it was pointed. It enabled Wiseman to record conversations that the ear could not pick up.[94] In one of his letters to film festivals, Wiseman stated that he had filmed "with no interference and relatively little consciousness on the part of the people that they were being photographed."[95]

Wiseman and his film crew, Marshall and Eames, were usually escorted around the Bridgewater grounds by Edward Pacheco, regularly a sanitation officer in the hospital's section for alcoholics.[96] Gaughan instructed Pacheco in Wiseman's presence that the film crew should be allowed to film anything they chose because the superintendent and commissioner would edit the film.[97] On a number of occasions when Bridgewater personnel protested subjects of the filming, Wiseman overcame the objections by pointing out that the commissioner and superintendent would have the right to censor the film later on.[98] From the start of filming in April 1966 until the announcement of the Lincoln Center showing in September 1967, Wiseman never gave any indication to the Commonwealth that he would not honor its right of approval.[99]

The process of editing the film footage and converting it into a finished product of about 3,200 feet took a year. On June 1, 1967, after completion of editing but before credits, title, and some sound features were entered, Wiseman showed the film to Superintendent Gaughan.[100] Gaughan "was very surprised at the trend or the new theme that the film had developed, . . . was amazed at that degree of nudity, . . . questioned whether the degree of nudity was legal under state or federal laws, [and also] questioned the representativeness of a number of scenes that were used."[101] He did not approve the film[102] and said it would have to be shown to the attorney general,[103] by then Elliot Richardson.

On June 27, Wiseman showed the film to Attorney General Richardson, accompanied by Assistant Attorney General Frederick Greenman and Superintendent Gaughan. The attorney general asked Wiseman whether he had obtained releases from all the people shown, and Wiseman replied that he had. The attorney general questioned whether these releases would be valid in view of the fact that any consents were obtained before the persons giving them had seen how they would be depicted in the film, and that some of the inmates who were filmed were evidently incompetent. He raised the possibility of obscuring the identities and private parts. He suggested that the lack of explanation of what was being shown made parts of the film misleading, and that this problem might be met by providing an opening statement and subtitles. As the meeting broke up, Richardson said he would have Greenman study the legal problems involved, and Gaughan reminded the Wiseman side that Commissioner Gavin would have to see the film so he could exercise his right of approval.[104]

At Richardson's request, Wiseman showed the film on July 13 to Franklin Flaschner, a special assistant attorney general appointed to study problems at Bridgewater, and to Albert Sachs, a Harvard Law School professor and chairman of the attorney general's Advisory Committee on Civil Rights and Civil Liberties.[105] Superintendent Gaughan followed up his verbal reminder of June 27 with a letter to Wiseman of July 5, 1967: "Let us keep in mind that at some point, the Commissioner will have to be drawn in."[106]

During the summer, unbeknownst to the Commonwealth, Wiseman was soliciting film festivals all over the world to show *Titicut Follies*.[107] He sent applications to events in London, Venice, Moscow, Acapulco, Leipzig, Budapest, Thessalonika, Cork, Edinburgh, Mannheim, West Berlin, San Francisco, and New York City.[108] The film was accepted in August for a fall showing at the Lincoln Center for the Performing Arts, New York City. The Commonwealth got wind of this planned showing a month later.

The scheduled Lincoln Center showing precipitated a meeting on September 21, 1967, in Attorney General Richardson's office. Wiseman was represented by attorneys Gerald Berlin and Harvard Law professor Alan Dershowitz. With Richardson were Greenman and First Assistant Attorney General Levin H. Campbell. At the meeting, Commissioner Gavin protested that he had a right of approval on the film, yet it had not been shown to him. Berlin responded that this was what could happen when an agreement was not put in writing. Campbell read aloud the account of Wiseman's assurances in the Brooke opinion and said that the Commonwealth expected the terms of the permission to be adhered to.

Greenman presented the results of his research—that the film invaded the privacy of the inmates, that some of the inmates shown were clearly incompetent, that the Commonwealth as *parens patriae* of the inmates had a duty to protect them, and that the scheduled public showing would have to be disapproved. Campbell asked for the written releases Wiseman claimed to have obtained, but Dershowitz advised that he saw no reason to produce them since the attorney general considered them invalid.[109] The meeting broke up. Wiseman showed the film to Commissioner Gavin that evening, and the next day the

Commissioner notified Wiseman and Berlin of his disapproval.[110] Wiseman ignored the disapproval and the attorney general's ruling. He went ahead with the proposed New York showing, and the Commonwealth sued.

Releases and Competency

Our proof was tight both that Wiseman had made the release-competency assurances and that he had failed to keep them. His agreement to these conditions was established by his opening letter of August 19, 1965, the repetition of these assurances in the attorney general's opinion of March 21, 1966, his awareness of the opinion and failure to dispute the assurances, and his this-means-we-can-go-ahead advice to his associate Eames.[111] At various times, Wiseman had releases distributed for signature to some of the subjects who had been filmed.[112]

That Wiseman had not carried out his promise to obtain a release "from each inmate and patient whose photograph is used" was undisputed. In his answer to the Commonwealth's bill in equity, he had admitted that he had obtained releases "from many, but not all" of the persons shown in the film.[113] Any releases from the "many" had been procured at the time of the filming and no one, at the time he signed a release, had seen the film or knew how he would be portrayed.[114] No consideration was paid to anyone for his release.[115] Wiseman never offered in evidence any of the releases he claimed to have secured.[116] When Hanify and I began to quantify the "but not all" by proving that there were 62 identifiable people in the film and that no releases had been obtained from the inmates most prominently displayed, Wiseman's attorneys offered a stipulation—that Wiseman had obtained releases from only 11 or 12 inmates shown in the film. We accepted.[117] There was no escaping, therefore, the fact that Wiseman did *not* "obtain a written release from each inmate and patient whose photograph is used in the film." Nor could one avoid the conclusion that Wiseman had knowingly misrepresented the facts to Lincoln Center when he told that organization in a letter of August 18, 1967, that "I have secured releases from those people who are in the film or from their authorized representatives."[118]

As for Wiseman's assurance that he would "only use the photographs of inmates and patients who are legally competent to sign releases," once he focused during the editing process on the inmates in Bridgewater's hospital for the insane, it was inevitable that he would not keep this promise either. One needed only to see the film to recognize that many of the inmates prominently pictured were incompetent. If additional proof were needed, it was provided by opinions of incompetency given by psychiatrists called by the Commonwealth,[119] by similar opinions drawn on cross-examination from expert witnesses called by Wiseman in his defense,[120] by inmate medical records,[121] and by the statement of Wiseman himself in letters he wrote to film festivals during the summer that "*Titicut Follies* is a film about various forms of madness."[122]

Breach of the promise to use only photographs of competent inmates was a subject of the Commonwealth's cross-examination of Wiseman. Hanify began: "Does the film show insane men?" Wiseman could not answer the question. The cross-examination continued with similar questions and a professed inability of the witness to answer them:

HANIFY: Based on your observation and in your judgment, does the film show insane men?

WISEMAN: I don't know what you mean by *insane men*, Mr. Hanify.

COURT: Well, do you say you are not qualified or did not make a judgment as to whether insane men appear in your film?

WISEMAN: My answer, your Honor—I cannot give a yes-or-no answer.

COURT: All right.[123]

Hanify pursued the subject of the incompetency of the inmates; Wiseman continued to take refuge in a claimed inability to apply or understand the vocabulary of mental disease—*incompetency, hallucinating, delusions, psychosis, neurosis, schizophrenia*:

HANIFY: Are there men in the film who are in your judgment mentally incompetent?

ST. CLAIR: Incompetent for what purpose?

COURT: Are you asking me? Your objection is based, I assume, on "competent for what purpose." I am going to let the witness answer. He says he is a lecturer in legal medicine. Is that right?

WISEMAN: I have been.

COURT: Do you understand the term? Is that in the vocabulary of legal medicine—mental competency or mental incompetency?

WISEMAN: It is in the vocabulary, yes, sir . . . I don't know what—the term *mental incompetency* has so many different meanings in so many different kinds of situations that I don't believe I can answer your question, Mr. Hanify.

HANIFY: Are there men in the film who are hallucinating?

ST. CLAIR: I object.

COURT: I will hear you.

ST. CLAIR: I don't think I have offered this witness as a medical expert. He is not a psychiatrist. This question would call for the opinion of a psychiatrist to answer, as I understand the question. Hallucinating is not any legal term with which I am familiar and I don't believe it is a proper question to be addressed to a lay witness.

COURT: He may answer . . . Do you know what the word *hallucinating* means?

WISEMAN: It is one of those words that in my view has so many different meanings that I cannot answer the question . . . I don't have any precise idea what the word *hallucinating* means, Mr. Hanify.

HANIFY: Are there men in the film who are acting under delusions?

WISEMAN: I don't know what the word *delusions* means in the context of your question, Mr. Hanify.

COURT: Do you know what the word *delusions* means as a straight word, without context in the field of psychiatry and/or legal medicine? . . .

WISEMAN: To my knowledge, sir, it is one of those words that is used in many different ways and in many different circumstances and has no fixed meaning.

HANIFY—WISEMAN:

Q. Do you, sir, recognize any difference between sanity and insanity?

A. If you could define for me how you are using those words, Mr. Hanify, I might be better able to answer your question. I can't answer the question as you put it.

Q. Do you know the difference between competency and incompetency?

A. My answer to that question would be the same as the answer to the previous question.

Q. Did you ever hear the term *psychosis* used?

A. I have heard the term used, yes.

Q. Do you know what it means?

A. No, sir.

Q. Did you ever hear the term *neurosis* used?

A. Yes.

Q. Do you know what it means?

A. No, sir.

Q. Did you ever hear the term *schizophrenia* used?

A. Yes, sir.

Q. Do you know what that means?

A. No, sir.[124]

Wiseman's professed inability during cross-examination to cope with the vocabulary of mental illness was hardly owing to a lack of qualifications. His mother had been an administrator of the psychiatry department at the Children's Hospital in Boston. His father had been a lawyer. He was a graduate of Williams College and of the Yale Law School. He had attended the John Jay College of Criminal Justice and had lectured on law at the Boston University Law School. He had been the recipient of a National Institute of Mental Health grant. When pointed in a different direction—supporting the defense of Grove Press in *Cullen v. Grove Press, Inc.*—Wiseman had emphasized his medico-legal background to the New York federal court. He had submitted an affidavit of this background and of an asserted desire to expose conditions in state institutions for the criminally insane. His credentials had been accepted in the opinion dismissing the guards' suit, where the court had said:

> The producer and director of the film, a law school graduate and former teacher of criminal law, psychiatry and legal medicine, has engaged in various research projects involving social science material and the law, including a study (pursuant to a grant from the National Institute of Health) of the relationship between crime and mental illness, and a report for the National Crime Commission dealing with social problems. He asserts under oath that the purpose of "Titicut Follies" was to give the general public a true and objective picture of typical conditions existing in

> many state institutions for the criminally insane, as reflected at Bridgewater. . . .[125]

It would doubtless have come as a surprise to the New York court, the National Institute of Health, and the National Crime Commission to learn that this "former teacher of criminal law, psychiatry, and legal medicine" could not recognize the presence of insane persons in his film of "typical conditions" in an institution for the criminally insane.

Several years later, in the course of defending a civil action for damages brought by guardians of Bridgewater inmates, the Wiseman side returned to the view that the film was indeed "about various forms of madness." One of the Wiseman defenses in that case was that the inmates, being incompetent, would not suffer the mental anguish requisite for payment of damages to victims of an invasion of privacy. Judge Robert Sullivan, who sat on the case, refused to award damages, saying "[t]his court has been asked to place a dollar value on an almost imperceptible change in degree of insanity. Such a task is impossible."[126]

Right of Approval

The documentary evidence did not wholly foreclose Wiseman denials that he had given the Commonwealth a right of approval over the film. Although his initial letter of August 19, 1965 came close—on questions of competency "we would completely defer to [the] judgment" of the superintendent and his staff (see Appendix III, 4A), it did not specify the point at which the judgment or deference would take place. The Gavin memorandum of his first encounter with Wiseman, advising subordinates that "it is also understood that nothing will be filmed or included that is not approved by the Department of Correction,"[127] was an internal department record not sent to Wiseman. Gavin's request for an attorney general opinion had mentioned only the release and competency conditions because Gavin thought these were the ones that presented legal questions.[128] The Gaughan letter to Wiseman of July 5, 1967 "Let us keep in mind that at some point, the Commissioner will have to be drawn in,"[129] had indeed been followed by the showing of the film to the commissioner on September 21, but by this time Wiseman had also scheduled the Lincoln Center showing.

The documents were supplemented, however, by the testimony of many witnesses to Wiseman's oral acknowledgment of the right of approval. Gavin and Gaughan testified to the initial conversations at which it had been agreed that the commissioner and the superintendent would have full rights of censorship over the finished product.[130] Half a dozen persons present at the meeting of key Bridgewater personnel prior to commencement of filming on April 6, 1966, testified to Gaughan's explanation, in Wiseman's presence and with his agreement, that Wiseman would be given *carte blanche* in filming whatever he liked because of the officials' right of approval at the end.[131] Guards testified to incidents in which their protests against filming had been overcome by Wiseman's reminders of this right of approval.[132]

As a practical matter, it would not have been possible for the superintendent to give up his general duties for the period of filming and marry himself to the film crew. Guards such as Pacheco, a sanitation officer, were not qualified to make determinations of competency and informed consent. The right of approval was a natural solution to the competing problems of allowing a private person to film within a state maximum security mental hospital, and, at the same time, protecting the rights of the facility's inmates. It was a means of assuring that the conditions of photographing and informed consent would be met.

The conflict of testimony between Wiseman and all the other witnesses—commissioner, superintendent, many guards—over the right of approval would have to be resolved by the judge. In making his choice, the judge had before him circumstantial evidence additional to the documents and direct testimony. Wiseman had showed the film to Gaughan on June 1, 1967, before it was even fully finished,[133] then to Attorney General Richardson on June 27, and then, at Richardson's request, to Sachs and Flaschner on July 13.[134] These showings to state officials and their timing were consistent with an agreed right of approval and, in the absence of such an arrangement, would have been surprising. Several facts involving Wiseman's cameraman, John Marshall, were significant. Marshall would have been present at the episodes where Wiseman had overcome guard opposition by referring to the Gavin-Gaughan right of approval. Marshall and his wife had resigned their positions in Wiseman's Bridgewater Film Company prior to the Lincoln Center showing in letters stating they were resigning in protest over the proposed showing and the contract with Grove Press.[135] Marshall did not appear as a witness.

Wiseman's claim of inability to answer questions about insanity and incompetency despite his background in teaching legal medicine and his letters to film festivals a few months earlier that his film was "about various forms of madness" was not likely to promote confidence in his testimony generally. Neither was his misrepresentation to Lincoln Center that "I have secured releases from those people who are in the film or from their authorized representatives."

Privacy

Wiseman was not necessarily finished if he was disbelieved and found to have violated agreed terms of the filming. He could lose on the facts, but still win on the law. We had to persuade the court not only that it should affirm a Massachusetts right of privacy, but also that the rights of the Commonwealth and inmates should be enforced in this instance, notwithstanding the clamor of "right to know" enthusiasts who insisted that freedom of speech was a super-right, entitled to precedence over lesser rights of privacy and contract.

At the time of the *Titicut Follies* case, the Massachusetts courts had not yet recognized a right of privacy. The existence of such a right had been first proposed in an 1890 *Harvard Law Review* article co-authored by Louis Brandeis, later a justice of the Supreme Court.[136] The article argued that legal principles behind the common law of England received by the colonies supported a right of privacy that state courts should recognize.

New York appears to have been the first state to entertain a claim of a right of privacy. Ten years after the Brandeis article, the Rochester Folding Box Company advertised the sale of its flour in circulars bearing an unauthorized picture of a comely young lady, Abigail Roberson, to attract attention and promote their flour. Abigail sued for violation of her right to privacy, alleging that her picture had been appropriated and put to public use without her knowledge or consent. She had "been greatly humiliated," she alleged, "by the scoffs and jeers of persons who have recognized her face and picture on this advertisement [so] that she was made sick, and suffered a severe nervous shock, was confined to her bed and was compelled to employ a physician."[137] The defendant demurred, contending that the plaintiff had not stated a case. The trial judge overruled the demurrer, Abigail won a judgment, the New York Appellate Division affirmed, and the Box Company appealed to the New York Court of Appeals.

The court of appeals debated the plaintiff's rights at length. Four judges came down on the side that acknowledgment—creation—of a right of privacy would be judicial legislation—"a step so far outside of the beaten paths of both common law and equity" that it would have to be left to the legislature. Three judges dissented. "That the exercise of the preventive power of a court of equity is demanded in a novel case, is not a fatal objection," the dissenters maintained. "The proposition is . . . an inconceivable one," they protested, "that these defendants may, unauthorizedly, use the likeness of this young woman upon their advertisement as a method of attracting widespread public attention to their wares, and that she must submit to the mortifying notoriety, without right to invoke the exercise of the preventive power of a court of equity."[138]

Inconceivable as the no-right-of-privacy proposition might be to the dissenters, it prevailed. The plaintiff had won over most of the judges who had considered her claim, but she had persuaded only three of seven at the final level of the court of appeals, and thus had lost her case. The next year, 1903, the New York legislature enacted the statute against unauthorized use of a person's picture. It was too late for Abigail, but the statute would be there for the Bridgewater guards.

As time went on, many states gave recognition to the Brandeisian right of privacy, either by statute or by judicial decisions recognizing it as part of state common law. On the federal side, the Ninth Circuit was the first court to hold, in 1963, that the U.S. Constitution conferred a right of privacy that states were forbidden to invade. In *York v. Story*, the court held that the state of California violated a constitutional right of privacy when a police officer of the town of Chino, California, by a subterfuge, took pictures of the plaintiff in the nude and then circulated them within the Chino police department (see Appendix I, Emergence of a Federal Constitutional Right of Privacy). Two years later, in the six disparate opinions of *Griswold v. Connecticut*, the Supreme Court found a right of privacy emanating from the Bill of Rights and the Fourteenth Amendment of the Constitution that prohibited the state of Connecticut from criminalizing the use of contraceptives by a married couple (see Appendix I). These decisions applied only to (mis)conduct by states, but their reasoning supported prohibition of major invasions of privacy by individuals.

In Massachusetts, plaintiffs in several cases had sought to invoke a right of privacy, but the Supreme Judicial Court had refused to rule on the issue because the offenses of which the plaintiffs were complaining were unremarkable.[139] "It will be time enough," the court said in a 1966 case, "to appraise these authorities and to deal with difficult questions presented by the assertion of such a right, when and if we are confronted with some substantial, serious, or indecent intrusion upon the private life of another."[140] Massachusetts thus appeared poised to recognize a right of privacy when a proper case came along. We expected a right of privacy to be declared once the courts were confronted with the indecencies of our case, and we believed that the battle would be fought, not over existence of the right, but over how strongly the courts should support it—whether rights of privacy and contract were outgunned in our situation by the constitutional right of free speech.

Free Speech

The Wiseman defense that the filmmaker's right of free speech overcame contrary rights of contract and privacy rested in part on *Time v. Hill*, the case that had done in the suit of Cullen and the other Bridgewater guards. On the precise issue before it, the decision of the New York federal court in *Cullen v. Grove Press* was undoubtedly correct. The guards claimed that in *Titicut Follies* they had been portrayed in a false light. *Time v. Hill* had held that allegations of falsity could prevail over constitutionally protected free speech only if the statements were false and the defendant could be shown to have known of the falsity or to have proceeded recklessly. The guards could prove neither. Because the essence of both *Time v. Hill* and *Cullen v. Grove Press* was falsity, they were more akin to defamation cases than privacy cases.

Commonwealth v. Wiseman, however, presented a pure right of privacy claim—that there had been, besides a breach of contract, an offensive invasion of private lives. Falsity was not an element of the claim and truth should not be a defense. Just as in *York v. Story* it would have been no defense that the photographs of the plaintiff in the nude were accurate representations, so also in our case it should not be a defense that the portrayals fairly represented inmate physiognomies and episodes. The rule in false-light cases that plaintiffs in such cases must show deliberate falsity had no relevance to the quite different intrusion case presented by *Titicut Follies*.

There was precedent, however, that public interest considerations could sometimes overcome rights of privacy. A formulation of privacy law in the *Restatement of Torts*, an authority used as a national guide of common law, declared that a plaintiff suing for offensive publicity of private matter had to prove that the matter publicized was "not of legitimate concern to the public."[141] The Wiseman side would claim that the display of the inmates as photographed was appropriate and necessary to understanding the institution MCI Bridgewater and deciding what should be done about conditions there. We would reply that the nude bodies and delusions of identifiable prison inmates were not of legitimate concern to the public, that their body parts and aberrations were not public issues, and that the Wiseman claim, carried to its logical conclusion, would justify treating all the inmates as human guinea pigs, subject to exploitation by anyone claiming to be socially motivated. The claim would appeal to some, but it should fail a test of common sense.

In a special note, the *Restatement of Torts* commented that even if a plaintiff met the not-of-legitimate-concern requirement for a right of privacy, "it has not been established with certainty that liability of this nature is consistent with the free-speech and free-press provisions of the First Amendment to the Constitution, as applied to state law, through the Fourteenth Amendment."[142] This disquieting passage reflected the notion of absolutists that free speech was a super-right to which all other rights must bow. We would have to trust that this contention too would fail a test of common sense.

How judges would decide on the *Commonwealth v. Wiseman* issue of privacy and contract versus free speech was likely to turn not on brilliance of argument or legal learning but on the predilections of the particular judges. Would the First Amendment absolutists have the votes? They would gather strength as they mounted the judicial ladder. To win on each rung, we would have to begin by winning the first. And the stronger the findings of facts by the trial court, the easier it would be to overcome the legal defenses at later stages.

The Decision

We completed testimony on December 12. I argued the case for the Commonwealth, and St. Clair argued for Wiseman. There was a lot of ground to cover, and the arguments took two days. Briefs were filed within two weeks, and Judge Kalus rendered a decision on January 4, 1968. He found for the Commonwealth (see Appendix III, 4C).[143] The labors of Hanify and Caner had not been in vain.

The first finding spelled out the conditions laid down to the permission to film. They were:

> (a) ". . . that the rights of the inmates and patients at Bridgewater are fully protected";
>
> (b) that Wiseman ". . . would only use the photographs of inmates and patients who are legally competent to sign releases";

> (c) that Wiseman ". . . will obtain a written release from each patient whose photograph is used in the film"; (the form and content of such release to be submitted to and approved by the Attorney General); and
>
> (d) that the film, after completion, would not be shown or released without first having been viewed and approved by the Commissioner and Superintendent.

(The court's quotes in finding 1 were from the opinion of the attorney general (see Appendix III, 4B).)

The court found that Wiseman had agreed to each of the conditions. Findings 1–4. Following agreement to the conditions, filming began. Wiseman and his crew, the decision continued, "roamed about the Institution . . . taking pictures indiscriminately of mentally incompetent patients in the nude while these persons were in the most personal and private situations." Finding 5. "The film product which Wiseman made . . . constitutes a most flagrant abuse of the privilege he was given to make a film." Finding 7. "The film . . . is a hodgepodge of sequences, with the camera jumping, helter-skelter, from the showing of an inmate in an act of masturbation to scenes depicting mentally ill patients engaged in repetitive, incoherent and obscene rantings and ravings. The film is excessively preoccupied with nudity, with full exposure of the privates of these persons. . . . No amount of rhetoric, no shibboleths of 'free speech' and the 'right of the public to know' can obscure or masquerade this pictorial performance for what it really is—a piece of abject commercialism, trafficking on the loneliness, on the human misery, degradation and sordidness in the lives of these unfortunate humans." Finding 7.

Judge Kalus contrasted the film Wiseman had made with the one he had described to the state officials. According to the statement of the proposed film that Wiseman had submitted at the beginning of his project, the film was to be an "educational documentary" called "The Bridgewater Story," featuring "three people"—a long-time Bridgewater inmate, a youthful offender committed for temporary observation, and a corrections officer. Finding 6.

"The plain import of Wiseman's representations" in the statement "was that his film was to be a non-commercial and non-sensational project, to be financed by one of the national charitable foundations. The film would be in the nature of a public service project. Wiseman's representations completely negated any thought of a commercial film . . . [T]he state officials could under no circumstances have given permission to make any such commercial film." Finding 6.

With *Titicut Follies*, the court said, "gone is the promise of 'The Three People' theme, and in its place is a new theme—crudities, nudities, and obscenities." "Just how such a contrived scenario squares with 'fidelity to truth' is most difficult to conceive." "None of the consultants . . . was ever consulted." The film "received no financial support from any of the national foundations. It was financed, in part, by private investors, for profit." "The film is a nightmare of ghoulish obscenities. It is a crass piece of commercialism—a contrived scenario—designed by its new title and by its contents to titillate the general public and lure them to the box office." Finding 7.

The court ruled that "the film is an unwarranted and illegal intrusion by Wiseman into the lives and right to privacy of each inmate and patient who is pictured there . . . [N]o person, whether mentally competent or not, can be dragooned or indentured into playing the part of an actor in a movie scenario whether as a star or in a supporting role. [The inmates] were virtually forced into exhibition of their nude bodies, and to suffer other indignities for the plain and manifest purpose of profitable box office receipts." Finding 17.

The procedure followed by Wiseman in procuring releases was, the court found, "a sham and a pretense." Finding 14. None of the releases assertedly obtained was produced, they were executed before the actual filming, and the signer never saw the actual film sequence in which he was pictured. Finding 14. Many of the inmates and patients "were, and still are, incompetent to give a release." Finding 9. Wiseman's letter to the Lincoln Center Film Festival stating "I have secured releases from those people who are in the film or from their authorized representatives" was noted. "This statement was not true, and the reference to '*their authorized representatives*' was made out of whole cloth." Finding 11 (emphasis the court's).

The court in findings 17 and 18 gave us all we could have asked to arm ourselves against the defense that Wiseman's free speech right overcame contract and privacy rights. "Many, if not all, of the scenes," it found, "embarrass and degrade these persons in a manner clearly not warranted by any legitimate public concern. . . . Assuming a matter of genuine public interest, and further assuming that the officials had authority to grant permission to make an educational documentary film, there is a heavy responsibility on these officials," the court said, "to protect the basic human rights of the patients and inmates who have been committed to their charge." The inmates at Bridgewater were "entitled to absolute protection against their commercial exploitation in any way for profit or gain. . . . The failure to give the patients such protection would be a most serious dereliction of duty."

The court took on the Wiseman defense that "no inmate of the M.C.I. Bridgewater has any privacy or any right of privacy."[144] "Apparently this contention is based in part on the premise that these inmates, by virtue of their confinement, are bereft of any vestige of personal privacy and human dignity. [Wiseman] says, in substance, that they are now public property and can be displayed as such in a commercial movie." Finding 19. To the contrary, the court declared,

> These patients have an absolute right, subject only to the necessary procedures for internal security, and for their care, custody and treatment, to be left alone. A legal pronouncement that, in the name of free speech, a person may be required, without his approval or agreement, to participate in a commercial, money-making

> movie or any other commercial enterprise would be shocking indeed. The right of the public to know and freedom of speech are not absolutes which, at all events and under all conditions, override the right of privacy. The court rules that the legitimate public interest, freedom of speech, and right of the public to know does not carry with them the unauthorized use of pictures showing persons, clearly identifiable, in such a manner as to outrage and cause mental suffering, shame or humiliation to a person of ordinary sensibilities. Finding 17.

The right-of-approval condition was reasonable and necessary, the court said, to assure that the rights of the inmates were fully protected, the first condition of filming. "The terms and conditions [of filming] including the right of approval to which Wiseman fully agreed, do not constitute 'censorship' in any pejorative sense . . . [They] were necessary precautions and safeguards in order that the State protect the civil and privacy rights of the patients and inmates." (Finding 20). The claim of violation of rights of free speech "is a complete afterthought, and was first raised by Wiseman when the Commonwealth instituted this suit. Wiseman seeks thereby to divert attention (a) from his willful violation of the express agreements he made . . . and (b) from his crass commercialism and venality." Finding 21.

The decision seemed almost too good to be true, a Matterhorn in the hills and valleys of litigation results. Ed Hanify's time as a special assistant attorney general ran out shortly after the decision. I devoted much of the year 1968 to securing a judgment against Grove Press and fencing with Wiseman over sporadic out-of-state showings of the film. After the Grove Press side of the case had been cleaned up, a final decree was entered permanently enjoining all showings of the film and Wiseman appealed.

The Civil Liberties Union of Massachusetts

On appeal, the Commonwealth picked up an ally in the Civil Liberties Union of Massachusetts. At the time of the Special Legislative Commission hearings, CLUM had issued a press release explaining its silence on *Titicut Follies* and implying that it would take a position after the facts had been established:

> The versions as to what actually happened, and under what agreements, are contradictory and confused, and until these facts have been clarified in a dispassionate forum, resolution as to the relative weight to be accorded to competing civil liberties are premature and indeed harmful. This in short is the reason, and the only reason, for the failure of the [CLUM] to add its voice to the hue and cry concerning the film. . . . The decisional process can be entrusted only to the judiciary.[145]

With the superior court decision, a dispassionate forum had spelled out what actually happened and "the relative weight to be accorded to competing civil liberties" could be resolved. The CLUM board designated a leading Boston civil liberties lawyer, Henry P. Monaghan, to file an *amicus curiae* brief with the Supreme Judicial Court in which CLUM supported a modified injunction against the film. The brief argued that if the invasions of privacy were as found by Judge Kalus, then the injunction did not violate the First Amendment, but that the injunction should be narrower. The reservation as to an invasion of privacy was because "the Union has not viewed the film, and it does not assume any conclusions with respect to its character."[146] The brief said that the Supreme Judicial Court must view the film for itself and make its own judgment, independent of the superior court.

The CLUM brief continued that "[s]hould the Court, after viewing the film, conclude that identifiable persons are depicted in a degrading manner (and, thereby, in violation of their constitutional rights), we submit that some adequate relief must be accorded."[147] Indeed CLUM argued, "It is a separate violation of the fourteenth amendment for a state not to provide a remedy to redress a substantive violation of the fourteenth amendment."[148] It rejected the contention of the Wiseman side that the Supreme Court case of *Time v. Hill* foreclosed an injunction where the subject was of public interest. *Time v. Hill* "itself indicates," CLUM argued, "that the Supreme Court would be willing to sanction relief where the invasion outrages accepted standards of human dignity."[149] In such a case, an injunction was in order.

Though CLUM described the injunction it advocated as "limited," its proposed injunction would apply to all public showings. It would be subject to an exception only for showings "to audiences of a specialized, professional character which are intimately concerned with conditions at Bridgewater and where it might fairly be assumed that the destructive impact which exhibition causes to the dignity of the inmates is at a minimum."[150] Though this exception was contrary to the conditions of the permission, Hanify and I had crossed this bridge to a lesser degree in our first court appearance when we invited the superior court to make an exception for the governor and legislature.

Some years after the decision, Wiseman advocates gained the upper hand at CLUM. The Union reversed its position and urged the film be shown. The facts had not changed, but the leadership had.

Appeal

Wiseman's appeal reached the Supreme Judicial Court of Massachusetts in the spring of 1969. I briefed and argued the case for the Commonwealth. The justices saw the film and decided the appeal in six weeks. Justice Ammi Cutter gave the opinion for a unanimous court.

"The Commissioner and the Superintendent," the court noted, "would have acted wisely" if everything had been put in writing.[151] But "we agree with the trial judge that Mr. Wiseman's wide ranging photography amounted to 'abuse of the privilege he was given to make a film' and a serious failure to comply with conditions reasonably imposed upon him." The appellate court agreed with the trial court's ruling of an egregious invasion of privacy. "There is a collective, indecent intrusion into the most private aspects of the lives of these unfortunate persons in the Commonwealth's custody." The state officials, had they known how the film would turn out and be shown, could not have allowed it:

> The Commissioner and Superintendent, under reasonable standards of custodial conduct, could hardly permit merely curious members of the public access to Bridgewater to view directly many activities of the type shown in the film. We think it equally inconsistent with their custodial duties to permit the general public (as opposed to members of groups with a legitimate, significant, interest) to view films showing inmates naked or exhibiting painful aspects of mental disease. See *York v. Story* . . . .

Wiseman must have known, the court declared, that the kind of film he had put together could not be commercially shown. "Mr. Wiseman could hardly have fairly believed that officials, solicitous about obtaining consent and releases from all inmates portrayed, could have been expected to approve this type of film for general distribution."

The Supreme Judicial Court found it unnecessary to consider the finding of a right of approval because it was plain that the fully documented conditions as to releases and competency had not been met. "There was ample basis for concluding that Mr. Wiseman had not fulfilled important undertakings clearly designed to assure that the film would show only those consenting in writing to their appearance in the film and competent to understand and to give such consent." It addressed Wiseman's claim that his failure to meet these conditions should somehow be excused because he assertedly took no pictures of people who objected to being photographed. "Even if . . . no pictures were taken of persons who did object, the requirement of releases from persons competent to give them does not seem to us unreasonable. . . . Indeed, in view of the character of the film, we would not be disposed to give a release (even from an inmate capable of giving one) substantial significance until the inmate giving it had seen the film and fully understood how he was to be portrayed."

The court addressed the defense contention "that no asserted interest of privacy may be protected from the publication of this film because the conditions at Bridgewater are matters of continuing public concern." It answered that presentation of Bridgewater conditions would not "justify . . . the depiction of identifiable inmates, who had not given valid written consents and releases, naked or in other embarrassing situations." No inmate shown "had any special news interest as an individual. . . . Recognizable pictures of individuals . . . were not essential." Free speech rights must yield to the right of privacy:

> In the circumstances, there will be no unreasonable interference with any publication of matters of public concern if showing the film to the general public is prevented (a) to protect interests of the inmates in privacy, and (b) because Mr. Wiseman went unreasonably beyond the scope of the conditional permission to enter, and take pictures upon, State owned premises properly not generally open for public inspection and photography.

"Mr. Wiseman's massive, unrestrained invasion of the intimate lives of these State patients," the court continued, "may be prevented by properly framed injunctive relief." Adopting CLUM's suggested exception, the justices directed that the injunction be modified to permit the showing of the film to "specialized or professional" groups. "The seemingly random and somewhat incoherent sequence . . . of scenes, probably designed to give to the film an impressionistic character, is not likely to confuse seriously interested professional and student audiences."

Wiseman has since been quoted in the *Civil Liberties Review* as claiming that "the Massachusetts Civil Liberties Union never supported the proceedings brought by the Commonwealth of Massachusetts."[152] The falsity of this statement is shown not only by the CLUM brief but also by another Wiseman assertion, also published in the *Review*:

> Despite Berlin's prior involvement, CLUM took a position in the case against the film. On appeal to the Massachusetts Supreme Court they filed an amicus brief written by five people who, to my knowledge, had never seen the film or read the trial transcript. They came up with the Solomon-like solution that I should cut out the faces of the inmates, and that the film should only be seen by audiences made up of limited groups, such as social workers and medical professionals. The latter was essentially what the Supreme Judicial Court decided, and remains the rule for showings in that state. The conditions under which I can show the *Follies* are so restrictive that I have not shown the film rather than comply with the terms of the restraining order. The moral insensitivity and cowardice of CLUM and its chairman were for me the worst part of the *Follies* case. The response of Richardson and most members of the Massachusetts legislature was at least consistent with their general, public, political behavior." [153]

The Commonwealth accepted the court's specialized groups exception without enthusiasm, fearing complications of administration and that it might undermine the basic injunction. As the quoted passage indicates, it turned out that Wiseman scorned the modification, continued to insist that he should be able to exhibit the film commercially to the general public, and for some time did not promote showings to specialized groups. The exception thus proved not to be a problem. Moreover, it probably worked in our favor at the next stage of the litigation—fighting off adverse action by the Supreme Court.

United States Supreme Court

After losing in the Supreme Judicial Court of Massachusetts, Wiseman re-enlisted Professor Alan Dershowitz to prepare a petition for a writ of certiorari to the Supreme Court of the United States. There was no absolute right to be heard; the case would be considered by the Supreme Court only if chosen by the Court for review.

The Supreme Court grants certiorari in less than 1 percent of the cases that apply for it. *Commonwealth v. Wiseman*, however, presented unique features making it an unusually strong candidate for Supreme Court review. Except for a very few films then banned for obscenity, *Titicut Follies* was the only film we knew of in the United States that was currently under injunction. "Prior restraint" of books and films always receives special appellate scrutiny and seldom survives. *Titicut Follies* also presented a classic conflict between important rights. The Supreme Court had noted in *Time v. Hill*, but had not passed on, the issue of whether "revelations . . . so intimate and so unwarranted . . . as to outrage the community's notions of decency [may] be constitutionally proscribed."[154] Had the Supreme Court exhausted itself on privacy issues in its extended *Griswold v. Connecticut* debate? (See Appendix I). If the Supreme Court took on our case, we would have to win the battle with Wiseman all over again.

Wiseman's petition for certiorari argued that because the film was of public interest, he had a constitutional right under the First Amendment to show it, notwithstanding the portrayals of the inmates and the violation of the terms of the permission to make it. "If the decision below is permitted to stand, it will represent the first instance in the history of this nation in which the Supreme Court has permitted a state to censor and suppress a film of conceded social value," the petition trumpeted, "the first case in which speech on a public issue has been banned for alleged violation of privacy or of a contract."[155] The familiar charge was repeated that the state was simply trying to suppress embarrassing conditions at Bridgewater. "Of course in reality it is not the privacy of the inmates of the Bridgewater institution," the petition announced, "but the privacy of the Commonwealth of Massachusetts and its officials, which is protected by the decision below."[156]

The petition for certiorari managed for its first 24 pages to avoid mentioning that the film portrayed incompetent prisoner-patients of the state nude, revealing confidences, hallucinating, and displaying other extreme mental aberrations. The petitioner's difficulty in grappling with the real reason the

Commonwealth had sued was also shown by the modest acknowledgment that finally appeared on page 25 of the petition:

> The film here in issue consists in part of scenes in which inmates of the Bridgewater prison who manifest indications of mental disturbances are shown. A few very brief scenes show inmates who are naked or only partially clothed. Such scenes are an integral and essential part of the film . . . .

This description contrasted with the findings of the Superior Court that the film jumps "from the showing of an inmate in an act of masturbation to scenes depicting mentally ill patients engaged in repetitive, incoherent and obscene rantings and ravings. The film is excessively pre-occupied with nudity, with full exposure of the privates . . ." and of the Supreme Judicial Court that the film was a "massive unrestrained invasion of the private lives of these state patients." The Wiseman rendition would stand only until the Supreme Court Justices saw the film themselves or reviewed the findings of the judges who had.

I filed an opposition to the petition describing the actual film content, giving the facts of the case, assembling authorities that First Amendment rights were not absolute, arguing that an injunction was the only way to protect the rights of the wards of the Commonwealth, and concluding that the Massachusetts courts had properly held the filmmaker to the terms of the permission to film; hence review was unnecessary.

The Supreme Court in passing on certiorari considers the importance of the case, any conflict with other cases, the need for establishing a definitive precedent, the apparent correctness of the decision rendered below, and the demands of competing certiorari applications. Under the unwritten "Rule of Four," Wiseman's petition for certiorari would be granted if four justices voted in favor.

Chief Justice Warren had just retired. We were probably fortunate in his replacement by Chief Justice Burger. We feared that Justices Douglas and Brennan would vote for certiorari and that they might be joined by Justices Harlan and Marshall. The newly appointed Justice Blackmun was an unknown quantity. How Justice Black would vote on Wiseman's petition was a particularly close speculation. Justice Black seldom missed an opportunity to expatiate on the importance of unrestricted free speech. One example: "Freedom to speak and write about public questions is as important to the life of our government as is the heart to the human body."[157] He questioned generally recognized free speech exceptions—for deliberate defamation, obscenity, and "fighting words."[158] In the Pentagon Papers case a year away, he would affirm that "the press must be left free to publish news, whatever the source, without censorship, injunctions, or prior restraints"[159] and would take the extreme, if not irrational, position that a court should not even enjoin a publication which threatens national security:

> The word "security" is a broad, vague generality whose contours should not be invoked to abrogate the fundamental law

> embodied in the First Amendment. The guarding of military and diplomatic secrets at the expense of informed representative government provides no real security for our Republic.[160]

Justice Black did, however, recognize some limits to free speech. In a case where the court majority permitted union picketing on a grocery store's privately owned pickup zone, Justice Black dissented. He would have sustained the employer's property right against the employees' asserted right of speech. "I think that . . . the lower court's injunction is valid under the First Amendment and that petitioners cannot, under the guise of exercising First Amendment rights, trespass on respondent Weis' private property for the purpose of picketing."[161]

How Justice Black would view *Titicut Follies* seemed to depend on whether he saw the Commonwealth's effort to block the invasion of the inmates' rights of privacy as analogous to a grocery store's right to keep trespassers off its property, or as a life-threatening assault on freedom to comment on public questions. How he would come out was anybody's guess.

The Supreme Court on June 15, 1970, denied the petition for certiorari. Court action rejecting petitions for certiorari is normally reported in one word, "Denied," without any statement of reasons, debate, or identification of who voted or how. In our case, however, the notice to the parties from the Court contained four announcements and a dissenting opinion. "The petition for a writ of certiorari is denied. Mr. Justice Douglas is of the opinion that certiorari should be granted. Mr. Justice Harlan, with whom Mr. Justice Brennan joins, dissents. Mr. Justice Marshall took no part in the consideration or decision of this petition."

The Harlan opinion dissenting from denial of certiorari declared that the film was "at once a scathing indictment of the inhumane conditions that prevailed . . . and an undeniable infringement of the privacy of the inmates filmed." It went on:

> The balance between these two interests, that of the individual's privacy and the public's right to know about conditions in public institutions, is not one that is easily struck. . . . I fail to see how, on a complex and important issue like this, it can be concluded that this Court should withhold plenary review. . . . I am at a loss to understand how questions of such importance can be deemed not "certworthy."[162]

Most of Justice Harlan's colleagues apparently disagreed: possibly they recognized the decision was right and should not be disturbed. By a process of elimination, Chief Justice Burger and Justices Black, Blackmun, Stewart, and White must have voted to deny certiorari. No reason was given as to why Justice Marshall had recused himself or why Justice Douglas did not join the Harlan dissent. At the time, it did not matter to us. On a 5-to-3 vote, with one abstention, we had prevailed.

But Wiseman was not through. Professor Dershowitz filed a petition for rehearing. He noted that Justice Marshall had not participated, although "so far as the petitioners are aware, he is not disqualified for any reason from participation in the matter." Since three justices had voted for the certiorari petition, "presumably the writ would have been granted if one additional justice had so voted."[163] This was more a complaint than an argument. It got no rise out of Justice Marshall, who continued in the role of a nonparticipant and never explained his inaction. Entitlement to a rehearing was claimed to rest on the (tenuous) ground that inmate guardians had just filed civil actions against Wiseman for damages.

Petitions for rehearing are not favored. Under Supreme Court rules, the respondents to such a petition (the Commonwealth and its officials in this instance) were not to reply to it unless specially directed to do so by the Court. I was soon shaken, however, by receiving just such an order. "The respondents are requested to file within 30 days a response to the petition for rehearing."[164] This "request" was ominous. What was going on? In my response I protested that the denial had been correct and should stand.

Surprisingly, the Supreme Court did reconsider. Even more surprising, Justice Blackmun changed sides. Blackmun had been on the Court only seven days when he first voted on certiorari, with the majority. The second time around he joined Justices Harlan and Brennan, who continued to vote for certiorari. (Had the Wiseman forces received a signal that this might happen?) Justice Douglas, however, at this point recused himself! We later learned that Grove Press's magazine, *Evergreen Re-*

view, had been running portions of Douglas's latest book, *Points of Rebellion*, in serial form. Douglas had been about to sit on two obscenity cases involving *I Am Curious-Yellow*, in which Grove Press was a party. Excerpts from *Points of Rebellion* in *Evergreen Review*, with pictures of nude women a few pages away, had been displayed on the floor of the U.S. House of Representatives. Threats of impeachment had been made on grounds of conflict of interest. Douglas had felt the heat and had withdrawn from participation in the *I Am Curious-Yellow* cases.[165]

Grove Press, of course, was a party in *Commonwealth v. Wiseman* as well. Yet Justice Douglas had passed on the petition for certiorari in our case, voting for the Wiseman-Grove Press side. When the Wiseman petition came up a second time, however, he conformed to his *I Am Curious-Yellow* recusal. Possibly he had become sensitized to the conflict just after the order that the Commonwealth respond to the petition for rehearing. The withdrawal of Justice Douglas left Wiseman still one vote short of certiorari.[166] The petition for rehearing was denied.[167] We had survived the Supreme Court.

Epilogue

The superior court entered a modified injunction reflecting the exception for specialized groups ordered by the Supreme Judicial Court. Wiseman appealed once again and I stayed on as an assistant attorney general to deal with the appeal. The final decree as approved permanently enjoined any showing of the film except to specialized groups and had no termination date. I resigned as a special assistant on March 7, 1972, and the case was thereafter the responsibility of regulars in the attorney general's office.

The injunction was to stand for 25 years. Wiseman would seek at intervals to have it vacated, but would be rebuffed. In time, many of the personalities involved in the film—officials and inmates—passed on. By 1987, the then attorney general of the Commonwealth, James Shannon, was leaving support for continuation of the injunction to lawyers for guardians of the Bridgewater inmates. In 1989 Superior Court Judge Andrew Meyer ordered that the film could be shown if the faces of the inmates were blurred so as to be unrecognizable.[168] The ruling was scornfully received by Wiseman and never acted upon. In 1991 Judge Meyer dissolved the injunction, saying that "as each year passes, the privacy issue of this case is of less concern to the court than the prior restraint issue. I am now convinced that the scales have tipped in favor of an unrestricted showing."[169] Wiseman was free to market his film, but it had lost its principal draw—our ban!

Chapter 5

Three Years of Judicial License to Infringe the "Boston Marathon" Name

Interest in the Boston Athletic Association's annual Boston Marathon starts to build in March. In the March before the 1986 Marathon, BAA President Frank Swift came to me with bad news. The market for our "Boston Marathon" T-shirts has been suddenly swamped with counterfeits, he told me. The rogue shirts undersell the shirts of our licensee Image Impact because the counterfeiters are paying nothing for use of our "Boston Marathon" name and the quality of their shirts is second rate. Image is making few sales and the BAA is getting no royalties. We have to do something.

Marketing Garments Under the "Boston Marathon" Name

Earlier that year, developments in the running world had led to a decision to market, for the first time, "Boston Marathon" T-shirts. An American win of the 1972 Olympic Marathon by Frank Shorter had heightened interest in United States road running, and Boston Marathon fields had increased from hundreds in the early 1970s to thousands in the 1980s. By 1986, managing a race of 10,000 runners and cleaning up behind a million spectators along the route had become a major operation. The BAA faced demands that it contribute to meeting the expenses of the eight cities and towns through which the Boston Marathon made its way.

Throughout its history, the Boston Marathon had been an amateur event. Anyone prepared to pay the $5 entry fee could enter, and the prize for winning was a laurel wreath and a bowl of beef stew. But times had changed. Professionals were competing in the Olympics, and the governing body of U.S. track and field had authorized cash prizes for "amateur" runners that would be paid into "trust funds." The money directed to an athlete's trust could be passed on to the athlete at a later date.

The Boston Marathon had just been blessed by the appearance of a new angel in the form of John Hancock Insurance Company, but the BAA still needed to be self-sufficient. In January 1986, the BAA had given an exclusive license to Image Impact, Inc., to market garments under the "Boston Marathon" name.

Under federal and Massachusetts statutes, registered trademarks enjoy special protections. An early Ropes & Gray project after Edward Hanify and I had taken on restoring the race to the BAA by invalidation of the agreement of sale made by BAA President William Cloney with Marshall Medoff (see Chapter 2) had been to register the names "Boston Marathon" and "BAA Marathon." Evidence had been submitted to state and federal trademark authorities that the names were understood by the public as referring to the race conducted since 1897 annually on Patriot's Day by the Boston Athletic Association. Certificates of registration had been issued in 1983. The registration of the names was by law prima facie evidence of the BAA's exclusive right to their commercial use. The Boston Marathon thus joined many other sporting events with familiar registered names, among them "Super Bowl," "Kentucky Derby," "Head of the Charles," "America's Cup," "Final Four," "Wimbledon," and "U.S. Open." It would be ruled in ensuing litigation that "the names 'Boston Marathon' and 'BAA Marathon' are the BAA's most valuable and important asset."[170]

It was a fact, however, that since the late 1970s, local merchants had been in the field selling T-shirts and other garments under the "Boston Marathon" name without BAA permission. But immersed in litigation with Medoff over ownership of the race, the BAA had put off taking on the infringers and enforcing its right to exclusive use of its name. In legal parlance, it had "slept" on its rights.

Past tolerance of the misappropriation of the name "Boston Marathon" was not thought at first to be a major problem. Under trademark law, acquiescence in past infringements prevented a name owner from complaining about the past, but it did not forfeit the owner's rights as to the future. The National Football League and Major League Baseball made a practice of granting exclusive licenses for the use of team names and logos on merchandise, and collected royalties on the sales. The New York Road Runners Club, which staged the New York Marathon annually in the fall, was profiting from the sale of "official" merchandise, particularly T-shirts, with the "New York Marathon" name imprinted on them. The BAA hoped to do likewise and that the courts could deal with any infringers.

BAA Adversaries

A trip to Washington Street in downtown Boston confirmed that street merchants there were indeed offering T-shirts that either tracked the "Boston Marathon" name *in haec verba* or featured a similar name (see Appendix III, 5A). For example, one offering bore the imprint "1986 Marathon" with the words "Hopkinton-Boston" underneath. The meaning and message—celebration of the race—was the same as that of an Image Impact "Boston Marathon" T-shirt, but the "Boston Marathon" name was split and reordered. Another had the imprint "Runnin' Marathon '86" followed by a sketch of a runner. Image Impact confirmed that such shirts were ubiquitous elsewhere.

Further investigation revealed that the merchandise came in part from an underground T-shirt industry that made a business of copying names of sports events and figures, flooding the market with counterfeit shirts just before an event or appearance, staying ahead of process servers, and disappearing when courts finally went into action. One would not expect these professional counterfeiters to attempt a defense in court; their success depended on getting the merchandise out on the street and sold before trademark owners could react and get effective judicial sanctions.[171] We could probably deal with this element through judicial seizure orders once a complaint was filed.

More of a problem were "Boston Marathon" garments being marketed under claim of right by the local merchants. Having for years sold merchandise with "Boston Marathon" indicia and having gotten away with the practice, they had come to view it as their right, just as a confirmed trespasser over time might consider his trespasses to have metamorphosed into a right.[172] The merchants had ignored the BAA's notice of Image Impact's exclusive rights and now challenged us to enforce them. The BAA would have to face off against this element in court.

Loss Number 1: The Suffolk Superior Court Denies a Preliminary Injunction

In a courtroom was the last place the BAA wanted to be. The superior court judge who had heard the BAA case against Marshall Medoff personally had just decided against the BAA on highly questionable grounds. The decision that Medoff could keep sponsor revenues he had scooped from his insolvent company IMI had robbed the BAA of any benefit from its success in the trial by jury (chapter 2, end). Besides this illustration of the hazards of litigation, some of the cases in the trademark field were not reassuring (see Appendix II, T-shirt Insignia

Trademark Law). But the BAA had no private army to enforce its rights and there was no alternative to resort once again to the courts.

On April 1, 1986, I filed a complaint for the BAA against six named defendants and various "John Does"—unidentified makers of various infringing T-shirts. For what then seemed to be sufficient reasons, I had opted for the state judicial system and the Suffolk Superior Court, rather than the equally available federal system. The court issued an ex parte seizure order for unauthorized shirts bearing the "Boston Marathon" mark and set April 11 as the date for hearing the BAA's application for a preliminary injunction against the infringements. Because of uncertainty as to how the court would rule at the hearing, I made only one seizure.

The courtroom on April 11 was packed with T-shirt entrepreneurs and their supporters. The professional counterfeiters made no appearance; they were lying low, waiting to see what would happen. Lawyers for the local merchants did appear and hotly opposed the injunction. I submitted evidence of the BAA's ownership and registration of "Boston Marathon" and a memorandum of trademark law. I argued that the BAA was entitled to an injunction halting infringements of its "Boston Marathon" name pending trial of the case on the merits. Defense counsel protested that their clients had used the "Boston Marathon" name for years without objection, claimed that through BAA acquiescence and inaction their clients had acquired prescriptive rights, and contended that it would be unfair for the defendants to lose the sales of the 1986 season without a trial. Sellers of T-shirts with close but nonidentical imprints argued dissimilarity. Others maintained that oral permission for their client's particular imprint had been given by BAA members.

There was an answer to each defense. The BAA's ownership of the name and its meaning was established by history and prima facie by registration. A necessary element of the acquiescence defense—prejudice to the defendants from the plaintiff's conduct—was not present. No BAA officer or member had authority to authorize use of the "Boston Marathon" name by any defendant.

The most plausible of the defenses was the claim of dissimilarity by merchants who had selected imprint wordings such as "1986 Marathon—Hopkinton-Boston." Most trademark cases involve a name designed by the defendant to be similar enough to the trademark to share its drawing power, but sufficiently dissimilar to provide a respectable defense in court. One case aptly describes the objective of the more subtle infringer: "to appropriate the good will and good name of the [plaintiff], while maintaining just sufficient a distinction between the marks to confuse, if possible, both the public and the courts."[173]

Until the 1988 decision of federal judge William Young against the BAA, which we will come to, every authority recognized that a trademark owner was entitled to protection not only against use of the owner's exact mark but also against use of any similar mark.[174] Both the federal and the Massachusetts trademark statutes imposed liability for deceptive use of "any reproduction, counterfeit, copy, or *colorable imitation* of a [registered] mark."[175] Under established law and these statutes, the question was whether "1986 Marathon—Hopkinton-Boston" was a colorable imitation of the "Boston Marathon" mark and thus likely to lead purchasers mistakenly to believe that the shirt was official merchandise, approved by the sponsor of the Boston Marathon. The merchant's T-shirt legend undoubtedly had been designed to imply such sponsorship, but to leave counsel some wiggle room if the seller was taken to court.

The superior court judge sitting on the injunction application, George C. Keady, Jr., took as a way out an asserted absence of irreparable harm to the BAA if an injunction was denied. "Since the BAA has never sought to enforce [its trademark] rights prior hereto, one more year of no enforcement by injunctive relief will not, it seems to the court, irreparably harm it." He ruled on the other hand, that issuance of an injunction would cause the defendants "irreparable harm":

> Conversely for a preliminary injunction to issue against the defendants will cause them irreparable harm. Most of them now have on their hands considerable product which on April 22, 1986, will rival in uselessness yesterday's newspaper.[176]

This finding, presumably of irreparable *legal* harm, wrongly assumed that the defendants had a lawful interest entitled to protection. The "useless" product, however, was the *infringing* merchandise that the defendants should not have been selling in the first place. The ruling ignored the statutory presumption from the BAA's registration of "Boston Marathon" and presumed that the defendants use of the name in past years carried with it a right to use the name in the future. The judge noted "the number of people who claim to have been dealing in the subject merchandise over the years with the acquiescence of the BAA," and "suggest[ed] that the matter should proceed to trial expeditiously so that the issues will be settled well in advance of the 1987 Marathon date."

Loss Number 2: On Appeals Court Review, the Superior Court Denial Stands

I petitioned for review of the ruling by an appeals court justice but struck out there as well. Judge Edith Fine ruled that "the motion judge did not abuse his discretion."[177] She also rested her decision on a supposed ability of the BAA to recover damages. "If the petitioners should prevail after a trial on the merits, they may recover damages from the respondents." The "matter is to be assigned for trial," she declared, "on a priority basis."

The asserted remedy of recovering damages was unrealistic. Proof of profits of individual defendants was unlikely to be cost effective. Legal damage would be impossible to prove where the BAA had as yet no track record of earnings itself and where the contribution of one defendant out of a dozen or so defendants and other infringers could not be apportioned. The threat of a modest money judgment in the distant future was unlikely either to impress a defendant or deter other infringers. As for the direction of trial assignment on a priority basis, Judge Fine ceased to have any jurisdiction over the case once she had acted on the appeal. Judge Keady too would never see the case again. Their directions for a "priority" and an "expeditious" trial had little meaning.

The denial of a preliminary injunction put the BAA in a position worse than it had been in before bringing the suit. Not only did the defendants now have free rein to continue their infringing sales until the case was tried and decided, but the professional counterfeiters, seeing that the "Boston Marathon" name was fair game, also returned in force to the field. The court decisions in effect had given our adversaries a license to infringe until the case was finally decided. Adding insult to injury, I had to return to one of the Washington Street peddlers counterfeit "Boston Marathon" shirts I had seized under the ex parte order.

The preliminary injunction proceeding had been a disaster, but the decisions rendered were interlocutory and not final. On the undisputed facts of this relatively simple case, the BAA, I firmly believed, should have been granted an injunction. Stubbornly, I convinced myself that if I could get a trial and develop facts and law in a more deliberate and thoughtful hearing, I could reverse the preliminary result. A presumption that ultimately justice will prevail may be naive, but it has kept me going over the years.

The time factor was critical. We had lost out on 1986. Now we had to get a trial on the merits and a decision in time to enforce the BAA's rights before the 1987 marathon. The rules gave the defendants generous periods within which they could file answers and engage in a full panoply of "discovery"—questioning of potential witnesses in oral depositions, propounding written interrogatories, demanding production of documents, and so forth. As it was, with numerous defendants and their awareness that they were best off with the status quo, by the fall my file of court papers had become three inches deep. And time was running out.

The system called for trial of cases in the approximate order in which they had been commenced. This meant that in the ordinary course trial of my case was several years away. No one was in charge of executing the direction of Judges Fine and Keady for a speedy trial; these judges were no longer in the loop.

To get a prompt trial, we would have to have our case put ahead of the many other court cases that had been commenced before ours. In the past, a case could be moved up simply by persuading the assignment session judge to allow a motion to advance the case for a speedy trial. But a supposed reform had been put into place assertedly to accelerate bringing cases in general to trial, which changed all the procedures. Under the cumbersome practice newly in effect, to get the case advanced I would have to get it specially assigned to a designated justice who could thereupon take hold of the case, try it, and decide it. Such an order had to come from the chief justice of the superior court and be preceded by a favorable recommendation by the assignment session judge. I filed a motion for special assignment seeking the necessary recommendation and designation. There were at that point outstanding in the case, not yet acted upon, BAA discovery motions seeking orders that the defendants answer deposition questions and produce documents. As I later learned, the clerk's office somehow positioned the assignment motion in the court file underneath the pending discovery motions so that the discovery motions were on top of the court file and the assignment motion was under them.

My motion for special assignment came up before the assignment session judge for his recommendation. The scene that unfolded could have come from *Alice in Wonderland*. The sitting judge was of advanced age. He had been retired by the system after reaching the age of seventy but had been brought back specially by the superior court chief justice to help with the superior court's backlog of cases. I explained to the judge the need for a speedy trial, noting that it would be a bench trial (since it was an "equity" case, seeking an injunction) and thus did not present the problems of a trial by jury. I pointed to the directions of Judges Fine and Keady and asked for a favorable recommendation on the assignment motion. His honor said there were discovery motions pending in the case and that he would decide them. I answered that the discovery motions were not before him. A transcript of testimony was on order that bore on the motions. The parties had agreed to await the transcript, I said, and when it came in, the discovery motions would be heard against the transcript by the designated judge, if by then there was one, or, if not, by the motion session judge. The only question presented now, I continued, was whether he would recommend special assignment of the case to a designated judge.

The judge responded that if I did not want to argue my discovery motions, he would deny them. I argued the motions. Opposing counsel was next. He protested that the matter before the judge was the judge's recommendation on specially assigning a designated justice to the case, not a ruling on the discovery motions. The judge said that if counsel did not want to argue the discovery motions, he would allow them. Defense counsel argued the motions. The judge said he would take the discovery motions under advisement and called the next case. End of "hearing."

Ultimately, through the intervention of the clerk, Tom Brophy, I got the recommendation of the assignment session judge and was sent to a trial session presided over by Judge John P. Sullivan with instructions to ask Judge Sullivan whether he could fit in my case. I explained why I was there and that I was seeking a trial in the fall. "Of what year?" was the response. I tried unsuccessfully to get away. Judge Sullivan sent the case off to a "conciliation" session, charged with promotion of settlements.

The detouring of my case into a conciliation session at first appeared simply another road block in the path to a trial. But as I had bounced around within the impenetrable state system, the conviction had been coming over me that I should cut my losses if I could, abandon the state court, and try my luck in the federal court. In the federal court, my case would be drawn to one of the district court judges, who would have permanent and exclusive responsibility for it from commencement to judgment. There was a rich body of federal trademark law that might serve as a stronger guide in the federal than in the state courts. Perhaps I had been wrong in opting for the state system to begin with. Moreover, a complicating aspect of a trial in the pending state case would be the claims that had been made by some defendants of specific BAA authorization for their 1986 supposedly dissimilar shirts. I could put this issue behind me by securing BAA board votes specifically renouncing any authorization that might be claimed, and by starting over the next year with 1987 infringements as my new target.

The conciliation session offered an opportunity to extricate myself from the state courts without initiating discussions or advertising my distress. By this time, legal expenses on both sides were considerable, and all parties were feeling the heat. I managed to negotiate injunctions by consent with some defendants and modest four-figure payments to the BAA with others. The most intransigent defendant agreed to a dismissal without prejudice. The action as a whole was dismissed on the same basis—without prejudice to renewal of infringement actions in the future. The trade was given notice that the BAA still intended to pursue its rights against infringers and that only Image Impact was authorized to use the "Boston Marathon" or similar name. The BAA licked its wounds and prepared for the next round.

The 1987 infringements began to appear in late March. This time none of the T-shirt imprints tracked the "Boston Marathon" name exactly; they all used variants. Principal offenders were Beau Tease, Inc., a Massachusetts imprinter, and Mark Sullivan, operator of the Hopkinton store Good Life. They were offering T-shirts with a three-line inscription: the first line "1987 Marathon"; the second line a sketch of three runners; the third line "Hopkinton—Boston."

Loss Number 3: The Federal District Court Denies an Effective Preliminary Injunction

On April 1, 1987, I filed a complaint in the U.S. District Court for the District of Massachusetts on behalf of the BAA and Image Impact, Inc., against Sullivan d/b/a Good Life and Beau Tease. The case fell to Judge William G. Young. Appointed by President Reagan to the federal bench in 1984, he was a graduate of Harvard College and Harvard Law School, and had served as chief legal counsel to Governor Francis W. Sargent and as a Massachusetts Superior Court justice. Ropes & Gray had experienced a more than two-year delay in a superior court case tried before Judge Young, non-jury, in December 1982 in which we represented the New England Patriots. Judge Young had taken 27 months after trial to decide the case, finally rendering his decision on April 24, 1985. In a footnote to the date of decision, he attributed his delay in part to lack of administrative support, including the fact that he had only "one-half a law clerk . . . as contrasted with the two law clerks available to each judge in . . . the U.S. District Court for the District of Massachusetts."[178] We had assumed the delay in the *Patriots* case was an isolated instance. And by the time of the draw in my BAA case, Judge Young had become a federal district court judge, supplied with the administrative support he had previously lacked.

An evidentiary hearing on the BAA's preliminary injunction application began April 13. I submitted detailed memoranda on trademark law, a statement of agreed facts I had worked out with defense counsel, affidavits, and witnesses. I presented testimony on the meaning of the "Boston Marathon" and "BAA Marathon" names—that they signified the race run annually on Patriot's Day sponsored by the Boston Athletic Association; on the confusion caused by the defendants' shirts—that customers mistakenly thought they were buying shirts made or sponsored by the BAA; and on comparative quality—that the defendants' shirts were inferior to the official Image Impact shirts. The facts were essentially the same as those in the Suffolk Superior Court case the year before but were developed in greater detail by oral testimony.

After several days of testimony, Judge Young announced he had heard enough to decide the preliminary injunction application. He dictated from the bench a bewildering opinion. He accepted most of the facts shown by the BAA but ruled that the BAA had largely failed to prove public appreciation that the Boston Marathon was sponsored by the BAA. He found on the one hand that people attending a sale of running equipment and memorabilia at the "Runners Expo," held in the Westin Hotel, Boston, would infer BAA sponsorship of the defendants' shirts:

> [T]he plaintiffs have shown a reasonable likelihood that those members of the public sufficiently interested in running in marathons to attend the Runners Expo sponsored by the Boston Athletic Association . . . and to purchase running and marathon gimmicks and materials at the Runners Expo, who there at the Runners Expo purchase the shirts with the logos described in Exhibits 1 and 2 manufactured by the defendant, Beau Tease, here, will conclude that those shirts are either licensed or authorized or in some way reflect upon sponsorship by the Boston Athletic Association.

He therefore enjoined further sale by the defendant Beau Tease of the "1987 Marathon" shirt at the Runners Expo, which had a day or two yet to run. But he further ruled that the public anywhere else, including shoppers on Washington Street and viewers along the race course, would *not* infer that the BAA stood behind the same defendants' T-shirts and, hence, that no broader injunction would issue:

> [T]he plaintiffs have failed to show that there is any reasonable likelihood that a person who buys the shirts with the logos Exhibits 1 and 2 in circumstances other than at the Runners Expo sponsored by the Boston Athletic Association and

> intimately connected with the registration process for the race itself will in any way come to infer that, while the shirt relates to a celebration of the Boston Marathon, the shirt, the defendant's shirts, Exhibits 1 and 2, that the Boston Athletic Association somehow authorizes, sponsors, or stands behind the shirts marketed from vendors on Washington Street in stores that are simply marketing marathon memorabilia either here in Boston or in Hopkinton or anywhere along the route.

The preliminary injunction would therefore be limited to one place, the Runners Expo floor at the Westin Hotel! It was useless. We now had two preliminary injunction rulings against us. Our grave had been dug a little bit deeper.

The judge's finding of no-inference-by-the-average-person of BAA sponsorship of the defendants' Boston Marathon T-shirts was contrary to the evidence, the law, and common understanding. To the extent the ruling rested on a notion that non-aficionados were ignorant of the fact that it was the BAA that sponsored the Boston Marathon, the law did not require a showing of knowledge of the identity of the sponsor, only that there was some sponsor standing behind the product,[179] and, moreover, the evidence showed that the public generally was familiar with BAA sponsorship of the Marathon. To the extent the ruling rested on the absence of an inference, even by knowledgeable people, of BAA authorization arising from the defendants' particular T-shirt imprints, it was contrary to the common understanding, at least of many, that use of a person's name or similar name on a product implies sponsorship by the name owner. It was as if the United States Golf Association's "U.S. Open" name and likeness had been protected against similar imprints at the site of the Open, but had been ruled fair game for use by anyone anywhere else.

Loss Number 4: The Federal Court of Appeals Refuses to Act

Judge Young's decision came on the Thursday before the Monday when the 1987 race was to be run. As in the state courts, there was a federal procedure for appellate review of a district court denial of a preliminary injunction. The timing and nature of the case made such an appeal a long shot, but it was our only hope. I appealed and moved for an injunction pending hearing of the appeal. My motion was promptly rejected. The Court of Appeals for the First Circuit refused "on short notice" to get into the case. Misunderstanding the history, it faulted the BAA for not filing sooner, remarking, cutely, "the race is sometimes to the swift."[180] Like the state courts, it also justified its ruling on the illusory right of the BAA, if it prevailed after trial, to recover damages or defendant profits.

Letting stand denial of an effective injunction continued the virtual license to infringe the "Boston Marathon" name. Just as had happened the year before, the 1987 marathon season was a field day for "Boston Marathon" infringers and counterfeiters.

Again I had to pick up the pieces. The court of appeals had not addressed the merits of the case. The district court's preliminary injunction decision confining the injunction to the premises at the Runners Expo was so irrational that I thought it possible Judge Young might be persuaded to change his mind. The case at that point had been only partially tried, and no final judgment had been rendered. The trial would have to be completed. Possibly, justice would then prevail. A decision against us could be appealed. If we were right that the facts required an injunction, we could hope for a better result on a second appeal.

Judge Young Directs Submission of Summary Judgment Motions

I went back to Judge Young with a motion for assignment of a trial completion date. He entered an order that "this case is scheduled for completion of trial at 2:00 p.m. on Tuesday, May 26, 1987," a date he later changed to June 11.

With the trial assignment, I focused on knocking out the defense that because the BAA had not sought to enjoin the T-shirt infringers before 1986, its rights had been lost. This defense was contrary to the established legal principle that past inaction by a tradename owner against infringements forfeited rights to future enforcement *only* if the infringer had been somehow prejudiced by the failure to enforce in the past. That is, if prolonged nonenforcement had legitimately led the defendants to infer that the BAA had abandoned its rights and the defendants had built a plant uniquely designed to manufacture "Boston Marathon" T-shirts, they could argue prejudice—that it would be unfair to prevent them from marketing the product of the plant. But the facts in this case were that the infringers' printing facilities customarily went into action only shortly before the marathon and could turn out any kind of imprint. The product changed from year to year. The defendants had ample notice of the intention of the BAA to enforce its rights. The case appeared to be squarely within the general rule laid down long ago by the U.S. Supreme Court in *Menendez v. Holt* that a trademark owner's *future* enforcement rights are not forfeited by acquiescence in past infringements:

> Where consent by the owner to the use of his trade-mark by another is to be inferred from his knowledge and silence merely, "it lasts no longer than the silence from which it springs; it is, in reality, no more than a revocable license." . . . So far as the act complained of is completed, acquiescence may defeat the remedy . . . but so far as the act is in progress and lies in the future, the right to the intervention of equity is not generally lost by previous delay.[181]

The BAA's failure to enforce its rights before 1986 was equivalent under the *Menendez* rule, I felt, to granting a revocable license. Revocation of any such "license" had simply taken away from the defendants (and other infringers) a profit source to which they were never entitled. They would not be prejudiced because they could keep their gains from prior years and, as for the present, they had advance notice that any implied "revocable license" had been revoked.

I brought the issue of the BAA's past nonenforcement to a head by filing a motion for a ruling that the defense of laches-acquiescence was insufficient in law. The motion was allowed by the court, giving the BAA its only success in two years of struggle. My pleasure at this ruling was tempered by a simultaneous notice from Judge Young's clerk that the trial date had been canceled. She advised that Judge Young considered the case might be suitable for summary judgment, that the trial was off, and that both parties were to file summary judgment motions.

In most litigation, the parties are at odds over the facts as well as the proper result. There are some cases, however, in which the critical facts are beyond argument and the only real question is the legal result required by these facts. In the case of the sale of the Boston Marathon, whether the agreement of sale was legally valid had presented such a case, and it had been decided by summary judgment without a trial. In a summary judgment situation, it is the job of the judge to decide who should prevail on the undisputed facts. The judge can but need not make findings or write an opinion. All the judge is required to do is endorse the summary judgment motion as "allowed" or "denied."

In calling for motions for summary judgment, Judge Young was suggesting the absence of any genuine issue of fact, and that one party or the other was entitled to judgment as a matter of law. I agreed that this was so; it had been my position from the beginning that the essential facts were beyond dispute and that the BAA was legally entitled to its injunction. With elimination of the laches-acquiescence defense, this conviction had become even stronger, and at the time of cancellation of the trial date, I had expected to take only a few hours to complete my case. All I needed to add, I felt, was further evidence (1) that the public was aware of the BAA's role in conducting the Boston Marathon and (2) that buyers had been actually confused by the defendants' T-shirts, thinking mistakenly that they were sponsored by the BAA. Point 1 evidence would be entirely documentary; Point 2 would involve short testimony by one witness. Proof of these points should require extension of the Expo injunction to the public at large.

Summary judgment motions and the affidavits that would have to accompany them would take longer for the parties to prepare and for the court to digest than the one-day trial I had anticipated. But the judge's direction that we take the summary judgment route implied an intention to render a speedy—"summary"—disposition. Indeed, this was the court's duty—Rule 56(c) of the Federal Rules of Civil Procedure provided that where a party was entitled to summary judgment "the judgment sought shall be entered forthwith." A "forthwith" judgment we sorely needed. A decision that went against us, if made promptly, could probably be acted on, and reversed, by the court of appeals before the running of the 1988 marathon.

Because of the judge's preliminary injunction ruling that only attendees at the Runners Expo would think that the defendant's shirts with their "Boston Marathon" likeness were sponsored by the BAA, so that an injunction should be limited to their protection alone, I intended to add to the proof that the public in general was quite aware that the Boston Marathon's sponsor was the BAA.

The record already contained considerable evidence of public awareness of which the court was required to take judicial notice. At the preliminary injunction hearing we had called Judge Young's attention to an *Encyclopedia Britannica* entry for the Boston Marathon:

> *Boston Marathon*, a 26-mile-385-yard (standard marathon distance) foot race from Hopkinton, Mass., to the Back Bay section of Boston. The race, held first in 1897 and annually thereafter, is among the most famous of the world's marathon races and is sponsored by the Boston Athletic Association. Runners come from all over the world to participate . . . .

In its 1984 opinion on the validity of the BAA contract with Medoff, *Boston Athletic Association v. International Marathons, Inc.*, the Supreme Judicial Court of the Commonwealth had referred to "the presentation of the Marathon" as "the most significant purpose of the BAA."[182] There had been no evidence offered of *absence* of public knowledge. To our minds the issue of public awareness had been a no-brainer. As one trademark case has said, "A court should not play the ostrich with regard to . . . general public knowledge."[183]

But the job of changing a court's mind generally calls for extreme measures. I made it a project to collect newspaper articles over the years that had referred to the BAA's sponsorship role. These articles not only reflected the writers' knowledge of that role but also exposed the fact of BAA sponsorship to millions of newspaper readers. This evidence turned out to be so prolific that we had to limit ourselves to representative samples. I eventually filed copies of sample newspaper articles (see Appendix III, 5C) published in the first year of the marathon, 1897, in each tenth year thereafter, and in 1986 and 1987.[184] To focus attention on the important passages, I also provided the court with summaries of the references in the articles to BAA sponsorship of the Boston Marathon (see Appendix III, 5D). The hundreds of newspaper and magazine articles submitted—only a tip of the iceberg—showed a continuous barrage of publicity concerning BAA sponsorship of the Boston Marathon each year during marathon season, so that the newspaper reading public could hardly remain unaware of the connection.

Filed additionally with the BAA's summary judgment motion were books on the Boston Marathon discussing the BAA role; contracts between the BAA and commercial sponsors permitting them to link their names with "Boston Marathon"; agreements between the BAA and the three Boston network television channels providing for the televising of the race; race videotapes showing along the course uninformed BAA officials, BAA control points, and BAA insignia; and miscellaneous BAA programs, brochures, and printed race materials (see Appendix III, 5E–5G).

As one example of public exposure to the BAA–Boston Marathon connection, my memorandum in support of the BAA summary judgment motion reviewed the publicity given BAA sponsorship for the most recent marathon, April 20, 1987. It called the court's attention to the dozens of running groups assisting the BAA in the conduct and administration of the race; the 2,500 BAA officials and volunteers at the start, finish, and along the route of the race wearing yellow jackets with "BAA" on the front and "Boston Marathon" on the back; the 7,000 competitors who had submitted applications to the BAA to enter the race; the hundreds of thousands of readers exposed to newspaper articles on the BAA and its race throughout April of that year; the approximately one million spectators lining the 26.2 mile race course, marshaled intermittently by BAA volunteers, and the millions more who had watched the race on Boston's three television stations; the viewing of the firing of the starting gun by long-time BAA figure Tom Brown; the first-aid and watering stations along the course displaying BAA insignia; the breaking of the BAA tape at the finish line; and the crowning of the winners with laurel wreaths at the finish line by BAA president Frank Swift (see Appendix III, 5E).

The submission of this prolific evidence of public knowledge of the BAA's sponsorship role elicited no response from the defendants. We considered the point established beyond question.

The second point to be covered was submission of further evidence of actual confusion. Trademark law required a trademark plaintiff to prove only that any colorable imitations of a mark were "likely" to cause confusion or mistake or to deceive. Episodes of *actual* confusion caused by the defendants' marks—in which purchasers had demonstrably been misled—would go beyond the statutory requirement that the trademark owner prove the imitation "likely" to cause confusion. Mickey Lawrence, president of Image Impact, had testified to several instances of actual confusion at the preliminary injunction hearing. This evidence was supplemented by an affidavit relating additional similar episodes.

The BAA's summary judgment motion, with exhibits showing public awareness, the affidavit of customer confusion, and a review of trademark authorities, was filed on July 13. My letter covering the filing called Judge Young's attention particularly to the many documents (on BAA sponsorship of the marathon) being added to the record. The next day the court entered an order that "the within [summary judgment] motion will be taken under advisement on the papers then on file on July 27, 1987." Within the intervening 14 days, the defendants filed their own motion for summary judgment and a supporting legal memorandum. Together, the motions relied on both the new and the old evidence, including the testimony, exhibits, and stipulations at the April 13–16 trial.[185] With the submission of the motions, the ball passed into Judge Young's court. The BAA could only await the result.

Judge Young Will Not Act on the Motions

Judge Young had known from the beginning that the case before him was a test case to establish the right of the BAA to exclusive commercial use of its names. He knew that time was of the essence, that after losing out on the 1986 and 1987 seasons, the BAA's objective was to get injunctive relief before the running of the 1988 marathon. He knew that entry of a final judgment in the case was a prerequisite to an appeal. He had complimented himself at the preliminary injunction hearing in April on the promptness with which he had handled the BAA's case, remarking, "And you certainly can't say that the court has given you anything else but absolutely first-class treatment to put the case to trial immediately so that you can get a final judgment."[186]

Getting a final judgment was key, as the judge had recognized. A judgment granting an injunction would prohibit further infringements by the defendants in the case and would virtually assure that preliminary injunctions could be obtained against any new infringers. A judgment denying an injunction could be appealed and possibly reversed.

A judgment pro or con, we could deal with; inaction, we could not. As long as the court held the case under advisement, we had neither won nor lost. An appeal lay only from a judgment. Without a judgment, and hence no right to appeal, we were dead in the water. Days, weeks, and months went by. Our worst fears were being realized.

The importance of prompt action in litigation is reflected in the dozens of rules of civil and criminal procedure prescribing due dates within which parties must act or lose their rights. Rule 1 of the Rules of Civil Procedure provides that the rules are to be "administered to secure the just, *speedy*, and inexpensive determination of every action." Rule 56(c) required that action on our motion be taken "forthwith." Canons of both the Massachusetts *Code of Judicial Conduct* and of the American Bar Association's 1984 *Model Code of Judicial Conduct* instructed that "a judge should dispose promptly of the business of the court."[187]

No enforcement mechanism was provided in either the rules or the canons to compel judicial action. Nevertheless, as winter approached, something had to be done. On November 24, 1987, I wrote the court:

> November 24, 1987
>
> Dear Judge Young:
>
> I hope you will not take it amiss that I should call to your attention the pendency of the summary judgment motions in the above case, which I do because my client had been hoping that it could secure a definitive result in the case prior to the running of next year's marathon on April 18, 1988.
>
> As the court is aware from the summary judgment papers, the BAA believes that it

> is entitled to judicial protection against the use of the name "Marathon 198X," etc., and it may well be that this issue will call for a ruling by the Court of Appeals. This is a test case and will affect the market for T-shirts relating to the Boston Marathon in March and April, 1988. The time is getting short to secure a district court judgment and review by the Court of Appeals prior to the 1988 Marathon.
>
> Very truly yours,
>
> George C. Caner, Jr.
>
> cc: Glen M. Shriberg, Esq.
> [Attorney for the defendants]

The letter was hand-delivered. There was no response.

Time passed. I made another move—a motion to amend my 1987 complaint to target several 1988 T-shirts that had unexpectedly appeared, and a motion for a preliminary injunction against their sale. One of the 1988 shirts was similar to the defendants' 1987 T-shirt—the first of three lines in a column carried the imprint "1988 Marathon," the second line carried figures of three runners, and the third bore the words "Hopkinton-Boston." A second 1988 shirt also had a three-line imprint—the first line read simply "Boston"; the second line depicted three runners; the third line said "1988."

INFRINGING BOSTON MARATHON T-SHIRT, 1988

Photo courtesy of the BAA.

In the past, infringers generally had waited until late March to come out with their products. This tactic of delaying publication of their "Boston Marathon" version that particular season, and thus putting off as long as possible their identification as BAA targets, assured the BAA would be criticized by courts for coming in and seeking orders at the last minute. But emboldened by their successes and the court's inaction, the defendants had put their 1988 shirts on display in February 1988 at the Good Life Hopkinton store. The BAA became aware of the 1988 imprints when BAA members visited the Good Life store and saw the two shirts hanging side by side. They were displayed with an arm carrying the imprint "Boston" obscuring the 1988 of the "1988 Marathon" shirt so that a customer could read "Boston Marathon" on the combination. Both BAA motions—to amend and for a preliminary injunction as to the 1988 shirts—were filed on February 4, 1988. The new infringements were described and pictured. The court's attention was called to the state court comments that the BAA's claim should be tried "expeditiously" and on a "priority" basis, and to the emphasis of the Court of Appeals for the First Circuit, in its negative action on the BAA's 1987 appeal, that "the race is sometimes to the swift."

Two weeks passed with no action. I wrote again:

> February 18, 1988
>
> Dear Judge Young:
>
> This will request on behalf of the plaintiffs, Boston Athletic Association and Image Impact, Inc., a hearing on the outstanding motions of the plaintiffs in the above-entitled action, particularly the motions for a Preliminary Injunction and to Further Amend filed February 4, 1988, and the opportunity to present oral argument thereon.
>
> The grounds for this request are that the defendants are currently infringing the plaintiffs' mark, and that in addition to its need for relief against these defendants, if the plaintiffs cannot secure relief in this in-

> stance, it will encourage other potential infringers and jeopardize the program of sale of merchandise under the plaintiffs' names. See Plaintiffs' Memorandum, filed February 4, 1988, pp. 1–3 and letter to the Court of November 24, 1987.
>
> Very truly yours,
>
> George C. Caner, Jr.
>
> cc: Glen M. Shriberg, Esq.

Although my letter of February 18 prompted no response from the court, it was noted by opposing counsel, who wrote the court the same day requesting that vacation plans he had between March 4 and 14 be honored. This gave me an opening, and the next day I delivered still another letter to Judge Young asking that a hearing on the BAA's motion be scheduled before March 4.

Nothing was heard from the court.

Since I had been unable to get any information from the clerk on judicial reaction to my letters and motions, I decided to look at the papers of the case to see if any endorsements had been made on them that had been overlooked by the court staff. The clerk's office advised that the judge had all the papers, so I asked for the docket entry sheet. To my surprise, the last docket entry save one was of August 17, 1987. The exception was "Ltr. to Judge from Mr. Caner dated 2-18-88, filed." There was no record of my letter of November 24, 1987, my motions of February 4, 1988, Shriberg's letter of November 18, 1988, or my letter of November 19, 1988.

Rule 79 of the Federal Rules of Civil Procedure requires the clerk to keep a "civil docket" on a prescribed form in every case. The rule provides that "[a]ll papers filed with the clerk . . . shall be entered chronologically in the civil docket. . . . These entries shall be brief but shall show the nature of each paper filed . . . and the substance of each order."[188] Docket entries are intended to present a chronological summary of events and the rulings in every federal case. Their maintenance is important. They are public records that tell the public what is going on. They reveal whether time requirements have been met, summarize actions taken by parties and by the court, and are a mandatory part of the record in every appeal. Virtually all courts must keep such records.[189]

All the papers seeking action had been delivered to the clerk's office for filing and submission to the court. Had they been docketed as required, the BAA's efforts to have a ruling made on the summary judgment motions the judge had called for, the BAA letters, the complaint of 1988 infringements and the motion for a 1988 injunction, and the judge's failure to act on any of the filings, would have been a matter of immediate public record.

In an attempt to smoke out the reason why my papers had not been docketed, and any involvement of the judge, I delivered yet another letter to the court:

> February 23, 1988
>
> Dear Judge Young:
>
> Having heard nothing from the court regarding the Plaintiffs' Preliminary Injunction Motions of July 14, 1987 and February 4, 1988 and my letters to the court of November 24, 1987 and February 18 and 19, 1988, I asked that the docket entries in the case be secured and, on receiving them this afternoon (copy enclosed), I find that the only activity listed after August 17, 1987 (allowance of Plaintiffs' Motion to Amend) was the filing of my letter of February 18, 1988.
>
> Because of the importance of my letter of November 24, 1987, copy enclosed, I attempted personally to deliver this letter to your clerk, Ms. Katharine Hart, but the 15th floor clerk's office refused to permit such a delivery and directed me to the 14th floor. At the 14th floor, I watched the clerk date stamp the letter and he assured me that it would find its way to you.
>
> My associate, Mr. Van Lonkhuyzen, personally delivered the February 4, 1988 filings (Motion to Further Amend, Motion for Preliminary Injunction and Sup-

> porting Memo) to the 15th floor clerk's office and saw them stamped.
>
> I notice that Mr. Shriberg's letter of February 18, 1988 has not been docketed. Also, there is no reference in the docket to the exhibits filed with the Motion for Summary Judgment and Preliminary Injunction July 13, 1987.
>
> Additional copies of the papers above referred to are, of course, available.
>
> Very truly yours,
>
> George C. Caner, Jr.
>
> cc: Glen M. Shriberg, Esq.

On the next day, I filed a motion to correct court record and for other relief, reciting the failures to docket my papers and attaching copies. Besides seeking correction of the record, the motion renewed the BAA's application for a preliminary injunction addressing the 1988 marathon eight weeks away. Nothing happened.

Boston Athletic Association Versus Young, J.

I was aware that throughout this period Judge Young was in town, apparently carrying out duties more important to him than the job of deciding *BAA v. Sullivan*. Still another year of judicially tolerated infringements was in the offing. The only remedy available would be a writ of mandamus by the Court of Appeals for the First Circuit ordering the judge to act. Seeking such an order would get the judge's attention, but it was not likely to promote a decision favorable to the BAA. It was also unlikely to advance the cause of client or counsel in appearances before other trial judges, who might not appreciate an assault on the judge prerogative of determining court agenda. Few litigators in their careers find themselves suing the judge sitting on one of their cases. This would be my second such enterprise.

The non-docketing of my papers, however, had been the last straw. I went to work preparing a mandamus petition. Another week passed with no action on any of my motions or letters. I entered my petition (see Appendix III, 5H) with the court of appeals praying for issuance of a writ of mandamus commanding Judge Young to act. The petition alleged the status of *Boston Athletic Association v. Sullivan* as a test case partially tried in April 1987, the cancellation of the trial completion date and direction of the judge to counsel in June that the parties file motions for summary judgment, compliance by the parties with that direction in early July, the judge's order of July 14 taking the motions under advisement, the importance that a final decision be made before the 1988 marathon season, the inaction of the judge on the motions for summary judgment and on the motion for a 1998 injunction filed in February 1988, the absence of any response by Judge Young to any of the BAA's letters and motions, and the unexplained and uncorrected failure to docket the papers showing the BAA's efforts to get the judge to act. The petition concluded that the "inaction of the district court constitutes an arbitrary refusal to exercise its authority in dereliction of its duty to do so and deprives the plaintiffs without due process of law of their rights to have their application for abatement of an ongoing trademark infringement adjudicated and to appeal any adverse decision."[190]

Loss Number 5: Judge Young Enters Summary Judgment for the Defendants

I filed the mandamus petition on Friday, March 4, 1988, and it was served on Judge Young that afternoon. Less than 72 hours later, on Monday, the next business day, we had our decision. It was a judgment for the defendants. Accompanying it was a nine-page memorandum of decision purporting to justify the judgment (see Appendix III, 51). Though by that time I had given the court over 75 pages of material summarizing the evidence and collecting all the relevant trademark authority,[191] the court's memorandum did not give the source or evidence behind any of its findings or cite to a single trademark case as a precedent. Without any reference to the law prohibiting infringement by use of similar marks—"colorable imitations"—Judge Young ruled that the rights of the BAA "do not sweep" beyond the precise marks "Boston Marathon" and "BAA Marathon." Curiously, even the precise names were said to be protectable only when used "in connection with the BAA's own distinctive unicorn logo" or with "prominence."

Under this do-not-sweep formation of the law, even the token preliminary injunction against sale of the defendants' shirts at the Expo was unwarranted—these shirts did not carry the precise marks "Boston Marathon" or "BAA Marathon," but only similar marks. According to Judge Young in 1988, these marks would not give rise to "an inference [of BAA sponsorship] even among those people who appreciate that the BAA sponsors the race;" they would never infringe "Boston Marathon." Judge Young's 1988 decision thus overruled the only feature of his 1987 decision favorable to the BAA. Our efforts in between had only made the situation worse.

Although the defendants had offered no evidence since the April 1987 preliminary injunction hearing, and the BAA had since provided additional affidavit evidence of customer mistake and a waterfall of documents showing awareness of BAA sponsorship, all of it pointing only one way, Judge Young's 1988 decision was even more adverse on these scores than his preliminary injunction decision had been the year before. He dealt with the proof that customers had been misled by ruling that "the affidavits . . . are hearsay and entitled to no evidentiary weight." On the issue of public knowledge of the BAA's sponsorship of the Marathon, he held that the existence of public knowledge was immaterial and questionable, and insinuated that the BAA's proof of that proposition rested on its *ipse dixit*: "Despite the BAA's apparent opinion of its own notoriety and its own promotional activities, there remains a genuine issue of fact concerning whether the average member of the purchasing public appreciates that the BAA sponsors the race run on or about Patriots Day commonly known as the Boston Marathon."

The BAA had rested its case not on its "opinion of its own notoriety," but on a multitude of largely unsolicited writings, oral accounts, tapes, photographs and videos authored by independent parties such as reporters, journalists, historians, runners, and radio and TV announcers attesting to the conduct of the Boston Marathon by the BAA—all thoroughly documented by exhibits submitted with the summary judgment motion and specially called to the judge's attention. Adding considerably to the injury of the ruling, there was no indication that the court had ever looked at any of this proof.

Court of Appeals Action

Judge Young's decision might be wrong, and it might be late, and it might have blown a third marathon season, but at least it was a decision. We now had a right to appeal. And the judge's rush to judgment in less than 72 hours after service on him of the mandamus petition, over a weekend, justified by a decision riddled with misstatements of fact and law, had presented us with a fat target.

A party appealing to a reviewing court must show error by the lower court so important that the decision below must be set aside or reversed. The appellant assembles the "record"—all the relevant testimonial and documentary evidence—and submits with it a brief arguing its side of the case. Ropes & Gray prepared a record of seven volumes containing all the pleadings, affidavits, and testimony and most of the documents. Special permission was granted not to duplicate the summary judgment newspaper articles, videotapes, photographs, T-shirts and similar exhibits; they were recovered from the district court and delivered in bulk to the court of appeals. That court now had all the materials that had been submitted to the district court. My brief repeated the trademark law previously given to Judge Young and contrasted it with his decision. The United States Golf Association, which had lost a round before District Court Judge Skinner against 1988 "U.S. Open" counterfeiters on the strength of the Young decision, filed an amicus brief supporting the BAA.[192]

On January 27, 1989, the court of appeals issued an opinion by Judge Hugh Bownes accepting the BAA's arguments of district court errors, ruling that the defendants' marks were confusingly similar to the plaintiff's marks, reversing the district court, and directing entry of a permanent injunction against the infringements (Appendix 5J). Stubbornness had prevailed over adversity.

The court of appeals opinion summarized Judge Young's decision before passing on it:

> The district court's March 7 decision found that BAA's marks were its most valuable asset and were at all relevant times valid and enforceable. It found that an av-

> erage person would infer sponsorship by someone of a product carrying the logo "Boston Marathon," and that defendants' logos referred to the marathon. The court stated that there was a dispute whether the public would associate BAA with the Boston Marathon but that this dispute was not material. It held that the public would not infer that the defendants' logos were sponsored by BAA. The court explicitly disregarded Lawrence's affidavit evidence of confusion because it was hearsay and the court found no other evidence that any "disinterested" person was confused as to the source of defendants' shirts. The court also held that BAA's rights did not extend beyond the use of its exact service marks. The court ruled as a matter of law that there was no confusion between the defendants' and plaintiffs' shirts. The court concluded its opinion: "More precisely, this court rules that the specific T-shirt logo challenged in this action does not, as a matter of law, give rise to any colorable confusion with products authorized by the BAA as part of its sponsorship of the particular road race in question."

The key ruling had been that the BAA's rights did not extend beyond the use of its precise marks. As Judge Young had put it, "beyond this, however, the legal rights of the BAA do not sweep." This unprecedented ruling, the court of appeals ruled, was wrong:

> The district court's holding that plaintiffs' rights did not sweep any further than their actual marks is not a correct application of trademark law. Such a rule would eviscerate trademark law because "few would be stupid enough to make exact copies of another's mark or symbol. It has been well said that the most successful form of copying is to employ enough points of similarity to confuse the public with enough points of difference to confuse the courts."

In a number of trademark decisions, the court of appeals had prescribed an eight-factor test for determining when a defendant's mark was a sufficient imitation of the plaintiff's mark to give rise to likelihood of confusion and a right to an injunction. The district court had spared itself from applying the test by ruling that only certain uses of the *identical* mark could be enjoined. When the court of appeals applied the eight-factor test to the defendants' marks, it found that each factor pointed to a likelihood of confusion.

On the factor of the similarity of the competing marks, the fact that the wording, characters, and arrangement of the defendants' imprints somewhat differed from "Boston Marathon" was more than overcome, the court of appeals held, by the common meanings of the marks. "Here, the meaning of the two marks is more than similar, it is identical. This overcomes any difference in appearance between them." On the factor of the similarity of the goods involved, the goods carrying the competing imprints—T-shirts and like garments—were virtually the same as the Image Impact goods and were sold in similar places at similar times.

On the factor of public appreciation of the meaning of the mark "Boston Marathon," the court ruled that the evidence showed beyond question that there was public awareness of BAA sponsorship of the race. The court noted the district court's initial division of the purchasing public into two classes—those "sufficiently interested in running" to attend the Runners Expo at the Westin Hotel in Boston and everyone else—and the district court's later assertion that there was a "genuine issue of fact" as to public appreciation of BAA sponsorship of the marathon. The court of appeals found no basis for the division between Runners Expo attendees and the public generally or for the claim of an outstanding issue of fact. It ruled that the district court's questioning of public knowledge of BAA sponsorship "is not supported in the record. Indeed, the evidence is to the contrary." This time, a court addressed the copious exhibits connecting the BAA and the Boston Marathon that I had filed with the BAA's summary judgment motion:

> Plaintiffs submitted voluminous, uncontradicted evidence, in the form of numerous newspaper and magazine articles dating back to 1897, videotapes of television broadcasts, and encyclopedia entries, all showing that the public was continually exposed to the fact of BAA's sponsorship of the Boston Marathon.

> We find that no genuine issue of fact exists as to the public's general awareness of BAA's sponsorship of the Boston Marathon; there was, therefore, no reason to divide the purchasing public into two classes.

Another factor in the court of appeals eight-factor test was whether there was evidence of actual mistake and confusion by purchasers. One could hardly deny "*likelihood*" of mistake and confusion if *actual* mistake and confusion had been shown. My proof of actual confusion—the testimony given in April at the preliminary injunction hearing (see Appendix III, 5B) and the additional affidavit averments submitted in July—had been ignored by Judge Young. He had ruled in his memorandum of decision that the affidavit averments were inadmissible and that "[t]here is, on this record, no evidence whatsoever that any disinterested individual purchased the defendants' offending T-shirt believing that he or she was buying a product sponsored or officially licensed by the BAA."

In fact, the record included abundant evidence of such a belief, admissible and admitted, in both courtroom testimony and affidavit form.

Abundant testimony given at the preliminary injunction hearing in April 1987, expressly invoked by the defendants' summary judgment motion, was in the record as a consequence of Judge Young's 1987 ruling that this type of evidence was *not* inadmissible. At the preliminary injunction hearing, the president of Image Impact, Mickey Lawrence, had testified to events at the Runners Expo, where the competing T-shirts were both on sale—the defendants' T-shirts at their booth and the BAA T-shirts at the BAA–Image Impact booth. Her testimony had been that many times people came over to the Image Impact booth after buying a "1986 Marathon" T-shirt from the defendants, sought to return the shirt to Image, and were indignant when they were told that it was not official BAA merchandise and therefore they could not return it at the BAA-Image Impact booth. The defendants' attorney had objected to the testimony and had moved strike it. Judge Young had admitted the testimony and had denied the motion to strike (see transcript of testimony, Appendix III, 5B). The testimony was not hearsay, and if it had been, it was within the hearsay exception for declarations showing state of mind; hence it was rightly admitted.

The record also contained an affidavit submitted with the BAA's summary judgment motion of other instances in which buyers showed an understanding that the defendants' shirts were sponsored by the BAA. In one episode, the purchaser of a defendants' "1986 Marathon" shirt complained to Mickey Lawrence because her shirt deteriorated after a few washings. In another, a purchaser of a defendants' "1987 Marathon" T-shirt expressed surprise and chagrin when advised that it was not an official T-shirt. The defendants did not contradict this evidence. Judge Young avoided the evidence by ruling it inadmissible in his memorandum of decision—treating it as a nullity and thus not in the legal record. Yet he had addressed the precise point a year earlier and had made the opposite ruling.

The court of appeals held that the "evidence shows that some people were actually confused as to who sponsored defendants' shirts." The court focused on the affidavit and ruled the district court wrong in treating the account of confusion in the affidavit as inadmissible hearsay:

> We think that the account was not hearsay, however, because it was not "offered in evidence to prove the truth of the matter asserted." Fed.R.Evid. 801 (c). The statement was made not to prove that the defendants' shirts were in fact officially authorized, but rather to show that the declarant, a member of the public, *believed* that they were officially authorized. [Emphasis that of the court of appeals].

The final factor of the eight-factor test was the strength of the BAA's mark. Returning to the "broad media exposure [of] the BAA's sponsorship of the Boston Marathon," the court of appeals found that "[t]he 'strength' factors militate in favor of a finding that the mark held by BAA in 'Boston Marathon' is a strong one. Therefore, broad protection of the mark is warranted. Based on the undisputed facts and the pertinent law, plaintiffs have proved that the purchasing public are likely to confuse defendants' shirts with those of plaintiffs."

My protests to courts in the past that it was unfair to permit the defendants to profit from their unauthorized use of the BAA's name had always before fallen on deaf ears.

This time the protest was heard. The court of appeals recognized that:

> Defendants' shirts are clearly designed to take advantage of the Boston Marathon and to benefit from the good will associated with its promotion by plaintiffs. Defendants thus obtain a "free ride" at plaintiffs' expense. In the oft quoted words of the Supreme Court in *International News Service v. Associated Press*, 248 U.S. 215 (1918), because the Boston Marathon has achieved its renown as a result of BAA's "expenditure of labor, skill, and money," such unlicensed use of BAA's mark would permit defendants to "reap where (they have) not sown." *International News Service v. Associated Press*, at 239. Like Rosie Ruiz, a notorious imposter in the 1980 Boston Marathon, defendants would be given a medal without having run the course.

After a further analysis of the case under the heading "The Promotional Goods Issue," reaching the same result, the court of appeals held that the defendants' shirts infringed the "Boston Marathon" mark. It reversed the district court and ordered a permanent injunction against "manufacturing or selling goods displaying the name 'Boston Marathon' or any other design which is confusingly similar to or a colorable imitation of 'Boston Marathon,' including goods which are imprinted with

'19xx Marathon; [runners]; Hopkinton—Boston,' or with 'Boston; [runner/s]; 1988.'"

This was substantially the same injunction, based on substantially the same facts, for which we had been battling since April 1986. It ended the competition of the infringing shirts.

The court of appeals awarded "costs" to the BAA. Unfortunately, under the system, these "costs" did not include six-figure attorneys' fees resulting from five successive erroneous judicial decisions and a mandamus action to compel a judge to do his duty, or three years of lost royalties. Few clients would have shown the tenacity and faith in counsel displayed by Frank Swift, president of the BAA, and the other BAA governors. They deserved a happy ending.

Appendix I

Emergence of a Federal Constitutional Right of Privacy

At the time of *Titicut Follies*, a right of privacy was in gestation not only as a Massachusetts common law right, but also as a federal constitutional right. No such right had been known to the law when the United States Constitution was ratified in 1788, but such a right could arguably be drawn from a combination of the 1791 Bill of Rights amendments and the Fourteenth Amendment, ratified in 1868 and decreeing "nor shall any State deprive any person of life, liberty, or property, without due process of law." Any such constitutional right would act only as a restriction on governmental action—for example, state abridgment of freedom of speech. A federal right of privacy would not ordinarily apply to violations of privacy by individuals—such as had been committed in *Titicut Follies*. But development of a federal constitutional right of privacy still had a bearing on the Commonwealth's case. Wiseman's principal defense was that the sacrosanct First Amendment constitutional right of free speech overrode violations of rights of privacy and contract. If privacy was recognized as a federal constitutional right, it would have achieved a status enabling it to face off on a more even basis with the competing right of free speech.

In *York v. Story*, 324 F.2d 450 (9th Cir. 1963), *cert. denied*, 376 U.S. 939 (1964), the Court of Appeals for the Ninth Circuit had been presented with the question of whether a woman tricked into being photographed in the nude by a California police officer had been deprived of a federal constitutional right of privacy. Angelynn York had gone to the police station of Chino, California, to file a charge that she had been assaulted. She was photographed nude by officer Story ostensibly to preserve evidence of bruises. Story later told her that the photographs had been destroyed, but instead he kept them and circulated them among the personnel of the Chino Police Department.

The federal Civil Rights Act imposes liability on any person who, under color of law, subjects any citizen "to the deprivation of any rights . . . secured by the Constitution." 42 U.S.C. § 1983. York sued under the act and charged that officer Story, acting under color of state law as a California policeman, had deprived her of a right to privacy—a liberty secured to her, she alleged, by the Fourteenth Amendment of the Constitution. The federal district court held that she had not stated a case and dismissed her suit.

The Court of Appeals for the Ninth Circuit reversed. It noted that in a Fourth Amendment search and seizure case the U.S. Supreme Court had held "the security of a person's privacy" to be a due process right "implicit in the concept of ordered liberty." *York v. Story*, 324 F.2d at 455 n.10. Applying this Supreme Court language a step removed from the Constitution itself, the Ninth Circuit held that "the concept of ordered liberty" included a right to "shield one's unclothed figure [ ] from the view of strangers" and that this Fourth Amendment limitation on federal action had been made applicable to the states by the Fourteenth Amendment. The court concluded that the state action of officer Story "constituted an arbitrary intrusion upon the security of [York's] privacy, as guaranteed to her by the Due Process Clause of the Fourteenth Amendment." At 456.

York was a great precedent both because it was a favorable constitutional holding and because of its factual similarities to our case. But it was a controlling authority only in the Ninth Circuit, a circuit prone to questionable rulings.

At about the same time that the *York* case was being heard, the State of Connecticut was prosecuting Estelle Griswold, executive director of the Planned Parenthood League, and a doctor charged as an accomplice, for giving advice on the use of contraceptives to a married couple. The defendants had defied an 1879 Connecticut criminal statute proscribing use of birth-control devices. They were found guilty as accessories for counseling use of such devices and were fined $100 each. Their defense was that the Connecticut statute violated a right of privacy of the married couple conferred by the U.S. Constitution and was void; hence there was no crime to which they could be accessories. They lost in three Connecticut courts—the trial court, the Appellate Division, and the Supreme Court of Errors. But their third appeal was taken up by the U.S. Supreme Court at about the same time that the Court was denying certiorari in

York. If the Supreme Court found a constitutional right of privacy in *Griswold* and reversed, this would establish a nationwide constitutional right of privacy and further increase the prestige of the right.

In grappling with the claimed constitutional right of privacy, the Supreme Court had several problems. It was a long stretch to work as the Ninth Circuit had in *York v. Story*, not from the Constitution itself, but from an unstated, supposedly implicit, "concept of [protected] ordered liberty." There was certainly no right of privacy spelled out *in haec verba* in the Constitution. One way to get to such a right was to derive it from the word "liberty" in the Fourteenth Amendment—to hold that freedom against governmental restraints in the marital bedroom was a "liberty" secured by that Amendment. But the Fourteenth Amendment does not protect against every state deprivation of "life, liberty, and property," only against a deprivation "without due process of law." To hold that there had been a deprivation of such a "liberty" without "due process," the Court would have to infuse into "without due process" a meaning akin to "without rational justification." It would have to apply a judicial rule of reason that had come to be characterized by its critics as "substantive due process." The Court would have to hold that a conviction by a jury acting under a statute duly passed by the Connecticut legislature, signed by the governor, and enforced by the Connecticut courts for 80 years, did not reflect "due process" because the Court considered the underlying statute unreasonable. For much of the century, progressives and the elite law schools of the country had inveighed against this kind of judicial activism. "Substantive due process" was anathema to every right-thinking judge in the country.

A rule of reason in due process constitutional law had not always been politically incorrect. From the turn of the century until the mid-1930s, the Supreme Court of the United States had frequently employed substantive due process doctrine to strike down state legislation considered unreasonable, unwise, arbitrary, or capricious. It was the Court that made the judgment on the wisdom of the legislation. *Lochner v. New York*, 198 U.S. 45 (1905), is generally cited as an especially invidious example of employment by the Supreme Court of substantive due process to invalidate reform legislation. New York had passed a statute providing that no employee of a bakery could be required to work more than 60 hours a week or 10 hours a day. Writing for a 5-4 majority of the Court in 1905, Justice Peckham held that the regulation was an unreasonable interference with the right of employers and employees to contract with each other:

> We think the limit of the police power has been reached and passed in this case. There is, in our judgment, no reasonable foundation for holding this to be necessary or appropriate as a health law to safeguard the public health of the individuals who are following the trade of a baker. If this statute be valid and, therefore, a proper case is made out in which to deny the right of an individual, *sui generis*, as employer or employee, to make contracts for

> the labor of the latter under the protection of the provisions of the Federal Constitution, there would seem to be no length to which legislation of this nature might not go. [198 U.S. at 58.]

Justice Holmes dissented. "This case is decided upon an economic theory which a large part of the country does not entertain. . . . The Fourteenth Amendment does not enact Mr. Herbert Spencer's [1851] Social Statics." Holmes became known as the "Great Dissenter" largely by reason of his dissents to substantive due process reasoning.

For 35 years much social legislation, including the New Deal's key National Industrial Recovery Act, had been invalidated as exceeding the powers of the federal government. In the mid-1930s, however, Justice Roberts, who had been voting with a 5-4 conservative majority, changed sides. The view expressed in the Holmes dissents became the law. The Supreme Court backed off from judgments of unreasonableness in economic contexts and turned to giving the strongest presumption of validity to state and federal economic legislation. Substantive due process was replaced by a new test—whether the challenged law had "a rational relation to a valid legislative objective" (see Chief Justice Rehnquist, dissenting in *Roe v. Wade*, 410 U.S. 113, 173 (1973))—sometimes (mis)called a "procedural due process" standard. During the second half of the century, the Supreme Court has repeatedly refused to strike down social and economic legislation claimed to be unreasonable, even outrageous, and thus a violation of due process.

But the defendants in *Griswold* were asking the Court to infuse substantive content into the Fourteenth Amendment due process clause and judge the Connecticut statute so unreasonable as to violate due process. Could the Court maintain its rejection of a substantive wisdom standard in economic cases if the standard was to be applied in personal rights cases? Wouldn't a finding that the Connecticut anticontraceptive statute violated due process risk reinstating the tool of substantive due process that reactionaries had in the past grievously misused?

Another problem in finding a constitutional right of privacy was Justice Hugo Black's version of the so-called "incorporation" doctrine. Under the "incorporation" doctrine, it was considered that the Fourteenth Amendment of 1868, "nor shall any State deprive any person of life, liberty, or property, without due process of law," made applicable to *state* action 1791 amendments to the Constitution known as the Bill of Rights. (The Bill of Rights as enacted imposed restrictions only on the *federal* government.) Thus, the Fourth Amendment's prohibition of "unreasonable searches and seizures" by the *federal* government was made applicable to *state* governments by the Fourteenth Amendment. Under the Black "incorporation" version, this enlargement of the Bill of Rights was accompanied by a matching restriction—the rights protected against state deprivation under the Fourteenth Amendment were *only* those spelled out against the federal government in the Bill of Rights. That is, if the liberty or property right could not be found in these beginning amendments to the Constitution, then the right was not one protected against state deprivation by the Fourteenth

Amendment. Under the Black "incorporation" doctrine, the constitutional right of privacy on which the *Griswold* defendants were relying had to be found in the Bill of Rights.

In a 7-2 decision, the Supreme Court reversed the convictions of Estelle Griswold and her accomplice. *Griswold v. Connecticut*, 381 U.S. 479 (1965). The case is an example of U.S. Supreme Court rights creation that is both illuminating and unsettling. Justice Douglas delivered the opinion of the Court, finding a right of privacy "emanating" from the Bill of Rights in general. Justice Goldberg wrote a concurring opinion, in which Justices Brennan and Chief Justice Warren joined, finding in the Ninth Amendment recognition of a right of privacy. Justices Harlan and White wrote separate opinions concurring in the result but not in the reasoning of their colleagues. Justices Black and Stewart joined each other in separate dissenting opinions. The new constitutional right of privacy was expounded and debated in six opinions stretching over 56 pages of the official report. Though the opinions cited hundreds of cases, no one, friend or foe, cited the only case that was directly relevant—*York v. Story*.

In rendering the opinion of the Court, Justice Douglas could not work from the "life, liberty, and property" language of the Fourteenth Amendment itself because he had accepted the Black incorporation theory. He would have to find a right of privacy somewhere in the Bill of Rights.

Justice Douglas began the job by purporting to reject a substantive due process standard. There could be no resort to a rule of (un)reason. "We do not sit," he began, "as a super-legislature to determine the wisdom, need, and propriety of laws that touch economic problems, business affairs, or social conditions." But the cases "bear witness," he said, "that the right of privacy which presses for recognition here is a legitimate one." He responded to the pressure. The absence of a right of privacy in the specific guarantees of the amendments, was not determinative. The "cases suggest," Douglas declared, "that specific guarantees in the Bill of Rights have penumbras, formed by emanations from those guarantees that help give them life and substance." Thus the First Amendment, prohibiting abridgment of freedom of speech, had been construed, Justice Douglas said, to include "the right to study the German language in a private school," "freedom of inquiry," "freedom of thought," "freedom to teach," and "freedom of the entire university community." "Without those peripheral rights," he asserted, "the specific rights would be less secure." "Several fundamental constitutional guarantees," such as the Third, Fourth, and Fifth Amendments, "create zones of privacy," including "the sacred precincts of marital bedrooms." When the State of Connecticut entered the protected zone of marital bedrooms with its anticontraceptive law, it had violated a federal constitutional right of privacy.

By this tour de force of "peripheral" rights, penumbras, and emanations from specific guarantees, Justice Douglas found the right of privacy that had been "press[ing] for recognition." He found it without identifying where it came from, and at the same time he was disclaiming status as a "super-legislature."

Justice Goldberg wrote a 14-page concurring opinion, in which Chief Justice Warren and Justice Brennan joined. Justice Goldberg argued that marital privacy was protected, not only as "within the protected penumbra of specific guarantees of the Bill of Rights," but also as a right recognized by the Ninth Amendment. That amendment provides that "[t]he enumeration in the Constitution, of certain rights, shall not be construed to deny or disparage others retained by the people." It had always before been considered a truism, meaning only what it said. Justice Goldberg argued that the amendment also implied the existence of "additional fundamental rights . . . which exist alongside those . . . specifically mentioned in the first eight constitutional amendments." To determine what these fundamental rights are, the Court "must look to the 'traditions and [collective] conscience of our people.'" "[A]pplying these tests, the right of privacy," he ruled, "is a fundamental personal right, emanating 'from the totality of the constitutional scheme under which we live.'" The Ninth Amendment prevented federal abridgment of this privacy right, and the Fourteenth Amendment (under the incorporation doctrine) prevented state abridgment of the right.

Next to hold forth in *Griswold* was Justice Harlan. He disputed the "incorporation" doctrine and declared that the Fourteenth Amendment neither republished—against states—the rights of the Bill of Rights, nor was it limited in scope to those rights. "The relevant inquiry," he said, "is not dependent on [Bill of Rights provisions] or any of their radiations. The due process clause of the Fourteenth Amendment stands, in my opinion, on its own bottom." Justice Harlan's opinion nowhere says that he finds a right of privacy in the Constitution, but it has to be implicit from his vote that he did, and that he considered the right flowed from the Fourteenth Amendment prohibition against state deprivation of liberty without due process of law. The evident mission of his concurring opinion was condemnation of Justice Black's version of the "incorporation" doctrine restricting Fourteenth Amendment protections to those spelled out in the Bill of Rights. "Judicial self-restraint," he concluded, "will . . . go farther toward keeping most judges from roaming at large in the constitutional field than will the interpolation into the Constitution of an artificial and largely illusory restriction on the content of the Due Process Clause."

The concurring opinion of Justice White in *Griswold* forthrightly invoked substantive due process. The Connecticut statute had to be matched against "the liberty guaranteed by the Fourteenth Amendment against arbitrary or capricious denials." "I find nothing," Justice White concluded after matching the two, "justifying the sweeping scope of this statute and therefore conclude that it deprives [married] persons of liberty without due process of law."

Justice Black dissented in a 20-page opinion rejecting any right of privacy, whether stemming from Justice Douglas's emanations, penumbras, and peripheral rights, from Justice Goldberg's Ninth Amendment fundamental rights, or from Justice White's construction of Fourteenth Amendment protected liberty. To Justice Black, the absence of any stated right of privacy in the Bill of Rights was decisive. "Connecticut's law . . . is not forbidden by any provision of the federal Constitution as that Constitution was written."

Justice Black contradicted the reasoning of each of the majority opinions. "I get nowhere in this case by talk about a constitutional 'right of privacy' as an emanation from one or more constitutional provisions." The Court had no right to construct Fourteenth Amendment rights from judge-made formulas. He condemned "catchwords" invoked by judges to invalidate statutes because they offend "notions of natural justice," "shock the conscience," run counter to the "decencies of civilized conduct," violate "some principal of justice so rooted in the traditions and conscience of our people as to be ranked as fundamental," constitute "an unreasonable, unnecessary and arbitrary interference," or are contrary to "canons of decency and fairness" or "civilized standards of conduct." He particularly scorned Justice Goldberg's argument that the Ninth Amendment implied the existence of unstated "fundamental" rights that were protected by the Constitution and awaited discovery. "Use of any such broad, unbounded judicial authority," Justice Black remonstrated, "would make of this court's members a day-to-day Constitutional convention."

The dissenting opinion of Justice Stewart agreed that the due process clause of the Fourteenth Amendment should not be invoked as a guide. "The day has long passed," he declared, "since the due process clause was regarded as a proper instrument for determining 'the wisdom, need and propriety' of state laws." Turning to the rest of the Constitution, Justice Stewart could find nothing in it establishing a right of privacy. The Connecticut statute, he said, is "an uncommonly silly law," but it was duly enacted and should stand until repealed by the elected representatives of the people of Connecticut.

Griswold was only indirect authority for us in *Commonwealth v. Wiseman*—its constitutional right of privacy protected only against adverse governmental action. We still had to persuade the Massachusetts courts that there was a Massachusetts common law right of privacy that individuals such as Wiseman must observe. *Griswold* furthered the cause, however, by adding another instance, and a constitutional one, in which the rights line had been crossed. (It would provide the foundation in 1973 for the Supreme Court decision in *Roe v. Wade*, 410 U.S. 113 (1973), that a woman has a constitutional right of personal privacy to elect an abortion in the early stages of pregnancy.) It was also significant for another reason. The discord on the issue of privacy revealed by the many and conflicting *Griswold* opinions carried a warning. If we ever found ourselves subject to Supreme Court review, anything could happen; the Supreme Court eggbeater could scramble our eggs.

Appendix II

T-shirt Insignia Trademark Law

The history of trademark law is marked by judicial ambivalence to enforcement of trademark rights. The reluctance of some courts to enforce rights in trademarks may be attributable to the fact that enforcement confers a monopoly in the commercial use of the words and symbols of the mark and to that extent restricts freedom of speech. To limit the restriction, turn-of-the-(twentieth) century decisions would often enforce the exclusivity of a mark only when it had been applied by a second user to a product directly in competition with the product of the first user—the name owner. Under these decisions, the BAA's rights would have been limited to preventing another *marathon* from appropriating "Boston Marathon" as the name of its race; T-shirt manufacturers who imprinted "Boston Marathon" on T-shirts could have claimed that they were free to do so because their product, T-shirts, was not competitive with the product, a *marathon race*, to which "Boston Marathon" applied.

Borden Ice Cream Co. v. Borden's Condensed Milk Co., 201 Fed. 510 (7th Cir. 1912),. illustrated the old doctrine. The plaintiff, Borden Ice Cream Co., was denied an injunction against use by the defendant of the word "Borden" in the defendant's adopted name, "Borden's Consolidated Milk Co.," because the plaintiff's product, *ice cream*, was not in direct competition with the defendant's product, *milk*. The court reasoned that the name "Borden"

> never had been associated with commercial ice cream. By making commercial ice cream the appellants do not come into competition with the appellee. In the absence of competition, [Borden Ice Cream Co.] cannot assert the rights accruing from what has been designated as the secondary meaning of the word "Borden."

Recognizing the illiberality of its decision, the *Borden* court claimed, obtusely, that its hands were tied by the circumstance that the products of the parties were not in direct competition:

> Doubtless it is morally wrong for a person to proclaim, or even intimate, that his goods are manufactured by some other and well-known concern; but this does not give rise to a private right of action, unless the property rights of that concern are interfered with. The use by the new company of the name "Borden" may have been with fraudulent intent; and, even assuming that it was, the trial court had no right to interfere, unless the property rights of the old company were jeopardized. Nothing else being shown, a court of equity cannot punish an unorthodox or immoral, or even

> dishonest, trader; it cannot enforce as such the police power of the state. [201 Fed. at 514.]

Over the years, judicial decisions such as the *Borden* case have required Congress and state legislatures to enact legislation to broaden trade name protection. *E.g.*, Mass. G.L. c. 110B, § 12 (absence of competition between the parties or absence of confusion as to source not a defense). A notorious recent example of judicial refusal to enforce trademark rights was the Ninth Circuit's "Monopoly" decision. The court ruled that the game had become so successful that the term "monopoly" had become generic, comparable to checkers or chess, and had ceased to be entitled to legal protection. *Anti-Monopoly, Inc. v. General Mills Fun Group*, 611 F.2d 296 (9th Cir. 1979), *appeal after remand*, 684 F.2d 1326 (9th Cir. 1982). The ruling had to be corrected —for the future—by federal legislation.

But other courts have participated in the liberalization of trademark law. Judge Learned Hand gave the reason for breaking away from the *Borden* doctrine in his classic statement:

> [I]t has of recent years been recognized that a merchant may have a sufficient economic interest in the use of his mark outside the field of his own exploitation to justify interposition by a court. His mark is his authentic seal; by it he vouches for the goods which bear it; it carries his name for good or ill. If another uses it, he borrows the owner's reputation, whose quality no longer lies within his control. This is an

> injury, even though the borrower does not tarnish it, or divert any sales by its use; for a reputation, like a face, is the symbol of its possessor and creator, and another can use it only as a mask. [*Yale Electric Corp. v. Robertson*, 26 F.2d 972, 974 (2d Cir. 1928).]

These principles were applied in a 1964 Massachusetts case in which Ropes & Gray had represented the jeweler Tiffany against a local restaurant that called itself "Tiffany Restaurant and Lounge." Federal District Judge Andrew Caffrey enjoined use of the "Tiffany" name by the restaurant as "a flagrant attempt to 'hitchhike' as it were on plaintiff's goodwill and reputation for quality." *Tiffany & Co. v. The Boston Club, Inc.*, 231 F.Supp. 836, 842 (D.Mass. 1964).

The application of a trademark designating a team, person, or event to promotional goods, as in the case of imprinting on T-shirts the name New York Giants, Michael Jordan, or Super Bowl XX, has been a post-World War II development. Several owners of such names litigated their rights with the U.S. Trademark Trial and Appeal Board against manufacturers who sought to trade on the names. A case involving a New York University T-shirt recognized that the university had an exclusive right to its name on T-shirts, and that the natural inference from the imprint "New York University" on the shirt was that the product must be sponsored or authorized by the university. The board said:

> [T]he name "New York University" and an illustration of the Hall of Fame, albeit it will serve as ornamentation on a T-shirt, will also advise the purchaser that the university is the secondary source of that shirt. . . . Where the shirt is distributed by other than the university the university's name on the shirt will indicate the sponsorship or authorization by the university. [*In re Olin Corp.*, 181 U.S.P.Q. (BNA) 182 (T.T.A.B. 1973).]

A similar ruling, though it involved cologne rather than T-shirts, had resulted from an effort to market "Wimbledon Cologne" without authorization from the All England Lawn Tennis Club, which conducts the Wimbledon tennis tournament. (A train station near the club was named "Wimbledon" and this name came to be applied to the club's world championship tennis tournament.) The name "Wimbledon Cologne" could not be registered by the cologne manufacturer, the Trademark Board decided, because

> [T]he mark sought to be registered by applicant clearly implies an association with these championships, especially in view of the design of a tennis player appearing below the words "Wimbledon Cologne." We conclude that purchasers of applicant's cologne would incorrectly believe that said product was approved by or otherwise associated with the Wimbledon tennis championships. [*All England Lawn Tennis Club,*

> *Ltd. v. Creations Aromatiques, Inc.*, 220 U.S.P.Q. 1069, 1072 (T.T.A.B. 1983).]

Advertising that merchandise is "official"—for example, billing Adidas as the official running shoe of the New York Marathon—proclaims a connection between the name owner and the product, implying that the former endorses the latter. Customers purchasing an "official" product are presumably motivated in part by approval of the connection. In an Eleventh Circuit decision, the court observed:

> [M]ost consumers who purchase products containing the name or emblem of their favorite school or sports team would prefer an officially sponsored or licensed product to an identical non-licensed product. Were this not true, the word 'official' would not appear in so many advertisements for such products. [*University of Ga. Athletic Ass'n v. Laite*, 756 F.2d 1535, 1547 n.28 (11th Cir. 1985).]

Some relatively recent T-shirt decisions, however, had been contrary to the name owner. One such ruling involved Champion, a large commercial imprinter of tee shirts, and the University of Pittsburgh. *University of Pittsburgh v. Champion Prods., Inc.*, 529 F.Supp. 464, 469 (W.D. Pa.) (judgment for Champion as to past and future), *reversed as to future and remanded for new trial*, 686 F.2d 1040 (3d Cir. 1982), 566 F.Supp. 711 (W.D. Pa. 1983) (judgment again for Champion as to future). For many years Champion had been imprinting, without permission, University of Pittsburgh insignia on soft goods Champion was marketing. In 1960 the university entered the T-shirt business, began to sell T-shirts under the Pitt insignia, and was soon in litigation with Champion. The federal district court found for Champion. On appeal, the Court of Appeals for the Third Circuit affirmed the decision as to the past but ruled that the University of Pittsburgh had a right to trademark protection as to the future and directed a new trial.

The district court came back with the same decision it had made to begin with, finding that because Champion had entered the market with the Pitt insignia before the university did, the university could not prove a secondary meaning that the shirts with Pitt insignia were sponsored by the university. The court declared that

> There is no historical custom or practice in the soft goods industry treating school, college or university insignia prominently emblazoned on the outside of soft goods as an indicator of source, origin, sponsorship or endorsement. [566 F.Supp. at 715.]

Pitt seems to have given up after this second loss in the district court; it did not appeal.

The *Champion* district court rulings were contrary to common understanding and the weight of authority even in the 1960s. That the law was quite clearly otherwise at the time of the 1986 Boston Marathon was established not only by the *Tiffany*, *New York University*, and *Wimbledon* cases just discussed but also by numerous other authorities holding that the name of a company, team, person or group on an unrelated product such as a T-shirt implies sponsorship by the name owner. Examples included *In re National Novice Hockey League, Inc.*, 222 U.S.P.Q. (BNA) 638, 640 (T.T.A.B. 1984) (appropriation of NHL mark by defendant likely to be "seen as a variation signifying a new and related field of activity sponsored by the senior user"); *Giant Food, Inc. v. Nation's Foodservice, Inc.*, 710 F.2d 1565, 1571 (Fed. Cir. 1983). ("A purchaser . . . would likely conclude that the word 'Giant' in applicant's mark refers to opposer as the sponsor, source, and origin of applicant's products"); *Dallas Cowboys Cheerleaders, Inc. v. Pussycat Cinema, Ltd.*, 604 F.2d 200, 205 (2d Cir. 1979) ("the public's belief that the mark's owner sponsored or otherwise approved the use of the trademark satisfies the confusion requirement"); *Estate of Elvis Presley v. Russen*, 513 F.Supp. 1339, 1382 (D.N.J. 1981) ("a potential attendee at The Big El Show . . . is entitled to know that the production has no connection with the plaintiff . . . the public interest favors our granting preliminary relief"); *National Football League Properties, Inc. v. New Jersey Giants, Inc.*, 229 U.S.P.Q. (BNA) 785, 787 (D.N.J. 1986) (NFL popularity and advertising "have combined to create a public perception and consumer awareness that merchandise bearing the NFL marks is sponsored or authorized by the NFL and its Member Clubs"; "New Jersey Giants" infringes name "New York Giants"); *Universal City Studios, Inc. v. Montgomery Ward & Co*, 207 U.S.P.Q. (BNA) 852, 856 (N.D. Ill. 1980) (movie company entitled to injunction to prevent misappropriation of its name "Jaws" on unrelated goods; "marks which are highly distinctive and have strong secondary meaning are likely to be associated in the public mind with wide breadth of products and services and are subject to being diluted when used by another on unrelated products or services"); *Boston Pro. Hockey Ass'n v. Dallas Cap. & E. Mfg., Inc.*, 510 F.2d 1004, 1011 (5th Cir. 1975) ("The sports fan in his local sporting goods store purchases defendant's fabric and thread emblems because they are embroidered with the symbols of ice hockey teams"); G. L. Battersby & C. W. Grimes, *Law of Merchandise & Character Licensing* 407 (1985) ("courts now recognize that unauthorized use of another's mark . . . even on unrelated goods or services can lead the public to believe that the property owner has authorized or sponsored such use").

Sometimes, however, backing by common sense and the great weight of authority is not enough. Pitt's difficulties in *Champion* were a warning of trouble ahead for the BAA.

Appendix III

Mandamus Petitions, Court Findings, Orders, Opinions, and Certain Exhibits

Re CHAPTER 1—WAR WITH JUDGE WYZANSKI

APPENDIX III, 1A—Prosecution's Motion to Vacate "Judgment of Acquittal" and for Reassignment for Trial (September 28, 1960) in United States v. Standard Coil Products Co., *Criminal No. 60-6-W (D.Mass.)*

UNITED STATES DISTRICT COURT
DISTRICT OF MASSACHUSETTS

Criminal No. 60-6-W

UNITED STATES OF AMERICA

v.

STANDARD COIL PRODUCTS CO., INC.
FONG FOO, and ROBERT KNUPP

MOTION TO VACATE "JUDGMENT OF ACQUITTAL" AND FOR REASSIGNMENT FOR TRIAL

The United States of America moves that the Court vacate its "Judgment of Acquittal" entered September 21, 1960 and reassign the above-entitled criminal action for trial.

As grounds for this motion, the United States says:

1. That the action of the Court in allowing motions for acquittal made on behalf of each defendant, ordering that each defendant be acquitted of the offenses charged in said action, and that each defendant be discharged, was beyond the authority of the Court at the stage of the trial then reached, since the evidence to be presented by the government had not closed. As the Court had been advised, the government had not completed its evidence, or called all its witnesses, either as to the case as a whole, or as to the date, which the Court described as "vital," of the Rosenholm-Teichman conversation. As the Court had been advised, only a few of many witnesses to be called by the government had been heard from. In a case charging falsification of tests, none of the principal test operators and only one of the co-conspirators named in the indictment, all of whom (save for the defendants) the government had subpoenaed and intended to call, had at the time of the Court's action been reached for testimony. The Court was not empowered, at the stage of the trial then reached to determine that the government's evidence was insufficient to sustain a conviction for the offenses charged.

2. That the Court's order, in so far as it was termed a "judgment of acquittal" was beyond the power of the Court and void, and the legal effect of the order, given its maximum possible scope, amounted to no more than the granting of a motion for mistrial.

3. That the grounds on which the Court relied in terminating the action were insufficient even to justify the granting of a motion for a mistrial.

4. That the United States of America has been unjustly deprived of its day in Court.

____

ELLIOT L. RICHARDSON
United States Attorney

____

GEORGE C. CANER, JR.
Assistant United States Attorney

Denied:
Wyzanski, J.

APPENDIX III, 1B—Petition for Writ of Mandamus in United States v. Hon. Charles E. Wyzanski, Jr., *No. 5755 Orig. (1st Cir. 1960)*

UNITED STATES COURT OF APPEALS
FOR THE FIRST CIRCUIT

UNITED STATES OF AMERICA,
Petitioner

v.

HONORABLE CHARLES E. WYZANSKI, JR.,
and the UNITED STATES DISTRICT COURT
for the DISTRICT OF MASSACHUSETTS
Respondents

PETITION FOR WRIT OF MANDAMUS

The petitioner, United States of America, petitioning herewith for issuance of a writ at mandamus directing the respondent Honorable Charles E. Wyzanski, Jr., Judge, United States District Court for the District of Massachusetts and the United States District Court for the District of Massachusetts, in the case of *United States v. Standard Coil Products Co., Inc. et al.*, Criminal No. 60-6-W, to vacate the "Judgment of Acquittal" entered September 21, 1960, in the said case, and to reassign the case for trial, respectfully alleges as follows:

1. On January 15, 1960 a federal Grand Jury returned an indictment in nine counts (a copy of which is attached hereto, marked "A") to the United States District Court, District of Massachusetts, against Standard Coil Products Co., Inc., a corporation, and two of its employees, Fong Foo and Robert Knupp, and the case was assigned to the respondent Honorable Charles E. Wyzanski, Jr. (hereafter sometimes referred to as "the Court"). A copy of the docket entries in the case is attached hereto, marked "B".

2. The first eight counts of said indictment charged that the defendants violated 18 U.S.C. § 1001 by concealing the material fact that tests of radiosondes, manufactured by Standard Coil Products Co., Inc., at its plant In North Dighton, Massachusetts, for the United States, under two contracts totaling $3,731,084.00, had been fraudulently conducted, and the results of the tests falsified. Count Nine charged that the defendants conspired with each other and with certain named co-conspirators, to conceal the material fact of the falsification of the tests, in violation of 18 U.S.C. § 371, and in the course of various overt acts committed in pursuance of the conspiracy, instructed certain test operators and co-conspirators to operate the tests on the radiosondes in such a way as to assure that the test results would not reveal any defects existing in the radiosondes being tested.

3. Motions to dismiss the indictment were denied by the Court on March 25, 1960 and August 30, 1960.

4. On June 7, 1900, the petitioner filed Particulars to the Indictment, a copy of which is attached hereto, marked "C."

5. Trial of the above case before a Jury commenced on September 8, l960. A transcript of the testimony at the trial and of such bench conferences as were recorded (hereafter cited "T") is filed herewith in support hereof.

6. In his opening, counsel for the government stated, *inter alia*, that the Government, following explanatory testimony as to test procedures and specification requirements to facilitate following the later testimony, would call the test operators as witnesses. Government counsel stated that these witnesses would testify that they ran the tests in a fraudulent manner at the direction of the defendants, who concealed the fraud from the government.

7. On September 12, 1960, following efforts by the government (T. 130–148) to comply with the Courts instructions (T. 130, 132, 148) to introduce into evidence a quantity of documents which the government did not consider relevant to its case (T. 130, 131, 150, 155 (A–31, 32)), the Government filed a Trial Memorandum, a copy of which is attached hereto, marked "D." The Trial Memorandum declared that the government would call the test operators as witnesses and set forth generally the nature and importance of their testimony.

8. After calling three witnesses for other purposes (Relzburg—contract documents, Pallotto—explanation, Fisher—agency), the government on September 19, 1960 called Robert

Rosenholm for testimony concerning the falsification of the tests. He was the first witness to testify as to the fraud. In the course of his testimony he stated that he believed a discussion he had had with a Mr. Teichman, a Standard Coil lawyer, took place in February, 1958 (T.681). The trial recessed at the end of the day, September 19, 1960, with Rosenholm's direct examination unfinished (T.692).

9. On September 20, 1960, when Rosenholm's direct examination was renewed, he was asked whether he was sure of the date of the Rosenholm-Teichman conversation (T.693). He testified that his best recollection was that it occurred in approximately September, 1957 (T.693). The Court inquired whether the witness had talked with counsel while testifying in the case (T.693-694), and the witness replied that he had (T.694). Thereafter, in the midst of cross-examination of Rosenholm, the Court excused the jury and inquired as to whether counsel for the government wished to make any statement (T.707). Counsel for the government stated that he had talked with the witness during the overnight recess concerning the correctness of the date, that he did not consider this improper, and that the date of the Rosenholm-Teichman discussion was a matter to which other witnesses would testify (T.710). Counsel for the defendants moved for judgments of acquittal (T.717). In argument opposing the motions, counsel for the government stated that there were many witnesses yet to be heard from, including the test operators (T.713). The Court then recalled the jury, declared that the government's witnesses had showed a lack of awareness or lack of capacity in connection with their

testimonial obligations (T.715), that the date or the Rosenholm-Teichman discussion was a very vital point (T.717), and that counsel for the government had admittedly conferred with the witness during the recess. Respondent Honorable Charles E. Wyzanski, Jr. stated that, in response to the motions of acquittal, he directed the Jury to return verdicts of acquittal (T.718). He then told the defendants that they had been acquitted by direction of the Court and by the Court (*Ibid.*). The next day, September 21, 1960, the Court entered a "Judgment of Acquittal;" a copy or which is attached hereto, marked "E."

10. Rule 29(a) of the Federal Rules of Criminal Procedure provides for the entry of a judgment of acquittal "after the evidence on either side is closed if the evidence is insufficient to sustain a conviction." Rule 57 authorizes a court, where no procedure is prescribed, to proceed "in any lawful manner not inconsistent with these rules." Both the quoted rules and Rule 23, providing that the consent of the government is a prerequisite to waiver of a jury trial in a criminal case, recognize the constitutional right of the government to a trial by jury (U.S. Const., Art. III, Sec. 2, clause 3), which includes the right of the government to present *all* its lawful evidence, when legally sufficient, to the jury for *their* consideration.

11. At the time the "Judgment of Acquittal" was entered, the government's case had not closed, nor had its evidence been concluded on any aspect of the case. As the Court had been advised, other witnesses were to testify to the date of the Rosenholm-Teichman conversation (T. 710), to the explanatory material

(T.370), and, particularly, to the fraud (T. 378-383, 713, opening, and government's Trial Memorandum, "D"). When the "Judgment of Acquittal" was entered, the government had under subpoena, and planned to call in its direct case fourteen additional witnesses, including the test operators and the co-conspirators (in addition to Rosenholm) named in the Indictment. It could not therefore have been determined, at the time the governments presentation was cut off, whether the government's evidence would or would not be sufficient to sustain a conviction of the offenses charged.

12. The Court's "acquittal" of the defendants and its entry of a "Judgment or Acquittal," was beyond the power of the Court at the stage of the case then reached. In so far as the Court's orders purported to acquit and to amount to a judgment, they were unlawful and null and void. Given their maximum possible scope, they amounted to no more than the declaration of a mistrial.

13. The said orders of the Court, and the declaration of a mistrial which they accomplished, were entered on the application and motions of the defendants.

14. No sufficient ground existed for the declaration, on application of the defense, of a mistrial. The credibility of the witnesses was a jury question. The conduct of government's counsel was not improper, did not prejudice the defendants, and did not warrant the action taken by the Court.

15. On September 28, 1960, the petitioner filed a Motion to Vacate "Judgment of Acquittal" and for Reassignment for Trial. A copy of said motion is attached hereto, marked "F." The motion was immediately denied, without a hearing.

16. Petitioner has been deprived of its day in court in violation of statute, rule of court, the Constitution and fundamental Justice.

17. Other than issuance of the writ of mandamus prayed for, no remedy is available to the petitioner.

18. Issuance of the said writ is necessary and would be appropriate in aid of this Court's jurisdiction under 28 U.S.C. § 1651, since respondents action in entering the "Judgment of Acquittal" and refusing to vacate the Judgment and refusing to reassign the case for trial has defeated the jurisdiction this Court would have had over the case upon an appeal from a judgment of conviction or other appealable order of the District Court. Moreover, under the exceptional circumstances presented here, intercession by this Court is necessary to preserve the integrity of the administration of criminal Justice below.

WHEREFORE, the petitioner prays:

(1) That this Court issue a writ of mandamus to respondents the Honorable Charles E. Wyzanski, Jr., and the United States District Court, District of Massachusetts, requiring, in *United States v. Standard Colt Products Co., Inc. et al*, Criminal No. 60-6-W:

(a) That the "Judgment of Acquittal" entered September 21, 1960, be vacated and

(b) That at the case be reassigned for trial.

(2) That this Court grant such other and further relief as it deems just.

UNITED STATES OF AMERICA,
By:

____

Elliot L. Richardson
United States Attorney

____

George C. Caner, Jr.
Assistant United States Attorney

____

Joseph S. Mitchell, Jr.
Assistant United States Attorney

(Attachments omitted.)

AFFIDAVIT

Commonwealth of Massachusetts
Suffolk, ss.

Elliot L. Richardson, United States Attorney, and George C. Caner, Jr. and Joseph S. Mitchell, Jr., Assistant United States Attorneys, being duly sworn, depose and say as follows:

That they have read the foregoing Petition for Writ of Mandamus and that the facts contained therein are true to the best of their knowledge and belief.

____

Elliot L. Richardson

____

George C. Caner, Jr.

____

Joseph S. Mitchell, Jr.

Subscribed and sworn to before me this 26th day of October, 1960.

____

Notary Public

My Commission expires: Sept. 15, 1962

APPENDIX III, 1C—Opinion of U.S. Court of Appeals for the First Circuit in In re United States, *286 F.2d 556 (1961), Directing that Mandamus Issue*

In the matter of
UNITED STATES OF AMERICA, Petitioner,
No. 5755, Original.

United States Court of Appeals
First Circuit.
Feb. 2, 1961.

Before WOODBURY, Chief Judge, and HARTIGAN and ALDRICH, Circuit Judges.

WOODBURY, Chief Judge.

This is a petition by the United States for a writ of mandamus directing a judge of the United States District Court for the District of Massachusetts, and also that District Court, to vacate a "Judgment of Acquittal" entered by the judge in a criminal case, to reassign the case for trial, and for such other and further relief as this court may deem just.

A grand jury in the court below returned an indictment in nine counts against Standard Coil Products Co., Inc., an Illinois corporation, which at the time covered by the indictment had a manufacturing plant in North Dighton, Massachusetts, and two individuals then employed by it at that plant, one as the Chief of its Quality Control Department and the other at first as a supervisor and later as the foreman in charge of the production of certain electronic instruments to be described presently, charging all three with the offenses of concealing material facts and conspiring to conceal material facts in a matter within the jurisdiction of an agency of the United States in violation of Title 18 U.S.C. § 1001 and § 371. More specifically the charges were that from September 1956 to November 1957 the accused had knowingly and wilfully falsified, and conspired between themselves and with others to falsify, tests of radiosondes[1] being manufactured at the time in the plant at North Dighton under two contracts entered into by Standard Coil Products Co., Inc., with the Army Signal Supply Agency.

Motions to dismiss the indictment were denied and the defendants were set to the bar to be tried by jury on their pleas of not guilty.

One of the two Assistant United States Attorneys who represented the Government at the trial made an opening statement to the jury in which he explained the general nature of the charges laid in the indictment and the evidence he proposed to introduce saying that the presentation of the Government's case would fall naturally into two parts, the first part consisting of evidence explanatory of the instruments and of the procedures for testing them and the second part consisting of

---

[1] These are electronic devices for furnishing weather data designed to be dropped from airplanes in remote places and while floating to earth by parachute to transmit continuous radio signals in Morse Code indicating the temperature, pressure and humidity of the air through which they pass.

evidence of deliberate and conniving falsification of the tests run on the instruments by the defendants. In carrying out this program the Assistant United States Attorney in charge at the trial called a witness through whom he introduced the contracts and related documents under which the radiosondes were manufactured by Standard Coil Products Co., Inc. He then called the "Quality Assurance Representative" of the Army Signal Supply Agency who had been stationed at the corporate defendant's North Dighton plant during the time involved for the purpose of supervising the inspection of radiosondes by plant personnel. An examination of the record shows that while this witness was on direct examination he was asked fully as many questions by the judge as by the Assistant United States Attorney. Moreover, the judge on several occasions, both during direct and cross-examination, ridiculed the witness with respect to his use of words, repeatedly corrected his grammar, and many times admonished him to remember that he should be careful in his statements since he was testifying in a criminal case. As the examination of this witness proceeded the questions and sometimes sharp comments of the judge clearly show that he considered the witness's testimony unworthy of belief.

The Assistant United States Attorney next called a witness who briefly identified certain charts to be used by subsequent witnesses as "chalks" and then called a witness to the stand who identified himself as having been the "final inspector of radiosondes" employed by the corporate defendant at its North Dighton plant during the period covered by the indictment.

The direct examination of this witness closely followed the pattern of the direct examination of the government inspector. Toward the end of a day, while still on direct examination, this witness was asked for the date of a conference he had been invited to attend at the plant office with counsel for the corporate defendant. He said at first that he did not remember the date but when pressed for his best recollection he said that he thought the meeting was early in 1958, he believed in February but was not sure. That is to say, he put the date of the conference after the period covered by the indictment. The next morning, while still on direct examination, the witness was again asked if he was certain of the date of the conference and he again said he was not. On being asked once more for his best recollection he said, "Approximately September 1957." The judge then asked the witness if he had talked with government counsel while testifying in the case, and the witness saying that he had, the judge remarked that in a criminal case that was not "correct."

A little while later, on cross-examination by counsel for the corporate defendant, the witness admitted that he had changed his testimony as to the date of the meeting as a result of a conference with one of the Assistant United States Attorneys during the preceding overnight recess. The judge then excused the jury and asked the Assistant United States Attorney involved if he wished to make any statement "as a matter of personal privilege." The latter answered that he was unaware of any reason why he should not talk with his own witness during a recess called in the course of the witness's direct examination and expressed astonishment that the judge should think that there was any impropriety in his having done so. The judge then ordered the witness to leave the courtroom and the Assistant United States Attorney, again having expressed ignorance of any impropriety in what he had done, the judge said, "You will very soon learn," and addressed the Assistant United States Attorney as follows:

> "You were here and you knew he was on the stand. You knew there was a recess. You know the principle that a witness must be examined in public. You know that, without suggesting for a moment that you offered any improper inducement, tampering with a witness is one of the most dangerous things in connection with a case, and particularly a criminal case, that a person should be left entirely alone during the course of his testimony. You must know that elementary fact and elementary rule."

During further colloquy in the same vein the judge said that he did not mean that counsel for the Government were "personally deliberately" doing something they "knew to be wicked," and that he was not "proposing to take any disciplinary action" against them but was only interested in finding out whether the "situation" was one in which he "must respond to a motion." After more colloquy in the course of which the judge again suggested that the "situation" might require him to act "in response to a motion," counsel for each defendant moved orally for judgment of acquittal. Counsel for the Government strenuously opposed these motions on the ground that the witnesses so far heard were not vital to the case but were primarily intended only to lay the basis for concrete testimony of guilt to follow and that there were many government witnesses in attendance in the courtroom yet to be heard for whose credibility he was ready to vouch. He suggested that the most that should be done would be to strike the testimony of the witness under examination.

At the conclusion of the Assistant United States Attorney's remarks the judge recalled the jury, ordered the witness back to the stand, and opened a statement to the jury as follows:

> "Mr. Foreman and Members of the Jury, before I say anything else, let me make it absolutely clear that counsel for the defendants as well as the Court are persuaded that neither the United States Attorney[2] nor either of his assistants consciously or deliberately violated any canon with which they were familiar. They were acting subjectively in good faith, and I do not mean at any stage of the remarks I am about to make to criticize them in the sense that I believe that they were conscious wrongdoers."

[2] The United States Attorney himself had joined his two assistants in the courtroom during the course of the trial.

Following this the judge implied that he considered the Assistant United States Attorney's conference with the witness during recess a serious infringement of the defendants' civil rights and that he regarded the testimony of the two principal witnesses so far produced by the Government to be wholly unworthy of belief, saying that both showed on the stand "a lamentable lack of awareness or lack of capacity in connection with their testimonial obligations" and that the witness then on the stand "has shown either lamentable lack of memory or an extraordinary power of inventiveness."

At the conclusion of his remarks the judge said to the jury that acting in response to the motions for acquittal made by counsel for the individual defendants and the corporate defendant, "I direct you at this stage to return verdicts of acquittal with respect to each of the individuals and with respect to the corporation." The judge then directed the defendants to stand up and announced, "You have been acquitted by direction of the Court and by the Court. Your bail is terminated. You are free."[3]

---

[3] On the next day judgment was entered as follows:

> "The Defendants, Standard Coil Products Co., Inc., Fong Foo, and Robert Knupp, having been set to the bar to be tried by a jury for the offenses of concealment of material facts and conspiring to conceal material facts in a matter within the jurisdiction of an agency of the United States in violation of 18 U.S.C. 1001 and 371 as charged in 9 counts, and
>
> "On September 20, 1960, upon the allowance of motions for acquittal made on behalf of each defendant, it is

We cannot be sure whether the judge directed acquittal of the defendants because he thought the testimony of two of the four witnesses put on by the United States at the outset of the trial was not entitled to belief or because he thought the action of the Assistant United States Attorney in talking with a government witness during a recess called while the witness was on direct examination deprived the defendants of some basic civil right. But whether the judge acted as he did for one reason or for the other, or for both reasons in combination, we think his action was not only plainly erroneous but beyond his jurisdiction.

The testimony of the two principal witnesses to whom we have specifically referred was certainly confused and conflicting. But, although to an appellate court the record of a trial may be "cold," it can nevertheless be clear; and it is clear from the record before us that the confusion and conflicts in these witnesses' testimony was due in no minor part to the trial judge's persistent, sharp and sometimes caustic cross-examination throughout their direct examination.

It is evident that the memories of the Government's witnesses were not entirely reliable, particularly as to details and it is also evident that they were not masters of the English lan-

---

"Ordered that each defendant be, and hereby is, acquitted of the offenses charged, and it is

"Further Ordered that each defendant be, and hereby is, discharged."

guage. But as every lawyer with trial experience knows, the witness whose memory is clear and sharp, who in court is neither over-awed nor cockily over-confident, and who has the capacity clearly to understand the questions asked and the command of language to answer briefly and accurately is indeed a *rara avis.* Cases can only be tried on the testimony of those who have knowledge of the issues, whoever they may happen to be, and all too often, indeed usually, witnesses, coming as they ordinarily do from the body of the general public, neither think nor speak with the clarity and precision of academicians. For the most part witnesses with only average education and intellectual capacity are the tools with which trial counsel must work as best they can. Moreover, every occupation has its own vernacular. Sailors, doctors, railroad men, engineers, not to omit lawyers, and others too numerous to mention, more or less unconsciously slip into the vocabularies of their callings. Naturally witnesses can and should be required to explain the words they use. It is hardly necessary, however, to do so with ridicule or caustic criticism, or repeatedly to check a witness's use of words in reasonably common use by reference to the Oxford English Dictionary, or to require strict adherence to the rules of grammar. The bench is not an appropriate rostrum from which to teach the niceties of English grammar and usage.

It may well be that solicitude for the essential rights of an accused requires the trial judge to cross-examine government witnesses when an accused with no capacity to protect his rights insists upon conducting his own defense or when an accused is represented by wholly inadequate counsel. No such situation is before us here, however, for the accused were skillfully represented by able and experienced trial counsel who were very well qualified to preserve their client's every interest. We think it would have been far better had performance of that function been left to counsel. Trial judges must not forget that questions from the bench naturally and properly fall with great impact upon ordinary witnesses and that counsel are reluctant to object to questions asked by a judge for fear of giving offense. There can be no even give and take in court between the judge and counsel for counsel on the floor do not stand on even terms with the judge on the bench.

[1] While performance by the trial judge of his function, indeed duty, to see that the truth is elicited ordinarily requires clarifying questions from the bench, and maybe on occasion sharp warnings, it is not his function or duty to take the conduct of a case away from counsel. Counsel, as in this case, who sees the examination of his witnesses taken over by the judge and led into matters the witnesses were not intended to cover in their testimony and so opened for cross-examination as to those matters by the other side, finds himself in a most difficult and embarrassing situation. In the first place, it is a delicate matter about which counsel think twice to object to any question asked by a judge. In the second place, if counsel objects to a judge's question on the ground that it leads the witness into matters he was not offered to testify about, counsel runs the risk, exemplified in this case, of comment by the judge before the jury implying that he is seeking to cut off legitimate inquiry. On the other hand, if counsel does not object he soon finds his witness

floundering and displaying ignorance and, again as in this case, provoking critical comments by the judge either on the witness's intelligence or on counsel's failure to prepare his case.

[2] We recognize that in the federal courts the trial judge is not relegated to the position of a mere moderator. He has the duty not only to make rulings of law but also to govern the trial to assure its proper conduct. Quercia v. United States, 1933, 289 U.S. 466, 469, 53 S.Ct. 698, 289 L.Ed. 1321. Moreover upon his shoulders rests the duty to see that the trial is conducted with solicitude for the basic and essential rights of the accused. Glasser v. United States, 1942, 315 U.S. 60, 71, 62 S.Ct. 457, 86 L.Ed. 680. But when the trial judge assumes the role of counsel the adversary system breaks down into confusion worse confounded as the record in this case clearly shows.

[3] This record provides a prime example of the consequences of overzealous participation in the examination of witnesses by the trial judge, for it is clear that the judge's sharp persistent, sometimes almost badgering, questioning and caustic remarks first made the witnesses wary and overcautious and then confused them into inconsistencies, and in addition disrupted the orderly presentation of the Government's case according to the plan outlined to the jury by the Assistant United States Attorney by taking its witnesses into matters they were not offered to cover in their testimony. Running cross-examination from the bench, particularly during a

witness's direct examination, is an innovation in trial practice which definitely does not have the approval of this court.[4]

[4] We are at a loss to understand the basis for the judge's criticism of the Assistant United States Attorney for talking with a Government witness during a recess. We are not aware of any rule of law, "elementary" or otherwise, or any canon of professional conduct forbidding the practice. Of course, as a matter of trial tactics, counsel ordinarily avoid talking with a witness during a recess called while the witness is on the stand so as not to provide opposing counsel with a point to argue to the jury. But tactics are one thing and rules of law and canons of ethics are quite another. There is nothing wrong that we know of in talking with a witness during intervals in his examination in court. Indeed in Frazer v. United States, 9 Cir., 1956, 233 F.2d 1, 2, counsel for the Government was commended for privately reminding a witness of a false statement in her testimony thereby causing her to change her testimony to conform to the truth.

The Assistant United States Attorney was not guilty of any misconduct or impropriety, and even if he had been it would seem that the most the defendants would be entitled to would be an order of mistrial[5]. Berger v. United States, 1935,

---

[4] If cases are to be tried by the judge instead of by counsel, the rules of procedure will have to be drastically revised.

[5] Conceivably, although we have no occasion to decide and do not decide, a judgment of acquittal might be warranted in the event that deliberate misconduct of

295 U.S. 78, 55 S.Ct. 629, 79 L.Ed. 1314. Moreover, the judge should have allowed the jury to pass on the credibility of the Government's introductory witnesses and allowed the Government to proceed with the presentation of its concrete evidence of the offenses charged. The question remains as to what, if anything, this court can and should do to correct the trial judge's error.

[5, 6] Certainly the judge's error was prejudicial to the United States. But the United States obviously cannot appeal. Nor may it resort to mandamus as a substitute for appeal. The writ is not available "to correct a mere error in the exercise of conceded judicial power." De Beers Consolidated Mines, Ltd. v. United States, 1945, 325 U.S. 212, 217, 65 S.Ct. 1130, 1133, 89 L.Ed. 1566. It is available, however, to correct judicial action which is not mere error but usurpation of power, id. One of the writ's two traditional uses "both at common law and in the federal courts has been, in appropriate cases, to confine inferior courts to the exercise of their prescribed jurisdiction." United States Alkali Export Ass'n, Inc. v. United States, 1945, 325 U.S. 196, 202, 65 S.Ct. 1120, 1124, 89 L.Ed. 1544. Therefore the distinction to be drawn is between an error in the exercise of a power conferred and an attempt to exercise a power not possessed.

Government counsel is so outrageous as not only to render the trial in progress unfair but also to make a fair trial in the future impossible.

There can be no doubt of the power of the court under Rule 29(a) of the Federal Rules of Criminal Procedure, 18 U.S.C.A., to order the entry of judgment of acquittal, either on its own motion or on motion of a defendant, as to one or more of the offenses charged in an indictment or information "after the evidence on either side is closed if the evidence is insufficient to sustain a conviction of such offense or offenses." In spite of the clear wording of the Rule, perhaps, as the Government concedes, although again we do not need to decide and do not decide, judgment of acquittal might properly be entered in some situations even before the close of the Government's case, as, for instance, when the Government's opening statement unmistakably shows that the evidence it proposes to introduce would not sustain a conviction, or when it produces evidence conclusively showing either that it has no case or that the accused has an iron-clad defense. But there is no suggestion of any such situation here, for the judge abruptly terminated the Government's case by ordering the entry of a judgment of acquittal on evidence showing no defense and long before the Government had had an opportunity to show whether or not it had a case; and, moreover, he did so in ignorance of either the exact nature or the cogency of the specific evidence of guilt which Government's counsel said he had available and was ready to present.

[7] Primarily on the basis of two cases to be cited and discussed presently, we think that under the circumstances of the case before us the judge had no power, that is to say, jurisdiction, to terminate the Government's presentation of its case

in midcourse by entering judgment of acquittal and that mandamus lies to correct the error.

In Ex parse United States, 1916, 242 U.S. 27, 37 S.Ct. 72, 74, 61 L.Ed. 129, the Court held that, practice in certain circuits including this one to the contrary notwithstanding, a district judge in the absence of statutory authority had no power permanently to suspend a mandatory minimum sentence of 5 years for bank fraud and that mandamus lay to require the judge to vacate his erroneous order of suspension.

In reaching this conclusion the Court adverted to the consequences of holding to the contrary, that is, of holding that an inherent judicial power could thwart a legislative determination of sentence saying:

> "[I]f it be that the plain legislative command fixing a specific punishment for crime is subject to be permanently set aside by an implied judicial power upon considerations extraneous to the legality of the conviction, it would seem necessarily to follow that there could be likewise implied a discretionary authority to permanently refuse to try a criminal charge because of the conclusion that a particular act made criminal by law ought not to be treated as criminal. And thus it would come to pass that the possession by the judicial department of power to permanently refuse to enforce a law would result in the destruction of the conceded powers of the

> other departments, and hence leave no law
> to be enforced."

A later case of the same name, Ex parse United States, 1932, 287 U.S. 241, 53 S.Ct. 129, 131, 77 L.Ed. 283, is more nearly in point. In that case the Court issued its writ of mandamus ordering a district judge to issue a bench warrant, which he had refused to do in the purported exercise of his discretion, for the arrest of one under an indictment "fair on its face" returned by a properly constituted grand jury. The case cited is particularly significant in that it shows that issuance of mandamus by this court in the present case would be in aid of our appellate jurisdiction, and also shows the jurisdictional limits of a trial judge's powers in criminal cases and the necessity for issuing the writ to confine trial judges within those limits.

[8] In the first place, since the Court in the case cited above was expressly exercising the original jurisdiction conferred upon it by § 262 of the Judicial Code (the forerunner of present § 1651 (a) of Title 28), we, as an intermediate appellate court, can safely rely upon it as direct authority for our issuance of the writ in aid of our appellate jurisdiction. See Chief Judge Magruder's discussion in In re Josephson, 1 Cir., 1954, 218 F.2d 174, 177–180. If, in spite of the fact that an accused may ultimately be found not guilty, the Supreme Court of the United States, in the exercise of its ultimate discretionary jurisdiction to review actions of the inferior federal courts by certiorari, has power in its discretion to issue mandamus to a federal district court ordering the arrest of one properly charged with crime by a grand jury, then this court, in the exercise of its direct appellate

jurisdiction, must also have discretionary power to issue mandamus to require a district judge, or court, to permit the United States to at least present its evidence of guilt when an accused properly charged with crime has been brought to trial. There is thus no need for us to consider whether authority to issue the writ in aid of our jurisdiction might also be found in Roche v. Evaporated Milk Ass'n, 1943, 319 U.S. 21, 63 S.Ct. 938, 87 L.Ed. 1185, or La Buy v. Howes Leather Co., 1957, 352 U.S. 249, 77 S.Ct. 309, 1 L.Ed.2d 560.

In the second place the considerations on which the Court relied in Ex parse United States, 1932, 287 U.S. 241, 249-251, 53 S.Ct. 129, 77 L.Ed. 283, for its conclusion that the district judge did not have jurisdiction to deny the Government's petition for a bench warrant for the arrest of one properly charged with crime support our conclusion that the district judge in the situation before us did not have jurisdiction to prevent the United States from going on with the presentation of its evidence of guilt. We have specific reference to the statement on page 250, 53 S.Ct. at page 131, that a proper indictment returned by a properly constituted grand jury[6] "conclusively" determined the existence of probable cause for holding the accused to answer to a charge of crime and also to the statement on page 249, 53 S.Ct. at page 131, that the effect of the refusal of the district court to issue a warrant for the arrest of one

---

[6] We can say the same for the indictment in the case at bar. At least there is no suggestion to the contrary and motions to dismiss the indictment were denied by the district judge.

charged in "an indictment fair upon its face and properly found and returned is equivalent to a denial of the absolute right of the government, as matters stand, to put the accused on trial. . . . The mere statement discloses the gravity and public importance of the question. It is obvious that, if a like attitude should be taken by District Courts generally, serious interference with the prosecution of persons indicted for criminal offenses might result."

These observations, and others we might quote from the same opinion and the cases cited therein, are pertinent here. If, under the circumstances disclosed by the record before us, a district judge for no good reason can halt the presentation of the Government's evidence in a criminal case and enter judgment of acquittal, the action of the grand jury in returning the indictment would be just as much flouted, and the Government fully as frustrated in the performance of its duty to prosecute persons regularly and properly charged with crime as though the judge at the outset had refused to issue a bench warrant for the arrest of the accused. The action of the trial judge in one situation falls as little short of a refusal to permit enforcement of the criminal law as in the other. See id. at page 250, 53 S.Ct. at page 131. Though the situations are different they are clearly comparable.

The industry of counsel and our own research has unearthed no case squarely in point. But if a trial judge does not have the power to prevent the arrest of anyone properly accused of crime, as held in the later case entitled Ex parse United States, cited above, or to refuse for no valid reason ever to try a criminal charge as indicated in the earlier case of the same name, also cited above, it seems to us to follow that a trial judge has no power arbitrarily to halt the trial of an accused when the government has only begun to present its evidence of guilt. We see no difference in principle between blocking a criminal trial at the threshold and blocking it when the government has barely had a chance to put its toe in the door.

The question of double jeopardy remains for consideration.

[9] Strictly speaking the defense of double jeopardy is not now before us. We can confidently anticipate, however, that the defense will be raised by the defendants by a plea of *autrefois acquit*, or former acquittal, when they are set to the bar to be tried again. Therefore, since issuance of mandamus, when within our power, is discretionary, and it would be pointless for us to issue the writ if it were a foregone conclusion that the plea of *autrefois acquit* would be good at another trial, it is appropriate here briefly to advert to the defense of double jeopardy. It will suffice for us to say that from our conclusion that the trial judge had no power, that is to say no jurisdiction, to enter judgment of acquittal, it follows under principles too well established to require citation of authorities that the judgment is void—a nullity—and hence affords no basis for the defense of double jeopardy. See Mitchell v. Youell, 4 Cir., 1942, 130 F.2d 880.

The United States in its application for mandamus has not specifically asked us to order that the case be reassigned for trial before another judge. Nevertheless we shall do so, for we do not see how a judge who has unnecessarily taken it upon himself to cross-examine witnesses not only extensively but also sharply can either listen to their testimony reflectively or weigh their testimony dispassionately.

Mandamus will issue directing that the judgment of acquittal entered in United States v. Standard Coil Products Co., Inc., Fong Foo and Robert Knupp, designated on the Criminal Docket of the United States District Court for the District of Massachusetts as CR. 60-6-W, be vacated and ordering that the above case be reassigned by that court for trial before another judge.

ALDRICH, Circuit Judge (concurring).

If I agreed with the court that one could not be sure of the reason why the district court ordered the acquittal I would have to disagree with its conclusion on the issue of double jeopardy. Since the subject is of some general importance, I will state my reasons.

I cannot think that a court is "without power," that is, "without jurisdiction,"[7] to order an acquittal in the midst of the government's case on the ground that evidence already introduced is so fatally defective that no jury could be allowed to convict. The court assumes, *arguendo*, that it may sometimes be

---

[7] The court apparently uses "power" and "jurisdiction" interchangeably. Certainly there is no question here about the district court's jurisdiction over the case and over the defendants. Accordingly, I will hereafter use the term "power."

appropriate for a district court to direct an acquittal prior to the closing of the government's case because of some evidentiary defect, but says it is unnecessary to decide. I do not think one can leave this matter hanging, but, rather, I believe its resolution to be all-important.

Not unnaturally, in view of the fact that the government has no general right of appeal, there is a paucity of authority with respect to the right of the court to acquit for evidentiary defects at any preliminary stage. In United States v. Dietrich, C.C.D. Neb.1904, 126 F. 676, at pages 677–678, Circuit Judge (afterwards Mr. Justice) Van Devanter said,

> "Where, by the opening statement for the prosecution in a criminal trial, and after full opportunity for the correction of any ambiguity, error, or omission in the statement, a fact is clearly and deliberately admitted which must necessarily prevent a conviction and require an acquittal, the court may, upon its motion or that of counsel, close the case by directing a verdict for the accused. The court has the same power to act upon such an admission that it would have to act upon the evidence if produced. It would be a waste of time to listen to evidence of other matters when at the outset a fact is clearly and deliberately admitted which must defeat the prosecution in the end."

I see no reason to say the court there erred in applying this well-recognized civil principle to a criminal proceeding. See McGuire v. United States, 8 Cir., 1945, 152 F.2d 577, 580. In like manner, in United States v. Maryland Cooperative Milk Producers, Inc., D.C.D.C. 1956, 145 F.Supp. 151, an acquittal was ordered when facts were stipulated during the course of the government's case which the court believed precluded any possibility of criminal liability. See also United States v. Weissman, 1924, 266 U.S. 377, 379, 45 S.Ct. 135, 69 L.Ed. 334.

In the absence of any contrary authority, it seems inherently reasonable to conclude that at whatever stage a fatal deficiency in the government's evidence irrevocably appears, the court is empowered to acquit.[8] Yet it must follow that if the court can make such a decision *in medias res* when its opinion of the damaging effect of particular facts is correct, it can equally do so when its interpretation is incorrect. If a court truly lacked jurisdiction, that would be one thing, but given power to decide, there must be power to decide erroneously. Therefore the question must be, was the nature of the ruling that the court made here so different that it must be said that the court was entirely without the power to make it.

---

[8] There is some suggestion in the court's opinion that Fed. Rule of Crim. Procedure 29(a), 18 U.S.C., permitting the court to acquit at the close of the government's evidence and allowing the defendant to move at that time without resting, impliedly indicates that the court may not acquit at any earlier stage. The rule contains, however, no positive prohibition to that effect. I believe the rule merely recognizes a common practice, and encourages it by not restricting the right of the defendant to move. See 5 Moore, Federal Practice ¶ 50.01 [2](2d ed. 1951).

There can be no doubt that even if a court found no conceded fact, as in the Maryland Cooperative case, fatal to the government, but nevertheless was of the opinion that the government's evidence was so unreliable and vacillating[9] as to be utterly unworthy of belief, it could order an acquittal at the close of the government's case. The government could not appeal, no matter how erroneous the court's determination. I cannot think that a court is entirely without power to reach the same conclusion before the last witness has testified. It is not always necessary to eat the whole of an egg to know if it is rotten. The fact that the court is obliged to put the defendant to the bar, Ex parse United States, 1932, 287 U.S. 241, 53 S.Ct. 129, 77 L.Ed. 283, seems a far cry from saying that it cannot, in a bona fide attempt to weigh evidence introduced, conclude that what it holds to be a vital part thereof is so irretrievably bad that no jury could properly convict.[10]

Suppose here that instead of ordering an acquittal forthwith the court had stated that under the circumstances then disclosed all of the remaining evidence offered by the government must be excluded as irrelevant. Manifestly, the power to exclude evidence as irrelevant exists at all times. The government, perforce, would then have rested, and the court's power to acquit

---

[9] The district court here (wrongfully, I agree) asserted that the witnesses continually and fundamentally contradicted themselves.

[10] Even accepting in full the government's suggestion that it is entitled to a trial by jury, such trial traditionally includes the right of the court to conclude that the evidence does not warrant submission. See Patton v. United States, 1929, 281 U.S. 276, 288, 50 S.Ct. 253, 74 L.Ed. 854.

would have become absolute. In what way was the court's ruling (if the unreliability of the evidence was its reason for acquittal rather than government counsel's alleged misconduct) other than that evidence already introduced so fatally infected the case that all further evidence was irrelevant in the sense that it could not cure the defect. To say that this was done without sufficient consideration is not to say that it was done without power. I believe the court has been misled by the relative magnitude of the district court's error into confusing a difference in degree with a difference in kind.

However, I think that a different question is raised by the other possible reason for the acquittal, the conduct of the Assistant U. S. Attorney in speaking to his witness during the recess. Here the court's assumption, *arguendo*, (note 5) is that "a judgment of acquittal might be warranted in the event that deliberate misconduct of Government counsel is so outrageous as not only to render the trial in progress unfair but also to make a fair trial in the future impossible." I find it difficult to imagine circumstances warranting such an assumption. Cf. Caldwell v. United States, 1953, 92 U.S. App. D.C. 355, 205 F.2d 879, 881, note 11, certiorari denied, 349 U.S. 930, 75 S.Ct. 773, 99 L.Ed. 1260. But in all events I agree with the court that it is totally inapplicable.

It must be conceded that it was within the power of the district court to determine, however, erroneously, that the conduct of counsel was improper. But I do not think it follows automatically that the court had power to acquit for that reason.

"A criminal prosecution is more than a game in which the government may be checkmated and the game lost merely because its officers have not played according to rule." McGuire v. United States, 1927, 273 U.S. 95, 99, 47 S.Ct. 259, 260, 71 L.Ed. 556. When a court acquits in the middle of the government's case because of what it believes to be an incurable defect in the evidence, it has made a judgment on the government's case as a whole. A ruling of misconduct, however, is only a judgment as to the procedure in the particular trial. What corrective steps the court should take after its determination of a procedural error is a separate question. To make the same assumption that the court makes in its opinion, that "deliberate," "outrageous" misconduct which would project its unfairness into a future trial would warrant an acquittal forthwith, does not advance the matter, because that is far from our case. The district court made it abundantly clear that the error, as it considered it, committed by the Assistant U. S. Attorney was based upon ignorance of the court's rule,[11] and was anything but deliberate. Nor was any question of prejudice to the defendants possibly involved. The only testimony which the witness had changed as a result of conferring with counsel was the date of a particular conference. The date was a preliminary matter. Nothing about the conference had been admitted in evidence. The present effect of this new testimony upon the trial was nil. Its future effect was entirely in the control of the court, who

---

[11] An understandable ignorance, since twice before during the trial the court had expressly invited a government witness to confer with counsel during recess about his testimony, and in one instance to "rehearse it with counsel."

could exclude any future evidence relating to this as yet undisclosed conference. This was not a question of degree. Prejudice to the defendants was entirely nonexistent.

Under these circumstances I do not think the court had any more power to order an acquittal than it would have had on the basis of some rule of thumb that more than three government questions, asked in good faith, but regarded by the court as irrelevant, had unduly delayed the trial.

While courts can do, and must be permitted to do, unwise and even foolish things, I think there must be some limit to naked, arbitrary power. As against a defendant's right to be free from double jeopardy, there is the interest of the public in the prosecution and conviction of criminals. See, e.g., Green v. United States, 1957, 335 U.S. 184, 216–219, 78 S.Ct. 221, 2 L.Ed.2d 199. (Frankfurter, J., dissenting). In some instances this has been permitted to override what, strictly, is a second jeopardy, or at least an extended jeopardy. Cf. Wade v. Hunter, 1949, 336 U.S. 684, 688–690, 69 S.Ct. 834, 93 L.Ed. 974; cases collected in United States v. Gori, 2 Cir., 1960, 282 F.2d 43, 48 (dissenting opinion), certiorari granted 81 S.Ct. 282. Whatever may be the correct philosophy of judicial power, I am unwilling to think that such a totally arbitrary act in the course of trial with no semblance of justification behind it,[12] should

---

[12] Unless one wanted to say it was to teach government counsel a lesson for not knowing the rules—which is scarcely a judicial function. It would be doubly inappropriate here in view of the court's prior instructions. See n.5, supra.

deprive the government of its day in court. This may be an exceptional ruling, but this is an exceptional case.

Since I think different consequences flow from the two suggested grounds of the district court's acquittal, it is essential to determine, if possible, which one was the actual basis of its action. With all respect, I do not share the court's expressed uncertainty. As soon as it appeared why the witness had changed his testimony the district court excused the jury and asked the Assistant U. S. Attorney, "As a matter of personal privilege do you want to make any statement?" The court stated that in talking to his witness counsel had violated an "elementary rule," and that it was "interested in whether this is a situation in which I must respond to a motion." The court then described counsel's conduct as "a violation of civil liberties." Subsequently the court called the jury, stated that counsel were acting "subjectively in good faith [but that] the standards of a criminal prosecution in the United States require a constant awareness of the rights and liberties guaranteed by the United States Constitution." It is true that thereafter the court mentioned the government witnesses' "lamentable lack of awareness or lack of capacity in connection with their testimonial obligations," and discussed the case generally. But it returned at some length to counsel's conference with the witness, discussed extorted confessions, unlawful search and seizure, and "the duty of a court to see that every man gets a fair trial," and concluded, "Bearing in mind these principles, and responding to the motions for acquittal made by counsel . . . , I direct you at this stage to return the verdicts of acquittal. . . ."

It may be that the district court would not have conceived of this "elementary rule" if it had not already been annoyed with the testimonial deficiencies of the witnesses, but I have no reluctance in concluding that the reason it granted the motions for acquittal was the same one that caused it to invite them—namely, counsel's violation of the "rule." Accordingly, I concur in the judgment of the court.

Re CHAPTER 2—UNDOING SALE OF THE BOSTON MARATHON

APPENDIX III, 2A—Order Approving Sale of Rights in BAA Names for $5.00 in In re Boston Athletic Association, *Proceedings for Reorganization, No. 57474 (Bankr. D.Mass. December 9, 1935)*

IN THE UNITED STATES DISTRICT COURT FOR THE DISTRICT OF MASSACHUSETTS

In the matter of
BOSTON ATHLETIC ASSOCIATION
(A Massachusetts corporation)

In Proceedings for Reorganization No. 57474

ORDER

On petition of William F. Garcelon, president of the Boston Athletic Association on behalf of himself and a group of Boston men desiring to perpetuate the name and activities of the Boston Athletic Association and asking that he and the group he represents be permitted to purchase for a nominal sum the name "Boston Athletic Association" and the initials "B.A.A.", and notice having been given to all parties interested, and nobody appearing in opposition thereto, it is hereby

ORDERED

That the Trustee, Harry H. Meehan, be and he hereby is empowered to deliver for the sum of Five Dollars, a Bill of Sale or other document to William F. Garcelon, giving to him as the representative of his group, the rights in and to the name "Boston Athletic Association" and the initials "B.A.A."

WITNESS the Honorable Arthur Black, Referee in Bankruptcy.

/s/ ______________________________

Date: December 9, 1935

APPENDIX III, 2B—Agreement Between International Marathons, Inc. and Boston Athletic Association Selling the Commercial Rights in the Boston Marathon to IMI (September 23, 1981)

THIS AGREEMENT made this 23 day of September, 1981, by and between (i) International Marathons, Inc. of Boston, Massachusetts, a Corporation organized under the laws of the Commonwealth of Massachusetts, and or its successors or assigns, hereinafter called "IMI", and (ii) Boston Athletic Association, hereinafter called the "BAA",

WITNESSETH THAT:

Whereas, the BAA is the organizer, manager and owner of the Boston Marathon, and its associated activities, hereinafter called the "event;"

WHEREAS, the BAA desires to obtain sponsorship of certain exclusive rights related to the event on the terms and conditions hereinafter set forth;

NOW THEREFORE, the BAA and IMI in consideration of the mutual covenants and agreements hereinafter set forth, hereby agree as follows:

Section 1. Representations and Warranties. The BAA represents and warrants to IMI as follows:

1.1 *Corporate Matters.* The BAA is a corporation duly organized, validly existing, and in good standing under the laws of the Commonwealth of Massachusetts, with the corporate powers to carry on its business and enter into this agreement.

1.2 *Authority to Execute Agreement.* The BAA by its president has full right, power, authority, and legal capacity to enter into, execute and consummate this agreement and the transactions contemplated hereby,

Section 2. Covenants of the BAA. The BAA covenants with IMI that:

2.1 The BAA understands and agrees that IMI shall use its best efforts to obtain parties, hereinafter called "sponsors", to acquire from IMI for such sums as may be agreed, any and all of those exclusive rights herein acquired by IMI from the BAA.

2.2 The BAA understands and agrees that IMI may under its agreements with sponsors provide for such of IMI's services and expenses as are mutually agreeable.

2.3 The BAA understands and agrees that IMI may make agreements with a maximum of 5 major sponsors, and offer among them any and all of the rights purchased herein.

2.4 The BAA understands and agrees that IMI may also make agreements with, in addition to five major sponsors, a maximum of five minor sponsors who do have on-site recognition, and a number of minor sponsors who do not have on-site recognition, as may be mutually agreeable; and offer among them any and all of the rights purchased herein, *excepting* the minor sponsors shall not appear on the official entry forms produced by the BAA, have free conference booth facilities at any exhibition sanctioned by the BAA, nor appear on the start or finish banners.

2.5 The BAA understands and agrees that it shall cooperate fully with IMI's efforts to negotiate with sponsors, and shall do all things reasonably necessary as may be requested by IMI to effectuate consummation of agreements with the sponsors.

Section 3. On the basis of the representations, warranties and covenants set forth above, and subject to the conditions, agreements and other terms and conditions hereinafter set forth, the BAA and IMI hereby agree as follows:

3.1 The BAA shall assign, and transfer to IMI, and IMI shall thereby acquire all right, title and interest to the exclusive use of the Boston Marathon and BAA Marathon logo(s) associated therewith (however, reserving to the BAA all right, title, and interest to the use of the Boston Marathon and BAA Marathon logos, which is not inconsistent with this agreement) together with the following exclusive rights to the event:

3.1.1 The event shall be exclusively promoted by IMI and the sponsor under language similar to "sponsored by" or "presented by". The exclusive right allowing for an appropriate sponsor identification of the event shall be without limitation excepting IMI or the "sponsor", as the term is hereinafter defined, shall not be allowed to change the name of the event as it has been traditionally named or known.

3.1.2 There shall be a right to place banners or other printed materials identifying the sponsorship of the event by the sponsor along, at, or near both the "start" and "finish" of the event, as may be appropriate.

3.1.3 The sponsor's name or logo shall appear on all bibs worn by participants in the Marathon but only when existing agreements with other parties relative to the material appearing on the bibs have expired.

3.1.4 The sponsor's and IMI's name or logo shall appear on all printed material of the BAA normally produced by the BAA in relation to the event, including information sheets, entry forms, advertising and the like. However, in 1982 only, the BAA shall not be so bound on any printed materials.

3.1.5 To the extent practicable IMI shall be granted by the BAA appropriate VIP seating at the event and parking adjacent to the event sufficient to accommodate eight persons for each of the sponsors to the event. If more seating is required by sponsors, same shall be erected by IMI at IMI's expense, but with the cooperation of the BAA.

3.1.6 The BAA shall provide three conference booth facilities for the major sponsors of the event at any exhibition sanctioned by the BAA.

3.1.7 The BAA shall provide IMI with event materials from its archives or records, and the BAA shall cooperate fully in the undertaking of IMI in its negotiations with sponsors.

3.1.8 The exclusive right for sponsor identification of the event at the prize ceremony, pre-event and post-event press conference, and each of the celebrations, festivities, and organized activities related to the event shall be granted hereunder to IMI, including the opportunity to develop such public relations and advertising as are appropriate to the promotion of the event, subject to the review and approval of the BAA which approval shall not be unreasonably withheld.

3.1.9 The BAA grants IMI and the sponsors exclusive sponsorship rights to the public relations, marketing, merchandising and advertising identification relating to the event by using the BAA Marathon or Boston Marathon name and logo, together with the sponsors or IMI's involvement with the event, subject to the review and approval of the BAA, which approval shall not be unreasonably withheld.

3.1.10 The BAA shall allow IMI or the sponsor without limitation to create celebrations and activities associated with the event, however, such celebrations and activities shall be in good taste and appropriate to the tradition and values of the event and subject to the approval of the BAA which approval shall not be unreasonably withheld.

3.1.11 The BAA grants such exclusive television, movie and radio rights of the event to IMI as may be allowed by law.

The BAA reserves the radio and TV broadcasting rights for Japan specifically and the exclusive right for such TV and radio production for the Japanese market.

3.1.12 The BAA shall, as part of its budget, reserve at the BAA's discretion, a fund to be used for clinics or prizes relating to the event and an additional fund for scholarships for such persons as may be qualified by the BAA or its trustee for such scholarships. Such funds shall be held by the BAA or its designated charitable trust for their identified purposes and subject only to the limitations set forth herein, may be allocated and used as the BAA or its designated charitable trustees deems appropriate to the purposes stated herein.

3.1.13 The BAA shall further allow identification by IMI or the sponsor by the language "sponsored by" or "presented by" or words of similar effect identifying the sponsor's involvement in the promotion of the event and its accompanying activities such as the clinics, scholarships, or activities separately identified by the BAA and IMI herein.

3.1.14 The BAA and IMI realize that a multiplicity of sponsors of the event would make less attractive and diminish its advertising and promotional value for the sponsors herein, therefore the BAA agrees with IMI that during the term of the Agreement it shall not enter into sponsorships other than those agreed to herein without the written consent of IMI. All now outstanding sponsor agreements with the BAA are accordingly to be provided to IMI under separate cover. The BAA warrants that any such agreements that now exist are not in conflict with or inconsistent with this agreement.

Section 4. The obligations of IMI under this agreement are subject to the satisfaction (or waiver by IMI) at its election, of each of the following conditions:

4.1 *The Event.* The BAA shall cause to be produced in essentially the same format as in prior years (the event). The event shall be scheduled as in prior years, but shall be subject to rescheduling at the sole discretion of the BAA.

The BAA shall have sole authority for the conduct or the event and shall cause the event to be properly advertised and promoted and do or cause to be done all other things necessary or advisable to make the event a success.

4.2 *Event Expenses.* The BAA shall pay all expenses directly pertaining to the production of the event and shall have sole and separate liability for same.

4.3 The BAA shall lend its cooperation and support to IMI and the sponsors to make the event successful.

4.4 All representations and warranties made by the BAA in this agreement shall be true and correct in all material respects.

4.5 The BAA shall have performed and complied in all material respects with all the covenants and obligations under this agreement to be performed.

Section 5. All understandings, representations and warranties of the parties shall survive the agreement and all are set forth and merged in this agreement and any exhibits attached hereto, and no other oral or written understanding, representation or warranty shall be deemed to be part of this agreement between the parties.

Section 6. All of the surviving representations, warranties, agreements and covenants of the BAA *in* this agreement shall be deemed to be material and shall be relied upon by IMI. The BAA shall indemnify and save IMI harmless from and against any loss, liability, damage, including reasonable legal fees and expenses, which IMI may incur as a result of any breach of any of the representations, warranties, agreements, and covenants made by the BAA herein, which as provided above, survive the execution of this agreement.

Section 7. The annual sponsorship fee due the BAA hereunder shall be as follows:

A. The annual fee shall be four hundred thousand dollars ($400,000) per year for each year of the event under this agreement. All payments from sponsors in excess of this amount shall be directly payable to IMI.

B. In the event that the Marathon is produced on a Sunday, and can be televised by a national commercial TV network, then the annual fee shall be six hundred thousand dollars ($600,000) per year for each year of the event under this agreement, commencing in a year when all agreements outstanding for the production of a Monday event have expired. All payment in excess of the amount due hereunder shall be directly payable to IMI.

C. Payment of the sponsorship fee shall be due and payable as follows: one quarter thereof at least three months prior to the running of the Marathon and the balance in full thirty (30) days prior to the event. Any payment made to the BAA will be returned to the sponsor should the BAA for any reason fail to conduct the Marathon for the year to which such payment is applicable. The sponsor shall agree not to make public the fact of its sponsorship of the event or to exercise its other rights under the sponsorship agreement prior to having made the first installment of the sponsorship fee for the Marathon as required above.

D. In the event that IMI cannot obtain sponsors agreements of four hundred thousand dollars ($400,000) per year, and thereby the BAA agrees to accept less than four hundred thousand dollars ($400,000) per year hereunder for the sponsorship of this event, then the BAA shall pay IMI a commission for its services of fifteen percent of the amount so accepted in the year involved. An agreement by the BAA to accept such a lesser amount in the year involved shall have the effect of automatically amending the payment requirement of paragraph 7 above, and in doing so, IMI shall be deemed to have performed as agreed in all respects under this agreement.

E. All fees paid by sponsors hereunder shall be kept by IMI in a separate escrow account in trust for the BAA and IMI. After IMI shall release to the BAA four hundred thousand dollars ($400,000) or such lesser amount as may be later accepted by the BAA as set forth above, then the escrow account for the year involved shall be dissolved and IMI shall release to its own account the balance of any fees received, as payment for its promotional services and expenses hereunder.

7.1 For the purposes of computation as set forth above, each year shall be deemed to run from the date set by the BAA for the event to the following year. The first year shall be deemed to have commenced on the date set for the event in 1982.

7.2 All fixed annual amounts as above set forth shall be payable out of the escrow account established hereunder. The amounts set forth above are total payments to be made to the BAA for the exclusive rights set forth herein.

Section 8. This agreement shall extend and renew itself automatically and shall continue year to year so long as the annual sponsorship fee due the BAA hereunder is paid as set forth herein. If sponsorship agreements amounting to four hundred thousand dollars ($400,000) have not been offered to the BAA for acceptance by January l, 1982, then this agreement shall expire without further obligation to IMI unless an extension is granted by the BAA. Every five years the annual sponsorship fee shall be adjusted by adding to the sponsorship fee stated above, an amount equal to the average change of the P.C.I. (Price Consumer Index) for the preceding five year term. In all other respects, the BAA and IMI shall be bound by the provisions of this agreement.

Section 9. The BAA shall provide IMI appropriate credentials of authority to introduce IMI to prospective sponsors of the event, and the BAA shall refer all inquiries regarding sponsorship directly to IMI.

Section 10. The BAA shall execute sponsorship agreements consistent with the terms and conditions stated herein, when IMI presents a sponsor ready, willing and able to execute and carry out the obligations of a sponsorship agreement substantially on the terms set forth hereunder. The BAA may decline to accept as a sponsor any or all sponsors; however, approval of a sponsor shall not be unreasonably withheld.

Section 11. Any contract between the BAA and a sponsor shall contain appropriate language to hold the BAA harmless against any loss, or liability arising to the BAA by reason of the activities of the sponsor.

Section 12. The BAA represents that it has been the producer of the annual marathon on Patriot's Day (covering the course from Hopkinton to Boston) for over 85 years, and that the BAA believes it has established through long and continued usage a right and claim to the names "BAA Marathon" and "Boston Marathon" and to the extent that this is true, the BAA executes this agreement.

Section 13. The payment provisions set forth in numbered paragraph seven (7) above, shall apply to the annual fee due the BAA. In any sponsorship agreement allowed hereunder subsequent to the execution of an agreement for the amount due the BAA under paragraph seven (7), it shall be required that such sponsorship payment be due and payable on a date agreeable to IMI only.

Section 14. Massachusetts Law. This agreement is made with reference to and shall be governed by and enforceable in accordance with the laws of the Commonwealth of Massachusetts.

Section 15. Nondisclosure. The parties shall not, without specific written authorization, either during the term of this agreement or thereafter reveal or disclose to any person or use for its own benefit, whether by private communication or by public address or publication or otherwise, any nonpublic information learned from the books and records of the other party.

Section 16. Notice. Any notice to be given hereunder by the BAA to IMI shall be deemed to be given if mailed to IMI by certified or registered mail, return receipt requested, postage pre-paid, to IMI, Marshall Medoff, President, One Boston Place, Boston, Massachusetts, and to the BAA at its address, 150 Causeway Street, Boston Massachusetts or in either case at such other address as may be provided by the parties to each other by notice in writing.

Section 17. Amendments. No change, edition or amendment shall be made herein or in any of the terms, covenants or conditions hereof except by written agreement signed by the parties hereto.

Executed as an instrument under seal this date,

____

International Marathons, Inc.
by its President

____

Boston Athletic Association
by its President

APPENDIX III, 2C—Memorandum of Decision and Order on Motions for Partial Summary Judgment in Boston Athletic Association v. International Marathons, Inc., *C.A. No. 57376 (Mass. Suffolk Super. Ct. August 29, 1983, Steadman, J.)*

COMMONWEALTH OF MASSACHUSETTS

SUFFOLK, ss. SUPERIOR COURT
CIVIL ACTION
NO. 57376

BOSTON ATHLETIC ASSOCIATION

vs.

INTERNATIONAL MARATHONS, INC.
and others[1]

MEMORANDUM OF DECISION AND ORDER ON MOTIONS FOR PARTIAL SUMMARY JUDGMENT OF (1) BOSTON ATHLETIC ASSOCIATION AND (2) INTERNATIONAL MARATHONS, INC.

I. INTRODUCTION

By this action, the plaintiff Boston Athletic Association (BAA) seeks, *inter alia*, a declaration that a contract executed for

---

[1] Marshall Medoff, Fidelity Daily Income Trust, Shaumut Bank of Boston, N.A., and Francis X. Bellotti, Attorney General. The Attorney General was joined as a party pursuant to G.L. c. 12, § 8G.

the BAA on September 23, 1981 (the agreement) by its then president, William T. Cloney, was entered into without authority and is unenforceable. The agreement purports to designate the defendant International Marathons, Inc. (IMI) as the exclusive promoter of the Boston Marathon, a sporting event conducted by the BAA since 1897. IMI has counterclaimed, seeking, *inter alia*, a declaration that the agreement is valid and binding on the BAA. Both IMI and the BAA have filed motions for partial summary judgment, requesting the court to determine the validity of the agreement and asserting that there is no dispute regarding the facts material to this issue. See Mass. R. Civ. P. 56 (a) and (b).

Based upon the pleadings, affidavits and authenticated documents[2] on file, the court finds that the following facts are not in dispute.

The BAA is a nonprofit corporation incorporated by Chapter 287 of the Special Acts of the General Court of 1887 and under Chapter 180 of the General Laws.[3] The principal activity of the BAA is the conduct of the annual Boston Marathon (the marathon). IMI is a Massachusetts business corporation

---

[2] These documents include a transcript of Proceeding 82-1 before the Massachusetts Division of Public Charities requested by IMI under G.L. c. 68, § 21. Cloney was called as a witness by IMI in that proceeding and was cross-examined by counsel for the BAA. The testimony has been authenticated by the stenographer and the exhibits have been authenticated by the assistant hearing examiner.

[3] The BAA was dissolved on November 28, 1972 for failure to file annual reports, and revived pursuant to G.L. c. 180, § 10A by petition filed on June 22, 1978 and approved on June 23, 1978.

organized on May 1, 1981 by the defendant Marshall Medoff, who has been its president since its inception. Its purpose is to carry on the business of sales and sports promotions.

In late 1980 and early 1981, Cloney and Medoff commenced having discussions regarding the future sponsorship of the marathon and the possibility that Medoff, through a corporation which he would later organize, might undertake the commercial promotion of the marathon. These discussions led to a meeting in March of 1981 between Medoff, Cloney, William B. Tyler and R.H. Kingsley Brown (the latter three all being members of the Board of Governors of the BAA [the board]). At this meeting, the possibility of Medoff becoming a promoter of the marathon was discussed, and a proposal prepared by Medoff was reviewed. Tyler voiced several objections to the terms of the proposal and the meeting ended with no agreement reached.[4]

Pursuant to due notice, a meeting of the Board of Governors of the BAA was held on April 27, 1981.[5] During the course of the meeting, R.H. Kingsley Brown presented a motion

---

[4] The propose discussed at the March, 1981 meeting contained a provision respecting duration which would have provided: "the term of this Agreement shall be a minimum of 5 years. The term may be extended beyond the five years for an additional period of 15 years in 5 years [sic] increments at the option of the representative [i.e., Medoff's yet-to-be organized corporation]." Thus, the term of the agreement under this proposal would have been a maximum of 20 years.

[5] The following governors were in attendance at the April 27 meeting: Cloney, Tyler, R.H. Kingsley Brown, Thomas J. Brown, Ellery P. Koch and Rodney McDonald. The seventh and final member of the board, George Brown, was not present.

seconded by Thomas Brown which sought to grant to Cloney authority to negotiate and execute agreements for the "presentation and underwriting of the marathon." The minutes of the April 27 meeting recite what followed:

> After considerable discussion concerning the extent of the authorization which such a vote would carry and its possible implications of future conduct of the Marathon, Mr. McDonald indicated his disapproval of the motion and asked that the matter be deferred. Mr. Tyler pointed out that Mr. Cloney would be empowered to seek out, negotiate and conclude a contract for the commercial sponsorship of the Marathon over the years ahead and that the Governors should appreciate that this might be the case. There followed expressions of strong confidence in Mr. Cloney and his judgment and discretion in the exercise of such a broad authorization and there appeared to be a general willingness to confer this responsibility on the President. Mr. McDonald continued to express reservations concerning the motion and Mr. Tyler suggested that because of the importance of the subject matter of the motion, the meeting stand adjourned until after dinner.
>
> The meeting reconvened following dinner with Mr. McDonald absent due to a conflicting commitment. The motion made by Mr. R.H.K. Brown was the subject of

> further discussion and it was voted by all Governors present as follows:
>
> VOTED: That William T. Cloney, as President of the Association, be and hereby is authorized and directed to negotiate and to execute in the name of and in behalf of this Association such agreement as he deems in the best interest of the Association for the perpetuation, sponsorship or underwriting of the Boston, A.A. Marathon.[6]

Further evidence of the circumstances surrounding the vote indicates that the members of the board were in general agreement that a sharp increase in sponsorship revenues would be required to sustain the prestige of the race. It appears, however, that there was no mention at the April 27 meeting of the possibility of hiring an exclusive promoter to whom major responsibility for sponsorship of the marathon would be delegated.

Prior to April 1981, the BAA had entered into several contracts for the sponsorship and broadcast coverage of the marathon. None of these contracts resulted in annual revenues to the BAA in excess of 525,000. Each such contract was negotiated by Cloney himself with the individual sponsor or broad-

[6] There seems to have been some confusion as to whether the vote included the singular term "agreement" or the plural "agreements". This court finds that the plural "agreements" was used, as this has been judicially admitted by IMI. See Answer and Counterclaim of IMI at par. 10.

caster. It is clear that the BAA had not at any time in the past engaged an independent promoter for the marathon.

After the April 27 meeting, and unbeknownst to the other members of the board, Cloney continued to negotiate with Medoff toward an agreement which would designate Medoff as promoter of the marathon. During this time, Cloney informed Medoff of the specific language of the April 27 vote. Finally, on September 23, 1981, the disputed agreement was executed by Cloney on behalf of the BAA and Medoff on behalf of IMI. The agreement was amended on January 13, 1982. The amendment also was executed by Cloney and Medoff.

Pursuant to the agreement, in the ensuing months Medoff negotiated and Cloney executed sponsorship contracts on behalf of the BAA. The existence of these contracts was not brought to the attention of the board. The sponsors IMI secured paid their fees directly to IMI. A majority of the members of the board did not learn of the existence of the disputed agreement until late in February of 1982. The board, by a vote taken on September 9, 1982, has declared the agreement to be beyond the authority vested in Cloney by the April 27 vote. The present action, by which the BAA seeks a declaration that the agreement is void, was commenced by the BAA on September 27, 1982.

II. DISCUSSION

A. The Agreement.

The primary focus of dispute in this case is the proper construction and characterization of the agreement. The court will therefore carefully review the agreement and state its conclusions with respect to the meaning and significance of its terms.

The agreement designates IMI as the exclusive promoter of the marathon. § 3.1.1. IMI may enter into five "major" (§ 2.3) and five "minor" (§ 2.4) sponsorship contracts and is permitted to contract with an unlimited number of companies which supply services to the BAA. § A3 (Amendment). In addition IMI is given the right to represent that the Boston Marathon is "presented by" IMI or its assignee. §§ 3.1.1, 3.3.13. With the exception of the Japanese market, all radio, television and movie rights in the Boston Marathon are assigned to IMI. § 3.1.11.

This "exclusive promoter" arrangement is accomplished through the transfer by the BAA to IMI of "all right, title and interest to the exclusive use of the Boston Marathon and BAA Marathon logo(s)." (§ 3.1) and name (§ 3.1.9), reserving to the BAA the right to use the name and logo only insofar as such use is not inconsistent with the agreement. § 3.1. This means, in effect, that the BAA retains its rights in the name and logo to the extent that it may use them in the actual conduct of the race. It has not been suggested that any further rights in the name and logo are to remain with the BAA.

Thus, the language of the agreement indicates a sale of intangible Personal property—the name and logo of the Boston Marathon—by the BAA to IMI, with the reservation by the BAA of certain rights to their use. This characterization is entirely consistent with the term respecting duration of the agreement, discussed below, which provides that IMI is to retain these rights in perpetuity, so long as it performs. § 8.

The agreement also governs the conduct of the parties in carrying out their contractual responsibilities. The agreement requires the BAA to "execute sponsorship agreements with the terms and conditions stated herein, when IMI presents a sponsor ready, willing and able to execute and carry out the obligations of a sponsorship agreement substantially on the terms set forth hereunder." § 10. The BAA is bound to "cooperate fully with IMI's efforts to negotiate with sponsors" and is required to "do all things reasonably necessary as may be requested by IMI to effectuate consummation of agreements with sponsors." § 2.5.

The BAA reserves the right to "decline to accept as a sponsor any or all sponsors" but "approval of a sponsor shall not be unreasonably withheld." § 10. Certain sponsors, however, are approved by contract (§§ A3, A4), and as to those sponsors, IMI itself "may execute on behalf of the BAA the sponsorship agreement, if the form of the sponsorship agreement is consistent with a form approved by prior BAA use." § Al.

It is clear, therefore, that a large measure of discretion in the sponsor selection process is delegated by the agreement to IMI. While the BAA does have a veto power, such power must be exercised reasonably in an atmosphere of cooperation and mutual goals.

The financial terms of the agreement are set out in Section 7. The "annual sponsorship fee" due the BAA under the agreement is $400,000. § 7A. The "fee" remains the same regardless of the amount actually paid by sponsors to associate their name with that of the marathon.[7] All sponsorship revenues in excess of the $400,000 "fee" belong to IMI. § 7A.

The most striking feature of these financial provisions is that they assign a static commercial value to the name and logo of the marathon for *all time*, so long as IMI remits this unchanging fee. See § 8. These arrangements also create at least the possibility that the name and logo of a nonprofit corporation (the BAA) will be utilized to create a potentially enormous profit for IMI.

Section 8 of the agreement governs its term, providing that "[t]his agreement shall extend and renew itself automati-

---

[7] The agreement provides one exception to this "fee" arrangement. If the marathon is produced on a Sunday and can be televised by a national commercial television network, the "fee" becomes $600,000. § 7B. Throughout the recent history of the race, it has been run on a local Monday holiday, Patriot's Day.

The agreement further provides that, at five year intervals, the "fee" is to be adjusted by adding to the $400,000 "an amount equal to the average change of the [consumer price index] for the preceding five year term."

cally and shall continue year to year so long as the annual sponsorship fee due the BAA hereunder is paid as set forth herein." The BAA contends that this provision renders the agreement perpetual at the option of IMI, in that it is renewed automatically and gives the BAA no right to terminate the agreement at any time in the future.

IMI contends, however, that § 8 must be read together with § 10, which permits the BAA to reject "any or all" sponsors upon reasonable grounds. The argument is that the BAA may return to its former practice of conducting the race with little or no assistance from sponsorship revenues, and in so doing "reasonably" refuse all proffered sponsors, thereby causing termination of the agreement by rendering remission of the $400,000 "fee" impossible. This, according to IMI, constitutes the BAA's right to terminate the agreement.

This argument must be rejected. The only tenable construction of the requirement that any BAA decision to refuse a sponsor be "reasonable," is that such refusal must be based on a negative impact on the BAA from association with the sponsor. For example, a cigarette manufacturer or liquor distributor might reasonably be deemed inappropriate as inconsistent with the purpose of the BAA to promote "athletic exercises." See Chapter 287 of the Special Acts of the General Court of 1887. See generally G.L. c. 180, § 4. A unilateral decision by the BAA to reject all sponsors of whatever character could not be so justified and would be anathema to the provisions of the agreement requiring it to cooperate in the execution of sponsorship contracts. See § 2.5. Such action would also be contrary to the "Whereas" clause of the agreement which states that "the BAA desires to obtain sponsorship . . . on the terms and conditions herein set forth." Put simply, the very action which IMI suggests the BAA could take to terminate the agreement would constitute a violation of the agreement.

As a practical matter, it likewise appears that IMI could effectively block any such action by the BAA. For example, pursuant to Amendment § A4 (contractually approved sponsors) IMI could by-pass the BAA's right of refusal completely by dealing only with such sponsors.[8]

In the opinion of the court, the agreement provides no mechanism by which the BAA may effect a termination. The agreement is therefore potentially perpetual, largely at the option of IMI.

B. Delegation of Authority by Board of Governors.

Section 4.2 of the By-Laws of the Boston Athletic Association (the by-laws) provides "The property and affairs of the

---

[8] In the years following 1982, IMI need not allow the agreement to terminate even if it does not procure sponsorship agreements amounting in the aggregate to at least $400,000. There is nothing in the language of the agreement to prevent IMI from making up any shortfall through use of its own funds if it should desire to preserve the agreement for future years. See § 8. Thus, the agreement now would terminate only if less than $400,000 in sponsorship revenues were raised *and* IMI did not or could not use its own funds to reach the $400,000 "fee." Note that even where IMI may be economically constrained to allow the agreement to terminate, the situation would in no sense involve a termination by the BAA.

association shall be under the direction, control, and management of the board of governors, which shall have and may exercise subject to limitations of law and of these By-Laws, all of the powers of the association. Section 12 of the by-laws provides that "[a]ll . . . contracts . . . to be made . . . shall be authorized by the board of governors . . . ." The corporation and its directors and officers are bound by and must comply with these by-laws. See *Mitchell v. Albanian Orthodox Diocese in America, Inc.*, 355 Mass. 278, 282 (1969). See generally G.L. c. 180, § 6A. See also *Morse* v. *Fall River Line Pier, Inc.*, 345 Mass. 681, 682–683; 8 Fletcher, Cyclopedia Corporations, § 4197 at 710 (1982) (business corporations).

Section 47 of Chapter 156B of the General Laws (Business Corporations) provides that "except as reserved to the stockholders . . . the business of every corporation shall be managed by a board of directors." Thus, the function of the board of the BAA is, in all material respects, the same as that of a board of directors of a Massachusetts business corporation. Likewise, the general rule adhered to by the great majority of States is that "the business and affairs of a corporation shall be managed by a board of directors." Restatement, Principles of Corporate Governance and Structure, § 3.02, Comment c. at 60, 61 (Tent. Draft No. 1 [1982]). Since the principles governing the conduct of the board of the BAA are the same as those controlling corporate boards generally, the Massachusetts and other appellate decisions enforcing such principles are applicable to the case at bar.

The leading Massachusetts decision concerning the extent to which corporate directors may delegate authority to officers is *Stoneman v. Fox Film Corp.*, 295 Mass. 419 (1936). In that case, a New York business corporation governed by bylaws similar to those governing the BAA (see id. at 421) was sued due to an alleged misrepresentation by its president in connection with the proposed purchase by the defendant corporation of a movie theater. Id. at 420, 422. The court determined that the principal business of the defendant corporation was producing and distributing films and noted that it had purchased only three theaters in the past. Id. at 423. The court found that the president had been without authority to bind the corporation in respect to the purchase of a theater, stating that such a "course of conduct manifestly was unusual and extraordinary in the conduct of a corporation. Id. at 425. In so deciding, the court ruled that "[t]he directors could not delegate to [the president] the entire control of the defendant because this would be inconsistent with the by-laws and the corporation law of New York.[9] Directors of a corporation are regarded as fiduciaries and are required to exercise their own independent judgment for the highest welfare of the corporation and its stockholders. "'The functions of directors may not be abdicated." Id. See also *Kanavos v. Hancock Bank Trust Co.*, 14 Mass.App.Ct. 326, 331, 333 (requirement of specific authority from board presumed for "major or unusual" transactions).

---

[9] The general corporation law of New York, effective at the time of the *Stoneman* decision, (Laws of 1929, c. 650, § 1) provided that the "business of a corporation shall be managed by its board of directors . . . ."

These same principles have been held applicable to trustees of charitable trusts and governors of charitable corporations. *Massachusetts Charitable Mechanics Assoc. v. Beede*, 320 Mass. 601, 609–610 (1947). See also *Boston v. Curley*, 276 Mass. 549, 562 (1931). Indeed, the powers of officers of charitable corporations to bind the corporation without ratification by its board of governors or directors are more strictly construed than are similar powers with reference to officers of business corporations. See *Boston Y.M.C.A. v. Royal Indemnity Co.*, 289 Mass. 391, 395 (1935) (treasurer) citing *People's Nat'l Bank v. New England Home*, 209 Mass. 48, 49–50 (1911) (president).

Assuming, *arguendo*, that the board intended by its vote of April 27, 1981, to confer sufficient authority on Cloney to enter the agreement, the above authorities compel the conclusion that such an attempted delegation was illegal and without effect. The ordinary business of the BAA is the presentation of the Boston Marathon. To the extent that sponsorship contracts come within the such ordinary business, they have been in the nature of the far more limited contracts discussed above, i.e., contracts by the BAA with individual sponsors. The agreement at issue in this case was clearly a major departure from the ordinary business of the BAA as established by past practice.

The circumstances of this case are to be contrasted with those of *Duby v. Baron*, 369 Mass. 614 (1976), in which the Supreme Judicial Court approved a delegation of authority by the governors of a charitable corporation to an officer. Id. at 621. In that case, the corporation was a hospital and the challenged delegation permitted an officer to temporarily suspend doctors for misconduct. Id. at 615. In approving the delegation, the court emphasized that "the exigencies of the everyday administration of a hospital often necessitate summary action to maintain the required quality of patient care." Id. at 621. In the present case, it is clear that no such justification existed to support the absence of specific review and approval of the agreement by the board. In no sense could a decision to forego such review be based on the "everyday exigencies" of administration of an annual event such as the marathon.

IMI argues that the vote of April 27 itself constituted the policy-making decision of the board necessary to prevent too broad a delegation. This argument fails to recognize, however, that the truly "extraordinary" or "major" character of the agreement derives from the nature of the agreement itself, which, of course, the board did not review.

For example, as concluded above, the agreement contemplates the sale of the major interest in the BAA's most valuable asset—its name. The sale of a corporation's most valuable asset has consistently been held to require a vote of the directors or governors. See, e.g., *Kanavos, supra*, at 331. See also Restatement, Principles of Corporate Governance and Structure, supra, § 3.02(a)(4). The agreement further contemplates its extension in perpetuity, so long as IMI performs. This alone would seem to render the agreement a "major" undertaking. Moreover, the combined effect of these two features is to assign a fixed value to the name and goodwill of the marathon for all time. Compare

Clarke Memorial College v. Monaghan Land Co., 257 A.2d 234, 240, 241 (1969) (express vote of directors divesting responsibility to value real estate invalid delegation by board).

This court concludes that to the extent that the vote of April 2 may be construed to delegate to Cloney powers broad enough to enter a contract such as the agreement at issue here, such vote constituted an illegal delegation of the board's fiduciary duties to the members of the BAA. Compare Milton *Frank Allen Pub. v. Georgia Ass'n of Pet. Ret.*, 162 S.E.2d 724, 729, 730 (Ga. 1968).

C. Apparent Authority.

IMI claims that the vote of April 27 conferred at least apparent authority upon Cloney to enter into the agreement. Thus, IMI seeks to characterize this case as one in which an innocent contracting party, IMI, is to be deprived of the benefit of its bargain through no fault of its own, but instead through the improper actions of the BAA. This contention is without merit.

Under the doctrine of apparent authority, a principal will be bound by the acts of another where representations or actions of the principal cause a third party to form the reasonable belief that the putative agent is clothed with authority to carry out such acts. See, e.g. *Kanavos, supra*, at 332, 333 and cases cited. See generally Restatement (Second) of Agency § 8 (1958). The vote of April 27 could not reasonably have been construed by Medoff, a lawyer, to authorize Cloney to execute on behalf of the BAA a contract in the nature of the disputed agreement.

The language of the vote is quite general. The vote authorizes Cloney to negotiate and execute agreements "for the perpetuation, sponsorship or underwriting" of the marathon. This would seem to encompass a broad variety of possible arrangements for the sponsorship of the marathon. The BAA contends, however, that the vote was intended merely to authorize Cloney to execute contracts similar in nature, if of greater magnitude, to sponsor contracts Cloney had executed in the past. In other words the BAA contends that under the vote, Cloney could only enter contracts directly with individual sponsors.

Were this the case, it would be difficult to explain the use by the board of such broad language. Instead, the factual setting indicates that the board indeed contemplated a "new departure," as IMI contends.[10] The minutes of the April 27 director's meeting indicate that the intent of the vote was to empower Cloney to "seek out, negotiate and conclude a contract for the commercial sponsorship of the Marathon over the years ahead . . . . Confidence was expressed "in Mr. Cloney and his

---

[10] The circumstances surrounding the adoption of the April 27 vote are admissible to elucidate its meaning. See *Fox v. Johnson's Wimsatt, Inc.*, 127 F.2d 729, 735 & n.l2 (D.C. Cir. 1942) to place resolution of directors in factual setting to explain terms does not violate parol evidence rule). Cf. *Robert Indus., Inc. v. Spence*, 362 Mass. 751, 755 (1973); *Shain Inv. Co., Inc. v. Cohen*, 15 Mass.App.Ct. 4, 13 (1982); Restatement (Second) of Contracts § 212(1) & Comment b (1981) (circumstances leading to execution of contract may be shown to elucidate its terms).

judgment and discretion in the exercise of such a broad authorization . . . ." These observations by board members were made at a time when the board had arrived at a new policy of utilizing its famous name and goodwill to generate far greater revenues in order to defray rising expenses and preserve the prestige of the event.

Construed in context, the intent of the vote appears to have been to authorize Cloney to devise a scheme by which to carry out this new policy "over the years ahead." The board appears to have intended to leave to Cloney the decision as to how to accomplish this.

Under this construction of the vote, it is not unreasonable to suppose that certain arrangements involving the use of an exclusive promoter might be within the authority the board intended to confer on Cloney. It is clear, however, that the vote may not be construed as authorizing Cloney to enter into a perpetual contract or to consummate what is in effect a sale of the major interest in the BAA most valuable asset. See *Braden v. Trustees of Phillips Academy*, 321 Mass. 53, 56 (1947) ("[I]t should not lightly be implied that [an agent] had apparent authority to bind his principal for a period which might be greatly in excess of his own tenure of office. . . .")

Since the vote of April 27 could not reasonably have been construed by Medoff to have empowered Cloney to enter into a contract in the nature of the disputed agreement, it did not confer apparent authority on Cloney to take such action. See Restatement (Second) of Agency, *supra*, § 8.

Even more fundamentally, the doctrine of apparent authority does not apply at all "where in the business context, the requirement of specific authority is presumed, e.g., the sale of a major asset by a corporation or a transaction which by its nature commits the corporation to an obligation outside the scope of its usual activity." *Kanavos, supra* at 333. Thus, the law charges persons dealing with corporations with the knowledge that extraordinary transactions, such as that embodied in the agreement, require the approval of the board of directors or governors of the corporation. To hold Medoff, a lawyer, to this standard is not unreasonable and does not unfairly deprive IMI of the benefit of its bargain.

D. Constructive Notice and Ratification.

IMI contends that Cloney's knowledge of the agreement and the sponsorship contracts executed thereunder constituted constructive notice to the BAA of these dealings, citing *Juergens v. Venture Capital Corp.*, 1 Mass.App.Ct. 274 (1973). IMI concludes that since the BAA failed to repudiate these undertakings in the face of such constructive knowledge, it ratified them.

IMI's reliance on *Juergens* is misplaced. In *Juergens*, the court decided that notice to one Shear, who was the defendant corporation's sole promoter, principal stockholder, president, treasurer, and one of only three directors was tantamount to notice to the corporation. Id. at 276, 277. The court accepted the *inference* of the trial judge that the board of the defendant knew of the disputed transaction and failed to repudiate it. Id. at 277.

In the present case, such an inference is precluded by the uncontroverted evidence that the board of the BAA did not become aware of the terms of the agreement until February of 1982 and has acted to repudiate the agreement at all times thereafter.

"Generally, in order to establish ratification of unauthorized acts of an agent, a principal must have 'full knowledge of all material facts.' . . . Ignorance of such facts will not lead to liability. . . . However, a qualification to this rule is that one cannot 'purposefully shut his eyes to means of information within his own control' . . . , having only that knowledge 'which he cares to have.'"

Perkins v. Rich, Mass.App.Ct. Adv. Sh. (1981) 270, 275 (citations omitted). Here the BAA did not have "full knowledge of all material facts," nor did it have such knowledge as would support an inference that it deliberately avoided learning of Cloney's execution of the agreement. This Court concludes that the BAA did not ratify the agreement, either by affirmative acts or by inaction in the face of knowledge of Cloney's acts.

III. ORDER

1. The motion of the Boston Athletic Association for partial summary judgment is *allowed*. An interlocutory summary judgment (see Mass. R. Civ. P. 54(b)) shall enter declaring that the agreement of September 23, 1981 is void, *ab initio*, and unenforceable.

2. The motion of International Marathons, Inc. for partial summary judgment is *denied.*

Robert L. Steadman
Justice of the Superior Court

Dated: August 29, 1983

Re CHAPTER 4—TITICUT TRAVESTY

APPENDIX III, 4A—Letter from Frederick Wiseman to John Gavin, Massachusetts Commissioner of Correction, August 19, 1965

WISEMAN FILM PRODUCTIONS
60 Martin Street
Cambridge, Mass. 02138
ELiot 4-2277

Cable Address: Wiseman
Cambridge, Mass.
August 19, 1965

John Gavin
Commissioner of Correction
Commonwealth of Massachusetts
120 Tremont St.
Boston, Mass.

Dear Commissioner Gavin,

I am enclosing a statement of the proposed film on Bridgewater.

The film would be made for showing on National Educational Television and also be available to organizations and institutions for teaching and training purposes.

I am negotiating for the film to be financed by National Educational Television or one of the Foundations particularly interested in this area such as Ford, Rockefeller or Russell Sage.

No people will be photographed who do not have the competency to give a release. The question of competency would in all cases be determined by the Superintendent and his staff and we would completely defer to their judgment.

Please let me know if you have need of any additional information.

Mr. Forsythe and I were most appreciative of the chance to talk with you on the 11th and are very grateful for the courtesies extended to us by you, Superintendent Gaughan and Mr. Canavan. I look forward to hearing from you.

Sincerely,

FREDERICK WISEMAN

APPENDIX III, 4B—Letter Opinion, Attorney General Edward W. Brooke to Commissioner Gavin, March 21, 1966

March 21, 1966

Honorable John A. Gavin
Commissioner of Correction
State Office Building
100 Cambridge Street
Boston, Massachusetts

Dear Commissioner Gavin:

In your recent request for an opinion, you provided the following information:

> "I have been asked by Frederick Wiseman of Cambridge for permission to make an educational film about M.C.I. Bridgewater. Mr. Wiseman is an attorney and an experienced film maker. I have told him that I would give him permission to make the film. Provided, however, that the rights of the inmates and patients at Bridgewater are fully protected. Mr. Wiseman has assured me that he will only use the photographs of inmates and patients who are legally competent to sign releases and that he will obtain a written release from each inmate and patient whose photograph is used in the film."

In light of the above, you have asked whether you may legally grant Mr. Wiseman permission to make such a film.

I direct your attention to G.L. c. 125, § 14 (relating to the Massachusetts Correctional Institution, Bridgewater), which reads as follows:

> "Subject to rules and regulations established by the commissioner and according to law, the superintendent shall be responsible for the custody and control of all prisoners in the correctional institution, and shall govern and employ them pursuant to their respective sentences until their sentences have been performed or they are otherwise discharged by due course of law, or they are removed by the commissioner, and shall also have the charge and custody of the institution and of the land, buildings, furniture, tools, implements, stock, provisions, and all other property belonging to it or within its precincts."

Unless your rules or regulations provide otherwise, the granting of the requested permission would be within the discretion of the Superintendent of the Institution at Bridgewater, who is a co-signer of your request.

There does not appear to be any provision, whether statutory, constitutional or common law, to the effect that a *consenting* inmate at the Institution may not be photographed (assuming that such inmate is mentally competent to give his consent). *Cason v. Baskin*, 155 Fla. 198, 200. *O'Brien v. Pabst Sales Co.*, 124 F.2d 167, 170 (C.C.A. 5), *cert. denied*, 315 U.S. 823. *Pallas v. Crowley, Milner & Co.*, 323 Mich. 411, 417–418. See 138 A.L.R. 454, 461; 14 A.L.R.2d 762, 770. "The care of a jail [or correctional institution] is entrusted to the jailer, whether he is the sheriff or another [in the case of the Institution at Bridgewater, the Superintendent]. It is his duty . . . to maintain order, as well as to exclude intruders therefrom. In the execution of this last duty the jailer [or Superintendent] has a large discretion in determining at what time, under what circumstances, and what persons not having legal authority may be permitted to enter the jail, or to have access to the prisoners." 41 Am. Jur. 888. See *Laughlin v. Cummings*, 105 F.2d 71, 73; *Shields v. State*, 104 Ala. 35, 37–38. I conclude that the Superintendent may, if he deems it advisable, permit Mr. Wiseman to make his film at the Institution.

Very truly yours,

EDWARD W. BROOKE

EWB:AMJ

APPENDIX III, 4C—Findings, Rulings, and Order for Decree in Commonwealth v. Wiseman, *Eq. No. 87538 (Mass. Suffolk Super. Ct. January 4, 1968, Kalus, J.)*

FINDINGS, RULINGS AND ORDER FOR DECREE

The following is a summary of the facts found by the court.

1. On January 28, 1966, the respondent Frederick Wiseman (Wiseman), in response to his request (after a denial of his previous request in September, 1965, Exhibits Nos. 1, 1A, 2 & 3), received permission from the petitioner John A. Gavin, Commissioner of Correction (Commissioner), and the petitioner Charles A. Gaughan, Superintendent of the Massachusetts Correctional Institution at Bridgewater (Superintendent), to make an "Educational Television Documentary" film at Bridgewater, subject, in the first instance, to a favorable legal opinion from the Attorney General that these officials had the power to give such permission, and subject further to the following conditions:

> (a) ". . . that the rights of the inmates and patients at Bridgewater are fully protected";
>
> (b) that Wiseman ". . . would only use the photographs of inmates and patients who are legally competent to sign releases";
>
> (c) that Wiseman ". . . will obtain a written release from each patient whose photograph is used in

> the film"; (the form and content of such release to be submitted to and approved by the Attorney General); and
>
> (d) that the film, after completion, would not be shown or released without first having been viewed and approved by the Commissioner and Superintendent.

Wiseman agreed to each of the foregoing conditions. See Exhibits Nos. 4 & 5. Exhibit 8.

2. Upon receipt of a favorable opinion from the Attorney General, dated March 21, 1966, that the Superintendent had the power to grant Wiseman permission to make the film, the Superintendent and the Commissioner gave Wiseman such permission (Exhibit #5A), subject to the previously stated conditions, to which Wiseman agreed.

3. The conclusion that Wiseman agreed to all of the foregoing conditions is buttressed (a) by the conditions expressly stated in the Attorney General's opinion, (b) by the testimony of the Commissioner and the Superintendent, and (c) by the testimony, of twelve security guards who severally testified that, upon objection by each of them to Wiseman on diverse and separate occasions during the filming of sequences involving nudity and obscenity and other situations they deemed improper, Wiseman assured the security guards that they had "nothing to worry about," that the officials of the department had the right to approve and edit the film after it was completed

and before it was shown. Wiseman further assured the guards when they objected to patients being photographed in the nude that he, Wiseman, would only show them from the waist up in the final film.

4. At no time prior to the bringing of this suit, during the many conferences between Wiseman and the State officials after the film was completed and was finally shown to the Superintendent and the Commissioner, did Wiseman deny the assertion by each of these officials, made in Wiseman's presence, that he had agreed to their right of approval before the film was to be shown. At no time during the conferences with the Attorney General, and in particular with Assistant Attorney General Frederick E. Greenman (Greenman), did Wiseman deny that the State officials had the right of approval of the film before it was shown. In telephone conversations between Wiseman and Greenman after the first showing of the film at Lincoln Center in New York City on September 8, 1967 (see Paragraph 11 for further findings concerning this showing), Wiseman agreed that he would not show the film again until the Attorney General had given his decision as to certain legal questions that arose concerning the showing of the film, and that neither party "would make any comment to the press until such decision was made."

5. Sometime in April, 1966, Wiseman and his film crew, Messrs. Eames and Marshall, started filming at the Institution, and they were given free access to all of the departments at the Institution, excepting The Treatment Center for the Sexually

Dangerous (which was made off limits as a result of the strong objections made by Dr. Harry Kozol, director of the Center, in his letter of May 2, 1966 to the Superintendent, Exhibit No. 14). Wiseman and his crew were accompanied by a security guard as they roamed about the Institution making their film. They were there, off and on, for about three months, shooting approximately 80,000 feet of film, taking pictures indiscriminately of mentally incompetent patients and inmates in the nude while these persons were in the most personal and private situations.

6. When Wiseman sought and secured permission to make a film, he represented that the film he was to make would be known as "The Bridgewater Story." It was to be an educational documentary, as set forth in detail in his five-page memorandum (Exhibit No. 1A). The following are the pertinent excerpts from this memorandum:

This will be a film about the Massachusetts Correctional Institution at Bridgewater. Bridgewater is a prison for (1) the criminally insane, (2) defective delinquents, (3) alcoholics, (4) narcotics addicts, (5) sexual deviates, (6) juvenile offenders. The prison therefore has a cross-section of the problems confronting the state in dealing with a wide range of behavior of individuals whom the state must (1) Punish, (2) Rehabilitate, (3) Treat, (4) Segregate. The purpose of this film is to give people an awareness and an understanding of these problems and the alternatives available to the state and its citizens.

"The story of the film would be that of *three people*—an inmate most of whose adult life has been spent at Bridgewater; a youthful offender committed from the Roxbury District Court for a 35 day observation period (Judge McKenney, Chief Judge of the Roxbury, Massachusetts, District Court, has granted us permission to photograph the sentencing); and a Correctional Officer intimately concerned with the day to day functioning of the institution. In showing the day to day activities of these *three people* it will be possible to illustrate the various services performed—custodial, punitive, rehabilitative and medical as well as the conflicting and complementary points of view of prisoner, patient, guard, family, legislature, etc."

"This will be a film about a prison and the people who are in it and those that administer it, as well as their families, friends, and the institutions, groups, agencies and forces within the community that either aid or hinder the custody, rehabilitation, punishment and return to community life of those who have been sentenced by the courts to prison." (Emphasis supplied.)

Wiseman further represented (Exhibit No. 12) that the film was to be shown on National Educational Television and would also be available to organizations for teaching and training purposes. The "consultants" on the film would be Charles A. Gaughan, Superintendent of Bridgewater, Professor John Seeley, Chairman of the Department of Sociology at Brandeis University, Professor Morris Schwartz, Professor of Sociology at Brandeis, and Professor Maurice Stein at Brandeis University.

The plain import of Wiseman's representations was that his film was to be a non-commercial and non-sensational project, to be financed by one of the national charitable foundations. The film would be in the nature of a public service project. Wiseman's representations completely negated any thought of a commercial film to be shown at movie houses throughout the United States, Canada and Europe. Indeed, the State officials could under no circumstances have given permission to make any such commercial film.

7. The film product which Wiseman made, and which the court viewed, constitutes a most flagrant abuse of the privilege he was given to make a film. It contravenes in every essential the stated and avowed purposes made by Wiseman, and as set out in his memorandum to the State officials. The film is no longer entitled "The Bridgewater Story." It is now entitled "Titicut Follies," to be shown to the general public in movie houses throughout the United States and Canada. By no stretch of the imagination can this film be deemed to be the kind of film Wiseman represented he was going to make. Gone is the promise of "The Three People" theme, and in its place there is a new theme—crudities, nudities and obscenities. The film is a nightmare of ghoulish obscenities. It is a crass piece of commercialism—a contrived scenario—designed by its new title and by its contents to titillate the general public and lure them to the box office. The film is 80 minutes of brutal sordidness and human degradation. It is a hodge-podge of sequences, with the camera jumping, helter-skelter, from the showing of an inmate in an act of masturbation to scenes depicting mentally ill

patients engaged in repetitive, incoherent and obscene rantings and ravings. The film is excessively preoccupied with nudity, with full exposure of the privates of these persons. There is no narrative accompanying the film, nor are there any subtitles, without which the film is a distortion of the daily routine and conditions at the Institution. Each viewer is left to his own devices as to just what is being portrayed and in what context. Even a professional film critic, who wrote a review of the film, was misled as to what is being portrayed in one of the nude (mob) scenes. Without any explanation it would appear (as it seemed to the critic) that the inmates are indiscriminately and unnecessarily stripped naked, and for no apparent reason. In fact, this scene is a "skin search," which is carried on whenever there is reason to believe that contraband smuggled into the Institution may be secreted on the person of the inmate.

Many of the naked inmates are shown desperately attempting to hide their shame by covering their privates with their hands. The camera, however, is in relentless pursuit—as a hunter stalks his prey—until the stark naked patients can elude the range of the prying eye and ear of the camera. There is a scene of the administering the last rites of the church to a dying patient, the preparation of a corpse for burial, the morgue where shrouded corpses are kept awaiting burial, and a burial scene. A mentally ill patient, grossly deformed by reason of congenital brain damage, is paraded before the camera. We have long since outlawed the exhibition "for hire" of an insane deformed person. See General Laws, Ch. 272, Sec. 33. "It is a film about various forms of madness." There are many other sequences depicting inmates in such a manner which compels the conclusion that the film is a "freak show," and in this connection it is interesting to ponder as to just what Wiseman had in mind when he wrote a letter to one of the film festivals, seeking to have the film shown, in which he volunteered the statement—using these very words—". . . nor is it a freak show." (See Exhibit #51 and #54). No amount of rhetoric, no shibboleths of "free speech" and the "right of the public to know" can obscure or masquerade this pictorial performance for what it really is—a piece of abject commercialism, trafficking on the loneliness, on the human misery, degradation and sordidness in the lives of these unfortunate humans.

None of the consultants previously mentioned was ever consulted, nor had they anything to do with the making of this film. Wiseman never showed the film to National Educational Television nor has he offered to make it available for education or training purposes. It received no financial support from any of the national foundations. It was financed, in part, by private investors, for profit (Exhibit #20). Practically nothing is shown about the other departments at Bridgewater. Wiseman concentrated his camera at the hospital for the criminally insane and, in particular, on those patients who were extremely disturbed and violent.

As bearing upon the question of whether Wiseman produced the kind of film he had promised to make, it may be pertinent to quote from his letter of April 26, 1966 (Exhibit #44), addressed to Russian officials, in his unsuccessful efforts to have the film shown at the Fifth Moscow International Film Festival. Wiseman's letter states in part:

> "The film is organized around an inmate-staff variety show in which the staff and the prisoner/patients exchange roles. For example, the prison psychologist will play the part of a murderer, and a murderer plays the part of a sheriff. Shots of the show are cut together with the "actors" performing their ordinary roles in the prison life—the psychologist as a psychologist, and the murderer as a clerk typist."

Whatever else may be implied in the term "educational documentary," it certainly must mean "fidelity to truth." Just how such a contrived scenario squares with "fidelity to truth" is most difficult to conceive.

We have seen 3200 feet of film. Wiseman has over 70,000 feet of film he took at Bridgewater, depicting many indecencies, and only he knows what else is portrayed in this footage.

8. Wiseman, without notice to the State officials, caused the Bridgewater Film Co., Inc. to be organized in November 14, 1966 (Exhibit #21). Its officers and directors were David Eames and Mr. and Mrs. John Marshall. The latter two resigned on September 25, 1967 when they first learned that the film was going to be shown to the public at Lincoln Center. Their letters of resignation contained strong protests and objections to the public showing of the film and, in particular, to the proposed sale of the distribution rights of the film to the respondent

Grove Press, Inc., a New York corporation, (Grove), (Exhibit #42). (The trial of this action against Grove and the respondent Titicut Follies Film Distributing Co., Inc., also a New York corporation, has been postponed on motion of the petitioners for severance.) The court finds that although Wiseman's name does not appear as an officer or director of this corporation,[1] he is the controlling mind and power in its operations. This corporation is nothing but an empty shell—it has no capital, no stockholders; never adopted any by-laws; never held any meetings (not even the first meeting of the named incorporators). It is merely an instrument created by Wiseman for the plain and manifest purpose of the unlimited commercial exploitation of the film. For the purposes of this case, the court finds no further need to refer to this corporation, except to say that Bridgewater Film Co., Inc. is Wiseman.

9. Wiseman violated each of the conditions to which he had agreed when he received permission to make the film at Bridgewater. He photographed many inmates and patients at the Institution who were, and still are, incompetent to give a release. He failed to obtain a written release from each of the inmates and patients shown in the film who are legally competent to execute such a release. He failed to show the completed film to, and secure approval from, the Commissioner and the Superintendent before releasing it. As soon as the film was completed, and before it was shown to the State officials, and without their knowledge, Wiseman, beginning in April, 1967,

---

[1] Bridgewater Film Co.

solicited practically every "Film Festival" (in 13 cities) in Europe and the United States in his effort to have the film publicly exhibited.[2] (See Exhibits Nos. 44 to 59, inclusive.)

10. After the Superintendent was first shown the film on June 1, 1967, he objected to the excessive nudity and the "new theme" in the film. He told Wiseman that, because of its content, he felt that the Attorney General should view the film. On June 27,1967, the Attorney General, accompanied by some members of his staff, and the Superintendent were shown the film by Wiseman. After viewing it, the Attorney General raised several questions—namely: the excessive nudity in the film; the right of privacy of the inmates; the legal competency of those from whom releases were allegedly obtained. He informed Wiseman, among other things, that he was going to have his staff do some legal research on these matters, and Wiseman agreed to do nothing further about showing the film until the Attorney General had given his opinion on these matters.

11. Without notice to the State officials, Wiseman showed the film on September 8, 1967 to a selection committee of the Lincoln Center Film Festival, and others, in New York

---

[2] The following is a list of the cities conducting "Annual Film Festivals" during the year 1967, at which Wiseman sought to make contacts and arrangements for the showing and ultimate commercial release of the film, prior to his deal giving Grove exclusive rights of distribution for the United States and Canada: *Manheim, West Germany; London, England; Venice, Italy; Moscow, Russia; Acapulco, Mexico; Leipzig, Germany; Budapest, Hungary; Thessalonika, Greece; Cork, Ireland; Edinburgh, Scotland; West Berlin, San Francisco, and New York City.* He sought maximum saturation exposure of the film to be shown on the screens of movie houses anywhere and everywhere.

City. In connection with this showing, Wiseman, by letter dated August 18, 1967 (Exhibit #58) informed the director of the festival that ". . . I have secured releases from those people who are in the film *or from their authorized representatives.*" This statement was not true, and the reference to ". . . *their authorized representatives*" was made out of whole cloth. (Emphasis supplied.)

12. On September 16, 1967, an article appeared in the Quincy Patriot Ledger (Exhibit #40) in which the Superintendent asserted that he had informed Wiseman that the film could not be shown at the New York Film Festival, scheduled for September 26, 1967, "until it is approved by the state's 'three censors'" (the Commissioner, the Superintendent and the Attorney General). On September 18, 1967, Wiseman called Greenman about the article and asked him if this meant that Wiseman would have "to withdraw" the film, to which Greenman replied by reminding Wiseman of his agreement not to show the film until the Attorney General had given his opinion. Arrangements were then made for the parties to meet at the Attorney General's office on September 20, which meeting was postponed on that date until the next day, September 21, at the request of Wiseman.

13. On September 21, 1967, there was a conference at the Attorney General's office, attended by Wiseman and his legal advisers, attorney G. Berlin and Professor Alan Dershowitz of the Harvard Law School. Wiseman was informed by the Attorney General that in his opinion the film constituted an

invasion of the privacy of the inmates shown in the film; that mentally incompetent patients were shown in the film, and that the releases, if any, obtained by Wiseman were not valid in view of the manner in which they were obtained. The Attorney General concluded by saying that he had a draft of a letter to the Commissioner incorporating these conclusions. As of the time of this meeting, the Commissioner had not yet been shown the film. He viewed it for the first time on the evening of September 21, 1967. On September 22, 1967, the Commissioner notified Wiseman by mail that the film could not be shown "in its present form." (Exhibit #7A.)

14. As to the releases allegedly procured by Wiseman from the mentally competent inmates and patients appearing in the film, the court finds and rules that the procedure followed by Wiseman was a sham and a pretense. Wiseman testified that he had procured about 170 individual releases, but none was produced in evidence during the trial (except as to a stipulation concerning ten of them). The releases were not shown to the Attorney General when he requested to see them. These releases, if they were obtained, were executed before the actual filming of the sequence involving the releaser, at that time had no idea of what was going to be portrayed, because it was to be "spontaneous and unrehearsed". He was never shown the actual film sequence concerning which his release was sought. Wiseman did not have any prepared list of the names of those whose pictures he had taken, and so it is impossible to tell from viewing the film as to the precise number or identity of the persons appearing therein who had purportedly signed releases. Furthermore,

there is indeed a serious question as to whether these patients were free to exercise any meaningful choice when they were asked to sign a release. These persons, being in custody, could well have been under psychological pressure or duress, when requested to sign a release, while in the presence of a security guard who accompanied the camera crew. As the consideration for the signing of a release, Wiseman promised to deposit "a few dollars" in the account (at the Institution) of each inmate or patient who signed. Wiseman neglected to keep his promises. The court finds and rules that such releases as may have been obtained are a nullity.

15. Sometime in August 1967, Wiseman, unknown to the State officials, started negotiations which culminated in an agreement in September 1967 with Grove, whereby Grove was given the exclusive rights to distribute the film "in all sizes and gauges of film for all purposes in the United States and Canada." This "memo" of agreement (Exhibit #22) amounted to an unlimited and unrestricted commercial exploitation of the film for its showing to the general public at movie houses throughout the United States and Canada. Under this arrangement, Wiseman is to receive an advance of $25,000 against the payment to him of 50% of the theatrical gross receipts, and 75% from any television sale in the territory. Grove agreed to spend $10,000 in the advertising and promoting of the film, with Grove having "complete control of the manner and means of distribution." The aforesaid arrangement was entered into surreptitiously, without notice to or knowledge of the State officials. In fact, the deal with Grove was being consummated

during the very period that Wiseman was having his conferences with the Attorney General's office—supposedly awaiting an opinion as to whether the film was to be approved.

16. On Thursday, September 28, 1967, the film "Titicut Follies" was shown at the Lincoln Center, New York City, before an audience of over two hundred people. Mr. Wiseman was present at the showing and gave a talk about the film after the film concluded. On October 3, 1967, the film commenced its exhibition, for profit, at Cinema 57 Rendezvous, a public theatre in New York City, and was shown five times daily, for two to three weeks. When it completed its showing at this theatre, it was exhibited for approximately two to three additional weeks at Carnegie Hall Theatre, for profit, with showings at 12:00 noon, 1:30 P.M., 3:00 P.M., 4:45 P.M., 6:30 P.M., 8:15 P.M., and 10:00 P.M. Both theatres advertised it as: "Makes Marat/Sade look like 'Holiday on Ice.'" A charge was made by these theatres to their patrons.

17. The court finds and rules that the film is an unwarranted and illegal intrusion by Wiseman into the lives and right to privacy of each inmate and patient who is pictured there. Many, if not all, of the scenes embarrass and degrade these persons in a manner clearly not warranted by any legitimate public concern. It would seem to be axiomatic that no person, whether mentally competent or not, can be dragooned or indentured into playing the part of an actor in a movie scenario whether as a star or in a supporting role. Assuming a matter of genuine public interest, and further assuming that the officials had

authority to grant permission to make an educational documentary film, there is a heavy responsibility on these officials to protect the basic human rights of the patients and inmates who have been committed to their charge. These patients have an absolute right, subject only to the necessary procedures for internal security, and for their care, custody and treatment, to be left alone. A legal pronouncement that, in the name of free speech, a person may be required, without his approval or agreement, to participate in a commercial, moneymaking movie or any other commercial enterprise would be shocking indeed. The right of the public to know and freedom of speech are not absolutes which, at all events and under all conditions, override the right of privacy. The court rules that the legitimate public interest, freedom of speech, and right of the public to know does not carry with them the unauthorized use of pictures showing persons, clearly identifiable, in such a manner as to outrage and cause mental suffering, shame or humiliation to a person of ordinary sensibilities. The court finds and rules that in the circumstances of this case these persons were virtually forced into exhibition of their nude bodies, and to suffer other indignities for the plain and manifest purpose of profitable box office receipts.

18. Those who are confined to state institutions under authority of law are entitled to absolute protection against their commercial exploitation in any way for profit or gain. This truth would seem to be founded upon the most elementary consideration of natural law and human decency, and it is the responsibility of the State to protect them against any such invasion or ex-

ploitation. The failure to give the patients such protection would be a most serious dereliction of duty.

19. Wiseman now takes the position that even if he agreed to the conditions, including the right of approval of the film by the State officials before it could be shown, this would constitute a violation of the right of free speech and of the free dissemination of news, and therefore the conditions cannot be enforced. He seizes upon this constitutional provision to permit him to exploit these unfortunate individuals through the medium of the film scenario he had contrived. Apparently this contention is based in part on the premise that these inmates, by virtue of their confinement, are bereft of any vestige of personal privacy and human dignity. He says, in substance, that they are now public property and can be displayed as such in a commercial movie.

20. The court finds and rules that the terms and conditions upon which Wiseman was given permission to make the film, including the right of approval, to which Wiseman fully agreed, do not constitute "censorship" in any pejorative sense. In the context of the problems necessarily involved in the making and subsequent showing of the film, these terms and conditions were necessary precautions and safeguards in order that the State protect the civil and privacy rights of the patients and inmates.

21. At no time during the period of almost two years since Wiseman was first given permission to make a film at Bridgewater and, in particular, after the film was viewed by the

State officials and during any of the conferences with State officials, did Wiseman or his attorney or his other legal advisers raise any question concerning "censorship" by the State or the violation of the rights of free speech, etc. This issue is a complete afterthought, and was first raised by Wiseman when the Commonwealth instituted this suit. Wiseman seeks thereby to divert attention (a) from his willful violation of the express agreements he made in connection with the permission given him to make the film, and (b) from his crass commercialization and venality, which are all so painfully obvious from the kind of film he made and exhibited, and from the sale of its distribution rights for unrestricted and public showing at movie houses throughout the United States and Canada. It is all too clear that Wiseman is now attempting to cast the Commonwealth of Massachusetts in the role of a malefactor seeking to suppress matters of legitimate concern; and to picture the State as trying to hide from public view and knowledge alleged unsatisfactory conditions at one of its institutions.

22. The court rules that the film is a violation of the natural and civil rights of the patients and inmates at the Institution, and in particular it is a violation of their respective rights of privacy. This right of privacy rests upon the most elementary principles of natural law, and its violation constitutes a trespass and a nuisance. Continued or continuing violations are a proper subject for injunctive relief. The true rule is that equity will protect the personal and intangible rights of an individual just as it will enjoin the violation of a person's property rights.

23. As to the status of the respective petitioners, the court finds and rules as follows:

(1) The Commissioner and the Superintendent, as individuals or as officials of the State, have no standing as petitioners. There is no allegation or any proof that the right of privacy as to either of them has been violated. On the issue of Wiseman's failure to observe and comply with the terms and conditions imposed on him when he was given the privilege to make the movie, the Commonwealth of Massachusetts is the proper party petitioner and not these two public officials who were then and there acting in the presumptive performance of their respective duties in behalf of the Commonwealth.

(2) Mr. Gaughan (Superintendent), as guardian of Mr. Bulcock, is a proper party petitioner in the trial of the issue of the invasion of the right of privacy of his ward, Mr. Bulcock. Mr. Gaughan's appointment as guardian cannot be collaterally attacked in these proceedings.

(3) The Commonwealth of Massachusetts has standing, in its sovereign capacity, to bring this bill of complaint, seeking an injunction based on the violation of the terms and conditions of the privilege given Wiseman to make a movie of the patients, inmates, and others committed to its care and custody at Bridgewater. This position may appear to rest

> upon the narrow ground of the breach of an "agreement," wherein equitable relief may be sought and obtained if the breach involves a continuing trespass or irreparable injury or damage. There is a further and much broader ground which gives the Commonwealth status as a party in these proceedings—namely: the obligation of the State to protect the right of privacy of those who are committed to its care and custody, and especially the mentally ill. While the right of privacy is generally considered to be personal, nevertheless, on the facts in this case, the Commonwealth may properly seek injunctive relief in their behalf. The Commonwealth not only has the power to protect the right of privacy of these patients and inmates, it has a bounden duty to do so.

24. In this proceeding, the petitioners do not seek any award of compensatory damages, as such, arising out of the violation by Wiseman of the right of privacy of the inmates and patients. With respect to the petitioners' prayers for relief concerning the disposition of the income and profits which have been derived from the showing of the film, the court reserves judgment thereon until the conclusion of this suit against the respondents Grove Press, Inc. and Titicut Follies Film Distributing Co., Inc.

25. Let a decree be entered substantially in accordance with paragraphs numbered 4, 5, 6, 11 and 12 and 13 of the prayers as set out in the substitute bill of complaint, modified,

however, by the deletion of the words "without prior approval in writing by the plaintiffs," as appearing at the end of said paragraphs numbered 5 and 12, respectively. The respondents Frederick Wiseman and Bridgewater Film Co., Inc. are further ordered to deliver to the Commonwealth forthwith, upon the entry of the decree, the balance of the film footage (the original negative and any and all prints thereof), together with sound tapes, taken by them at Bridgewater.

HARRY KALUS
Justice of the Superior Court

Entered: January 4, 1968

(The foregoing Findings, Rulings and Order for Decree has been amended in compliance with the court's Report of Material Facts, R. 59-60.)

Re CHAPTER 5—THREE YEARS OF JUDICIAL LICENSE TO INFRINGE THE "BOSTON MARATHON" NAME

APPENDIX III, 5A—Bogus "Boston Marathon" T-shirts, 1986

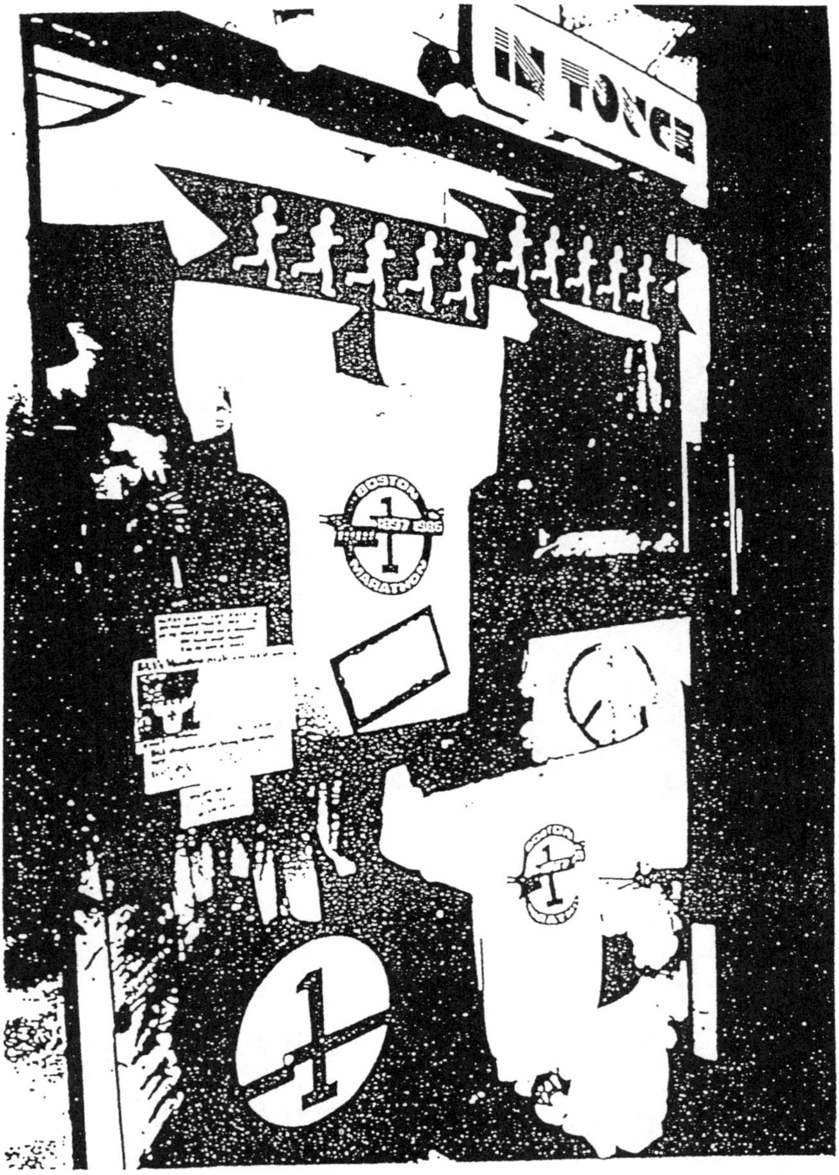
BOSTON
1897 1986
MARATHON

RUNNIN'
MARATHON '86
Collector's Item

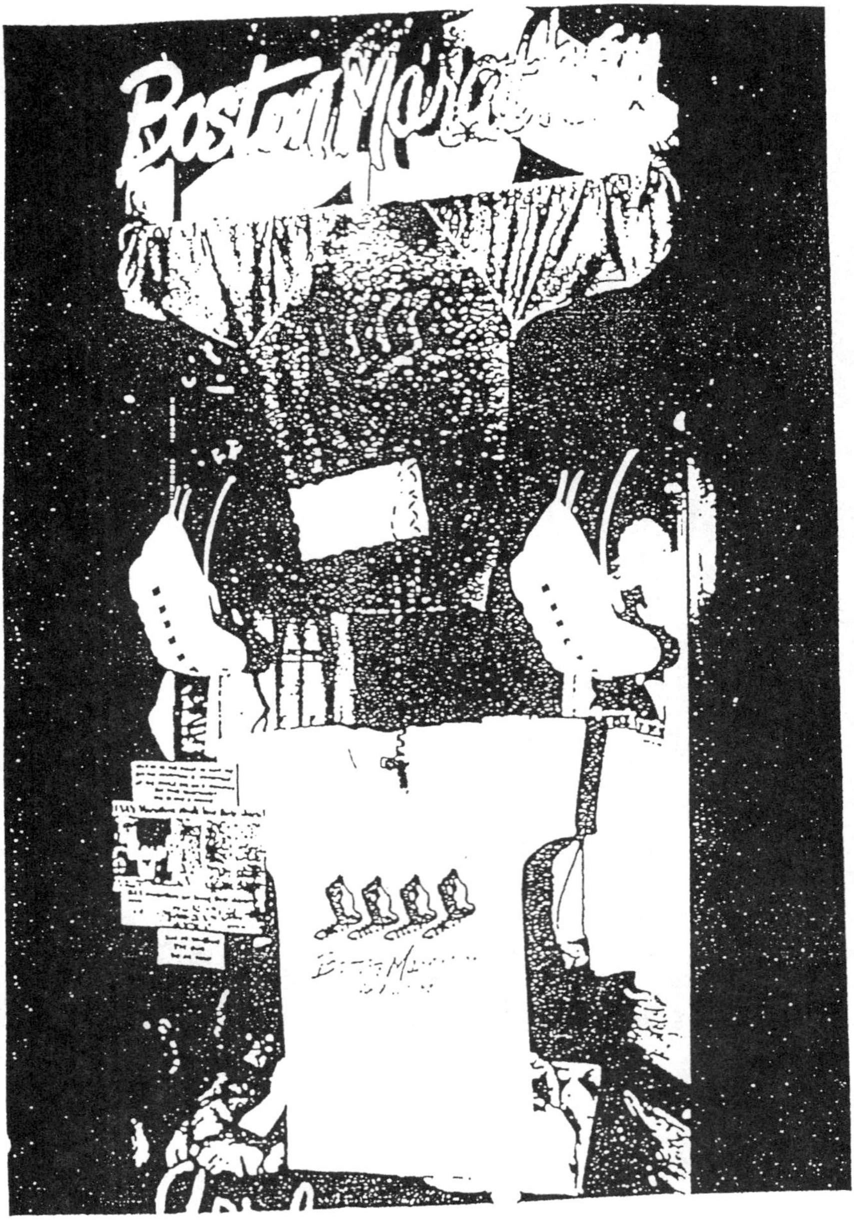

APPENDIX III, 5B—Testimony on Purchaser Mistake and Confusion at June 1987 Preliminary Injunction Hearing in Boston Athletic Association v. Sullivan, *C.A. No. 87-0802-Y (D.Mass. 1987), 2T. 43–44, 62–63*

Q. . . . Now, you were telling us that Mr. Rubenstein had brought this shirt at the Westin Hotel?

A. Yes.

Q. And he showed it to you?

A. Yes.

Q. And what did he say when he showed it to you?

MR. SHRIBERG: Objection, your Honor.

MR. CANER: Not offering it for the truth of the matter asserted but as something that came to her attention which will bear on the matter of confusion.

THE COURT: Oh well, I don't know, he certainly doesn't sound to me like he was confused, but we'll listen to what he has to say and then I'll make the ruling. What did he say?

THE WITNESS: He said I was giving the merchandise at the expo and he didn't want to take it anymore, I wasn't charging him, so he took the T-shirt and a jacket and then he went to another booth figuring that it was a licensed T-shirt and he bought it there feeling better about it because he didn't want to take any T-shirt that I was giving to him. A few weeks later, he came by wearing this T-shirt, and I said, "Where did you get that?" He said, "It's one of your Boston Marathon T-shirts," he said, "and it's not wearing too well. You should think of using another T-shirt." And I looked at it, and I said it wasn't our T-shirt and it's not a Boston Marathon T-shirt, it is—and of course, he was embarrassed and surprised.

THE COURT: So much of the answer as includes what he said is admitted. All of his feelings and his knowledge, that's all stricken and I'll disregard it. What he said is admitted.

. . . .

Q. In the course of sale of T-shirts at the Expo, was there anything like the episode as to Mr. Rubenstein that you have just related?

. . . .

A. People would come over after they had been shopping. They would get to our booth and they would say, oh, I think I like that T-shirt better. Can I exchange this one? And they would take out a 1987 Marathon Hopkinton to Boston shirt.

Q. '86?

A. '86.

Q. Yes.

A. And I would tell them or one of my salespeople would say, that isn't one of our shirts. You will have to return it where you bought it. And then there would be indignation of, well, it's a Boston Marathon shirt. Why can't I return it at a Boston Marathon booth? This happened many times to many of the people who were selling, all of the people that we had hired to do it. And it happened throughout the course of the race—of the expo.

MR. SHRIBERG: I move to strike.

THE COURT: No. The motion to strike is denied. That may stand.

APPENDIX III, 5C—Sample Newspaper Articles Reporting on Boston Marathon and Its Sponsorship by BAA Submitted to District Court with BAA Motion for

Journal Readers will be interested in the Readers' Census, page 5.

Boston Morning Journal

ESTABLISHED 1833. BOSTON, TUESDAY, APRIL 20, 1897.

THE TWO NATIONS COMPARED.

HORSE SHOW.

Second Annual Event Opens Splendidly.

Society Out in Force Last Evening.

Summary of Awards of the First Day.

RECORD GONE.

McDermott of New York Marathon Winner.

Time 10 Secs. Faster Than the Greek.

Nine of the 15 Starters Finished.

CAPTAINS KILLED.

Spaniards Mow Down the Cubans.

Several Spanish Victories, With Many Killed.

Demonstration Celebrating the Pacification.

A CLOSE CALL.

Bostons Narrowly Avert

GREEK VALOR.

Nine of the 15 Starters Finished.

Yesterday the B. A. A. had an innovation in the shape of a Marathon run 25 miles over the roads. There were 15 starters, and nine finished. The time was 10 seconds better than that made by Loues, the Greek, in the Olympic Games, at Athens, in the spring of '96. The winner is J. J. McDermott, Pastime A. C., New York—Time, 2.55.10. He finished a mile ahead.

BEAUTIFUL MODERN

The Technical Story.

Summary Judgment

Boston Morning Journal, April 20, 1897

THE BOSTON HERALD

LATE CITY EDITION

ROOSEVELT SPURNS AID SLASH

Young, Canadian, Wins B. A. A. Marathon

KELLEY, TAKEN ILL, IS SECOND; PAWSON THIRD

OSHAWA MOTOR STRIKERS KILL PEACE OFFER

$1,500,000,000 SET FOR RELIEF IN 1938 BUDGET

Reporter with Aching, Blistered Feet Decides First Marathon is His Last

SPIRIT OF 1775 REDEDICATED

Police Squad Sets Trap for Capture Of Slain Gang Leader's Lieutenant

BEES DROP TWO TO PHILS, 2-1, 1-0

PROF. WHEELER, HARVARD, DIES

Today's Herald

No Party for Race Victor, Says Wife; Hard Enough to Get Food to Live on

FINANCIAL WORRIES?

Showdown in Tiff Between Hurley, O'Dea on 'Fixing' Cases Due Today

THINK!

Boston Herald, April 20, 1937

MARATHON EDITION

The Boston Globe

RACE ENTRIES ON PAGE 2

Vol. 229; No. 111 MONDAY, APRIL 21, 1986 62 Pages • 25 cents

90th BAA: Off and away

Men to watch

1—Rob de Castella, Australia
2—Kunimitsu Ito, Japan
3—Greg Meyer, Michigan
5—Orlando Pizzolato, Italy
6—Peter Butler, Canada
7—David Edge, Canada
8—Dave Gordon, Oregon
9—Paul Cummings, Utah
10—Art Boileau, Canada
11—Peter Pfitzinger, Wellesley
14—Bill Rodgers, Dover
15—Mehmet Terzi, Turkey
16—Kirk Pfeffer, Colorado
17—Esa Tikannen, Finland
18—Ken Martin, Phoenix
19—Pertti Tiainen, Finland
20—Rich Brownsberger, California
21—Domingo Tibaduiza, Columbia
23—Dennis Rinde, California
24—Jarme Sippola, Finland
25—Hiroshi Nagashima, Japan

Women to watch

F1—Ingrid Kristiansen, Norway

Marathon Prize Structure

Open Division

Place	Men	Women
1.	$ 30,000	$ 30,000
2.	20,000	20,000
3	15,000	16,000
4.	12,000	12,000
5	10,000	10,000
6	8,500	8,500
7	7,000	7,000
8	5,500	5,500
9	4,000	4,000
10.	2,500	2,500
11.	1,400	1,400
12.	1,300	1,300
13	1,200	1,200
14	1,100	1,100
15	1,000	1,000
Total	$120,500	$120,500

Masters Division

Place	Men	Women
1	$ 2,500	$ 2,500
2	1,500	1,500
3	500	500
Total	$ 4,500	$ 4,500
Totals	$175,000	$125,000

Wheelchair Division

Place	Men	Women
1.	$ 2,500	$ 2,500

Bonus Money

(World Record)	(Current Record Holder)	(Bonus)
Men : 2:07:12	Carlos Lopes Portugal (1985)	$50,000

Boston Globe, April 21, 1986

APPENDIX III, 5D—Sample Summaries of Newspaper Articles Reporting BAA Sponsorship of Boston Marathon Submitted to District Court with BAA Motion for Summary Judgment

SUMMARY

1907

Date	Publication & Page		Author	Subject Matter - Excerpts
4/18/07	BOSTON JOURNAL,	p. 9	--	"...the B.A.A. Marathon run..."
4/18/07	BOSTON JOURNAL,	p. 9	--	[runners'] "arrival yesterday at the B.A.A. Club...."
4/18/07	BOSTON TRAVELER,	p. 9	--	"...tomorrow's annual Marathon race from Ashland to this city, which as in former years, will be under the auspices of the B.A.A."
4/18/07	BOSTON TRAVELER,	p. 9	--	"...will be run over the route of former years from Ashland to the B.A.A. clubhouse at Exeter St."
4/19/07	BOSTON JOURNAL,	p. 1	--	"The race is the eleventh annual Marathon run under the auspices of the Boston Athletic Association, and is now recognized as the greatest long distance event in the world."
4/19/07	BOSTON JOURNAL,	p. 8	--	"The men will... finish in front of the B.A.A. clubhouse."
4/19/07	NEW YORK TIMES,	p. 10	--	"The annual Marathon run of the Boston Athletic Association will be held to-day..."
4/19/07	BOSTON POST,	p. 1	--	"The event-Eleventh annual B.A.A. Marathon race."
4/19/07	BOSTON POST,	p. 1	--	"The course-From Ashland to the B.A.A. clubhouse..."
4/19/07	BOSTON POST,	p. 1	--	"Today the greatest race in the history of the Boston Athletic Association's Marathon runs is expected to take place over the 25 mile course from Ashland into the B.A.A. clubhouse."
4/20/07	BOSTON GLOBE,	p. 1	--	"Thomas Longboat...won the famous B.A.A. Marathon race..."

4/20/07	BOSTON POST,	p. 1	Howard G. Reynolds	"Thomas Longboat...won the great Marathon race held by the Boston Athletic Association yesterday."
4/20/07	BOSTON TRAVELER,	p. 7	--	"Over 250,000 people who lined the roads from...Ashland to the B.A.A. clubhouse...saw Longboat...run the grandest Marathon race ever...."
4/20/07	NEW YORK TIMES,	p. 10	--	"Thomas Longboat...to-day won the Marathon road race...finishing at the Boston Athletic Association house..."
4/20/07	BOSTON EVENING RECORD,	p. 7	--	"Longboat's amateur standing, according to Col. Billings of the B.A.A., who was in charge of the race, was found to be perfectly satisfactory to the officials."
4/20/07	BOSTON JOURNAL,	p. 1	--	"The Boston Athletic Association, which supervises the contest..."
4/20/07	BOSTON JOURNAL,	p. 4	Thomas E. Burke	"...the Marathon race held under the auspices of the Boston Athletic Association yesterday."
4/20/07	BOSTON JOURNAL,	p. 4	Thomas E. Burke	"Caffrey...twice winner of the Boston Marathon...."
4/20/07	BOSTON JOURNAL,	p. 4	Thomas E. Burke	"...never in the history of a B.A.A. Marathon have men finished in such excellent physical condition."

4/18/17	BOSTON TRAVELER,	P. 10	A.J. Rooney	"...the finish line, directly in front of the B.A.A. clubhouse on Exeter Street."
4/18/17	BOSTON TRAVELER,	P. 10	A.J. Rooney	"Sidney Hatch...has won Marathon runs in nearly all the large cities of the United States and now he expects to win the B.A.A."
4/18/17	BOSTON HERALD,	P. 5	-	"Gov. McCall and A. Paul Keith will act as honorary referees of the American Marathon of the Boston Athletic Association tomorrow. Mr. Keith is president of the B.A.A...."
4/18/17	BOSTON EVENING TRANSCRIPT,	P. 6	-	"...the long-distance classic which was started by the Boston Athletic Association back in 1897..."
4/18/17	BOSTON EVENING, TRANSCRIPT,	P. 6	-	"George V. Brown, athletic manager of the B.A.A., has made arrangements for a special train...Runners...will be on the scene in time by taking this train."
4/18/17	BOSTON EVENING AMERICAN,	P. 7	John W. Moran, Jr.	"...the twentieth renewal of the classic B.A.A. marathon run..."
4/18/17	BOSTON EVENING AMERICAN,	P. 7	John W. Moran, Jr.	"...George V. Brown of the B.A.A. confidently expects that the number of entrants will approach seventy."
4/18/17	BOSTON EVENING RECORD,	P. 10	-	HEADLINE: "...The 1917 B.A.A. Marathon"
4/18/17	BOSTON EVENING RECORD,	P. 10	-	"...arrived in town for the B.A.A. race of April 19."
4/18/17	BOSTON EVENING RECORD,	P. 10	-	"Hannes Kolehmainen, the...outstanding favorite to win the B.A.A. marathon tomorrow..."
4/19/17	BOSTON GLOBE,	P. 1	Lawrence J. Sweeney	"...the 21st annual running of the B.A.A. classic."
4/19/17	BOSTON GLOBE,	P. 1	Lawrence J. Sweeney	"Hannes Kolehmainen...will make his American debut in a Marathon race over the B.A.A. course today..."
4/19/17	NEW YORK TIMES,	P. 12	-	"...the American Marathon road race tomorrow."
4/19/17	NEW YORK TIMES,	P. 12	-	HEADING: "BOSTON MARATHON TODAY"
4/19/17	NEW YORK TIMES,	P. 12	-	"This twenty-first renewal of the country's leading long distance running event..."
4/19/17	BOSTON POST,	P. 11	Charles E. Parker	"...to uphold its sterling record in the B.A.A. event."

4/19/17	BOSTON POST,	P. 11	Charles E. Parker	"...the 21st annual American Marathon..."
4/19/17	BOSTON POST,	P. 11	Charles E. Parker	HEADLINE: "MARATHON RACE TO BE RUN TODAY"
4/19/17	BOSTON MORNING JOURNAL,	P. 8	Jack Keleher	HEADLINE: "300,000 will watch B.A.A. Marathon"
4/19/17	BOSTON MORNING JOURNAL,	P. 8	Jack Keleher	"...the 21st B.A.A. classic..."
4/19/17	BOSTON HERALD,	P. 1	John J. Hallahan	HEADLINES: "MARATHON WILL BE RUN TODAY" "SIXTY-EIGHT OF FASTEST LONG DISTANCE MEN OF THE COUNTRY NAMED IN B.A.A. EVENT"
4/19/17	BOSTON HERALD,	P. 1	John J. Hallahan	"...the 21st annual American Marathon of the Boston Athletic Association."
4/19/17	BOSTON HERALD,	P. 1	John J. Hallahan	"The objective...will be a little piece of yarn...in front of the Boston Athletic Association..."
4/19/17	BOSTON DAILY ADVERTISER,	P. 8	-	"...the B.A.A race today"
4/19/17	BOSTON DAILY ADVERTISER,	P. 8	-	"Hannes Kolehmainen...favorite to win the B.A.A. marathon today..."
4/20/17	BOSTON GLOBE,	P. 1	Lawrence J. Sweeney	HEADING: "...B.A.A. CLASSIC"
4/20/17	BOSTON GLOBE,	P. 1	Lawrence J. Sweeney	"...William J. ('Bill') Kennedy, winner of the 21st annual American Marathon run, held by the B.A.A."
4/20/17	BOSTON GLOBE,	P. 2	Lawrence J. Sweeney	"...his fifth B.A.A. race..."
4/20/17	BOSTON GLOBE,	P. 2	Lawrence J. Sweeney	"...the stiff B.A.A. course."
4/20/17	BOSTON GLOBE,	P. 7	Lawrence J. Sweeney	"...yesterday's exciting B.A.A. Marathon run..."
4/20/17	BOSTON GLOBE,	P. 7	Lawrence J. Sweeney	"Kennedy is perhaps the most original and modest man to win a Boston Marathon race."
4/20/17	BOSTON GLOBE,	P. 7	Lawrence J. Sweeney	"...he never said he was going to win the B.A.A. race."
4/20/17	NEW YORK TIMES,	P. 10	-	HEADLINE: "KENNEDY CAPTURES BOSTON MARATHON"
4/20/17	NEW YORK TIMES,	P. 10	-	"William J. Kennedy...won the annual Boston A.A. Marathon road race..."
4/20/17	NEW YORK TIMES,	P. 10	-	"Kennedy...had twice previously figured in the American Marathon..."

4/20/17	BOSTON POST,	P. 1	Charles E. Parker	"Bill Kennedy...won the 21st annual American Marathon yesterday..."
4/20/17	BOSTON POST,	P. 16	Bill Kennedy (Winner)	"I had a sense all along that I would win the big B.A.A. Marathon..."
4/20/17	BOSTON POST,	P. 16	Bill Kennedy (Winner)	"...let me thank the people of Boston and the officials of the B.A.A. for the treatment that I received in the race. I have run in Marathons all over the country - 23 to be exact, but never was I treated better or raced in a better conducted race than the Boston race."
4/20/17	BOSTON POST,	P. 16	Bill Kennedy (Winner)	"...I started training for the Boston race several months ago."
4/20/17	BOSTON POST,	P. 16	Bill Kennedy (Winner)	"...no Marathon runner's career is complete without winning a Boston race."
4/20/17	BOSTON TRAVELER,	P. 11	A.J. Rooney	HEADLINE: "WINNER OF B.A.A. MARATHON RETURNED TO WORK TODAY"
4/20/17	BOSTON TRAVELER,	P. 11	-	HEADING: "PREFERRED WINNING B.A.A. CLASSIC TO AN OLYMPIC MARATHON"
4/20/17	BOSTON MORNING JOURNAL,	P. 1	Jack Keleher	HEADLINE: "YOUTH NOT SERVED WHEN KENNEDY WINS WITH HATCH SECOND IN B.A.A. CLASSIC"
4/20/17	BOSTON MORNING JOURNAL,	P. 1	Jack Keleher	"...William Kennedy...won the B.A.A.'s 21st marathon..."
4/20/17	BOSTON HERALD,	P. 10	-	"...George B. Billings of the athletic committee of the B.A.A. who was referee."
4/20/17	BOSTON HERALD,	P. 10	-	"'I would rather win the Boston event than any five Marathons,' was the way Kennedy talked after the race."
4/20/17	BOSTON EVENING TRANSCRIPT,	P. 2	-	"...the twenty-first annual American Marathon of the Boston Athletic Association."
4/20/17	BOSTON WEEKLY TRANSCRIPT,	P. 1	-	"...William J. Kennedy...won the twenty-first annual American marathon under the auspices of the Boston Athletic Association."
4/20/17	BOSTON DAILY ADVERTISER,	P. 8	-	"The annual Boston Athletic Association classic, 25-mile Marathon race..."
4/20/17	BOSTON DAILY ADVERTISER,	P. 8	-	"William Kennedy...has been an entrant in the B.A.A. marathons for several years."
4/20/17	BOSTON DAILY ADVERTISER,	P. 8	-	"The B.A.A. prizes consisted of ten loving cups and twenty-five medals."
4/20/17	BOSTON EVENING RECORD,	P. 10	-	"...the American Marathon, the greatest annual road race classic held by the B.A.A..."
4/21/17	BOSTON GLOBE,	P. 4	Lawrence J. Sweeney	HEADLINE: "Action on Runner Protested in B.A.A. Marathon"

APPENDIX III, 5E—Sample 1987 Boston Marathon Photographs Featuring BAA Sponsorship Submitted to District Court with BAA Motion for Summary Judgment

BAA Marathon Watering Station

Crowning of Female Winner, Rosa Mota, by BAA President Frank Swift

"BAA Marathon" and "Boston Marathon 1987" Finish Indicia

APPENDIX III, 5F—BAA Boston Marathon Logo Used in 1987 Race Events Submitted to District Court with BAA Motion for Summary Judgment

APPENDIX III, 5G—BAA Certificate-of-Finishing-Boston Marathon Form Submitted to District Court with BAA Motion for Summary Judgment

Hopkinton Green

BOSTON ATHLETIC ASSOCIATION

ANNUAL BOSTON MARATHON

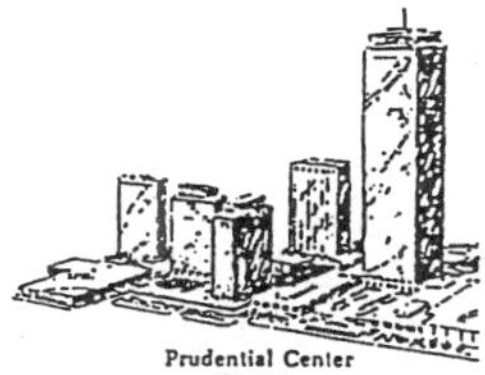

Prudential Center
Boston

This is to certify that

____

finished______________ in______________

in the ________ Annual Boston Marathon

from Hopkinton to Boston, 26 miles 385 yards

____
Date

Will Cloney
President, Boston Athletic Association

APPENDIX III, 5H—Petition for Writ of Mandamus to Young, J. in Boston Athletic Association v. United States District Court, *No. 88-1178 Orig. (1st Cir. March 4, 1988)*

UNITED STATES COURT OF APPEALS
FOR THE FIRST CIRCUIT

No. 88-1178

In re BOSTON ATHLETIC ASSOCIATION
and IMAGE IMPACT, INC.,
Petitioners,

PETITION FOR WRIT OF MANDAMUS
TO THE UNITED STATES DISTRICT COURT
FOR THE DISTRICT OF MASSACHUSETTS

District Court Civil Action No.87-0802-Y:

BOSTON ATHLETIC ASSOCIATION and
IMAGE IMPACT, INC.,
Plaintiffs,

v.

MARK SULLIVAN d/b/a GOOD LIFE
and BEAU TEASE, INC.,
Defendants.

---

1. This is a Petition for issuance of a Writ of Mandamus to a Judge of the United States District Court for the District of Massachusetts, William G. Young, D.J., to require the Court to act in the pending action *Boston Athletic Association and Image Impact, Inc. v. Mark Sullivan d/b/a Good Life and Beau Tease, Inc.*, C.A. No. 87-0802-Y (D.Mass).

2. The issues presented by this Petition are:

1) Whether the District Judge, under the circumstances of this case, had a duty to act currently upon the repeated requests by the plaintiffs (July 13, 1987, November 24, 1987 and February 4, 18, 19 and 24, 1988) for a preliminary injunction against continuing and current infringements of its registered name "Boston Marathon" and to render a decision upon which the plaintiffs could seek review under 28 U.S.C. § 1291; and

2) Whether under the circumstances of this case—viewed as a test case by the plaintiffs and apparently also by this Court and, for a time, by the District Court —the District Judge had a duty to act on the merits prior to the commencement of 1988 March–April Boston Marathon season.

3. The plaintiffs Boston Athletic Association (BAA) and its licensee, Image Impact, Inc., commenced the District Court action March 31, 1987 seeking preliminary and permanent

injunctive relief against infringement of the BAA's registered name and mark "Boston Marathon" by defendants' use of similar or colorably imitative marks and the profits of the defendants derived from such use, under the Lanham Act, 15 U.S.C. § 1114 and 1125, principles of unfair competition, the Massachusetts anti-infringement and dilution statutes, G.L. c. 110B, §§ 11, 12 and 13, and G.L. c. 214, § 3A, the Massachusetts statute respective use of another name without consent.

4. The District Court consolidated the application for a preliminary injunction with trial of the action on the merits and promptly commenced trial. After trial sessions during the week of April 13, 1987, the Court issued Findings and Rulings on Motion for Preliminary Injunction, April 16, 1987, a copy of which is attached hereto marked "1" (hereafter "F & R"). Though the court found a reasonable likelihood (l) that the Boston Athletic Association owned the mark "Boston Marathon" which at all material times had been valid and effective (F & R at 2); (2) that use of the name "Boston Marathon" in commercial products would cause the average observer to infer that the product was sponsored by a sponsor which stands behind the race (F & R at 2–3); (3) that an average member of the public purchasing the defendants' shirts with the logos "1987 Marathon"—3 runners—"Hopkinton-Boston" would appreciate that the writing and logo taken together referred to and celebrated the race known in New England and worldwide as the "Boston Marathon" (F & R at 3); (4) that the plaintiffs' T-shirts were of higher quality than those of the defendants (F & R at 3–4); and (5) that persons attending the Runners Expo

sponsored by the Boston Athletic Association who purchased shirts with the logos described would conclude that those shirts were licensed, authorized or sponsored by the Boston Athletic Association (F & R at 4); it then went on to conclude that no such inference would be drawn by persons buying shirts with the same logo on Washington Street, Boston, or in Hopkinton, or anywhere along the route (F & R at 5); wherefore, the Court, until April 10, 1988, enjoined the defendants from marketing their T-shirts at the Runners Expo, but otherwise denied a preliminary injunction (F & R at 8).

5. The plaintiffs appealed the April 16, 1987 decision of the District court the next day and moved for an injunction pending appeal, which was denied by this Court the same day in an Order suggesting that the suit might have been filed sooner and remarking that "the race is sometimes to the swift." No. 83-1317 (1st Cir. April 17, 1987) (Attachment "2").

6. In its order of April 17, 1987, this Court noted that "the sale of shirts relating to the Boston Marathon generally is, like the race itself, an annual event" and recognized that "trademark infringement or dilution inflicts intangible injuries, such as loss of reputation and good will and encouragement of additional infringes, that are not easily quantified in a damages award." Order at 1. This Court then implied that it expected the District Court would have decided the case by the start of the 1988 Boston Marathon shirt season:

> If permanent injunctive relief is ultimately obtained, appellants' position *in 1988* and

> in the years following will be largely unaffected by any infringement that might be found to have occurred in 1987.

Order at 1 (emphasis added).

7. On April 24, 1987, the Plaintiff-Appellants moved to dismiss their appeal, giving as reasons the conclusion of the 1987 Boston Marathon season, the desirability that review by this Court be on a full record on a final judgment on the merits, and the possibility that the final decision might differ from the Interlocutory Order, whereupon this Court dismissed the appeal. The expeditious handling of the action to that point by the District Court led the plaintiffs to believe that the action would be decided and ripe for review well prior to the 1988 Marathon season. Simultaneously, the trial on the merits being only half completed, the plaintiffs moved for completion of the trial and the Court below set May 26, 1987 as the date for resumption of trial (Attachment "3"), an apparent recognition that the case warranted prompt disposition. The Court thereafter changed the assigned trial resumption date to June 11, 1987, but then cancelled the assignment.

8. On June 11, 1987, the District Court allowed the plaintiffs' Motion for a ruling that the defense of laches-acquiescence was insufficient in law in light of the proof to date and affidavits and a stipulation on file. Attachment "4." Thereafter, through its clerk, the Court instructed the parties to file motions for Summary Judgment.

9. On July 13, 1987, the plaintiffs filed a Motion for Summary Judgment Entering a Permanent Injunction or, Alternatively, for a Preliminary Injunction. The motion was supported by memoranda, affidavits and exhibits, including hundreds of newspaper and magazine articles, and TV programs, and other publications showing that the name "Boston Marathon" and its connection with the Boston Athletic Association was at all times prominently before the public during the Boston Marathon season on Washington Street, Boston, in Hopkinton, and elsewhere along the route, as much as at the Runners Expo. The Court entered an order on July 14, 1987 that the plaintiffs' Motion for Summary Judgment would be taken under advisement on the papers then on file July 27, 1987. Attachment "5." The defendants filed their Motion for summary Judgment on July 23, 1987. See Attachment "8–A2."

10. The District Court has never taken any action on the plaintiffs' Motion for Summary Judgment Entering a Permanent Injunction or, Alternatively, for a Preliminary Injunction, or on the defendants' Motion for Summary Judgment.

11. Having heard nothing from the Court below and recognizing that when they did hear the result might well be adverse, and being aware that the period within which an appeal might be taken and a definitive result obtained from this Court was becoming very tight, the plaintiffs on November 24, 1987 addressed a letter to the District Court and delivered it to the clerk's office and witnessed that it was date stamped. This letter, Attachment "8–A3," expressed the hope of the plaintiffs that a

result be forthcoming in the case, pointing out that "this is a test case and will affect the market for T-shirts relating to the Boston Marathon in March and April, 1988. The time is getting short to secure a District Court judgment and review by the Court of Appeals prior to the 1988 Marathon." The Court never responded to the letter and the clerk's office, as of February 23, 1988, had not docketed it.

12. On February 4, 1988, the plaintiffs filed a Motion to Further Amend their Complaint, with the proposed Amendment, by adding allegations that the defendants were currently infringing the plaintiffs' name by sale of "1988 Marathon" T-shirts with imprints similar to those sold in 1987 and seeking preliminary and permanent injunctive relief. The Motion to Amend was accompanied by a Motion for Preliminary Injunction against infringement by the defendants of the name "Boston Marathon" and by a supporting memorandum. The Court has taken no action on the Motion to Further Amend or the Motion for Preliminary Injunction and, as of February 23, 1988, the motions and the memorandum had not been docketed.

13. Having heard nothing from the Court respecting the motions filed February 4, 1988, the plaintiffs wrote the Court a letter of February 18, 1988 (Attachment "6"), requesting a hearing on the Motions to Further Amend and for a Preliminary Injunction of February 4, 1988. This letter was docketed. It was followed by a letter from the defendants to the Court also of February 18, 1988 concerning vacation plans between March

4 and 14, 1988 (Attachment "8E"), and another letter from the plaintiffs of February 19, 1988 (Attachment "7"), requesting a hearing prior to March 4, 1988. There has been no response from the Court and no hearing.

14. On February 23, 1988, the plaintiffs obtained from the clerk's office the docket entries in the action (Attachment "8-A2"), learned that no papers other than the plaintiffs' letter of February 18, 1988 had been docketed in the action since August 17, 1987, and wrote the Court to that effect. The next day the plaintiffs filed a Motion to Correct the Court Record and Renewal of Preliminary Injunction Application, a copy of which is attached hereto marked "8." This Motion contained among its attachments the plaintiffs' letter to the Court of November 24, 1987 ("A3"), and the Motion to Further Amend and Proposed Amendment, Motion for Preliminary Injunction and the Memorandum in support filed February 4, 1988, marked "B," "C," and "D."

15. By reason of the failures of the District Court to act, the plaintiffs have effectively been deprived of their statutory and common law rights to injunctive relief against infringement of their name and of their further right to judicial review by this Court of refusal of injunctive relief under the Interlocutory Appeals Act 28 U.S.C. § 1291. In addition, by failing to act the District Court has undercut the basis of this Court's conclusion that intangible injury to plaintiffs in 1987 was not sufficient to warrant an injunction pending appeal, that basis being the assumption that the matter of permanent injunctive relief would

be decided by the 1988 season. The District Court has at all relevant times had before it the facts in undisputed form, contained in a stipulation of the parties, affidavits, and real and documentary exhibits, and a detailed exposition of the law in four separate memoranda. The inaction of the District Court constitutes an arbitrary refusal to exercise its authority in dereliction of its duty to do so and deprives the plaintiffs without due process of law of their rights to have their application for abatement for an ongoing trademark infringement adjudicated and to appeal any adverse decision. Issuance of the Writ of Mandamus prayed would be appropriate in aid of the jurisdiction of this Court and is necessary in the light of the circumstances.

16. Factual statements herein are made by the undersigned under the penalties of perjury.

WHEREFORE, the plaintiffs pray that the Court issue a writ of Mandamus to the United States District court for the District of Massachusetts, William G. Young, D.J., commanding him:

1) Forthwith to hear and determine the plaintiffs' applications for preliminary injunctive relief against infringement of their name; and

2) Seasonably to decide the action on the merits, either upon the summary judgment motions or after resumption of trial, if necessary.

By its attorneys,

____

George C. Caner, Jr.
John W. Van Lonkhayzen
Ropes & Gray
225 Franklin Street
Boston, Massachusetts 02110
(617) 423-6100

March 4, 1988

(Attachments omitted.)

APPENDIX III, 5I—Memorandum of Decision Accompanying District Court Judgment in Boston Athletic Association v. Sullivan, *C.A. No. 87-0802-Y (D.Mass. March 7, 1988)*

UNITED STATES DISTRICT COURT
DISTRICT OF MASSACHUSETTS

CIVIL ACTION No. 87-0802-Y

BOSTON ATHLETIC ASSOCIATION
and IMAGE IMPACT, INC.,
Plaintiffs

v.

MARX SULLIVAN d/b/a GOOD LIFE
and BEAU TEASE, INC.,
Defendants

MEMORANDUM OF DECISION

YOUNG, D.J. March 7, 1988

This matter comes before the Court upon cross motions for summary judgment after an extensive evidentiary hearing upon the plaintiff's motion for a preliminary injunction. Each of the cross motions is supported by comprehensive and thorough affidavits. Review of the entire file reveals that there exists no genuine issue of material fact in dispute between the parties and the case is accordingly ripe for Judgment pursuant to Fed. R. Civ. P. 56.

The plaintiff Boston Athletic Association ("BBA")* is a charitable corporation duly organized under the laws of the Commonwealth of Massachusetts with a usual place of business in the City of Boston, Massachusetts. The corporate purpose and principal activity of the BAA is the presentation, annually on Patriot's Day, of a road race known as the "Boston Marathon" which for many years has originated in Hopkinton, passed through Ashland, Framingham, Natick, Wellesley, Newton, and Brookline, and ended in Boston. The Boston Marathon will be presented this year on April 18, 1989.

The plaintiff Image Impact, Inc. is a corporation duly organized under the laws of the State of New York and doing business in the County of Suffolk.

The defendant Mark Sullivan, a resident of Hopkinton, Massachusetts, is engaged in selling merchandise including apparel in a retail store under the name "Good Life" in Hopkinton, Massachusetts.

The defendant Beau Tease, Inc., a corporation organized under the laws of the Commonwealth of Massachusetts with a place of business at 67 Rogers Street, Cambridge, Massachusetts,

---

* Editor's note: The Boston Athletic Association was wrongly abbreviated in this document as "BBA" and not "BAA."

is engaged in imprinting and distributing merchandise, including T-shirts, to the trade.

This Court has subject matter jurisdiction of this action by virtue of section 39 of the Lanham Act, 15 U.S.C. § 1121, 28 U.S.C. §§ 1331 and 1338(a) & (b), and the doctrine of pendant jurisdiction.

Although when staging the race the BAA receives assistance in vehicle and crowd control, aid and water stations, and clean-up from the Commissioner of Public Safety, the State Police, the cities and towns through which the race passes, and private organizations, whose activities it coordinates, the BAA has been solely responsible for the organization, composition, and conduct of the race since it was first organized and presented by the BAA in 1897. The BAA maintains a permanent staff and offices in Boston and Hopkinton devoted year round to planning for the race. Its officers and governors serve on an unpaid basis. Spectators consisting of much of the population of the Greater Boston area view the race without charge along its route or on local television. Runners are drawn from, and the event is televised, all over the world. The ever increasing expenses of the race have in recent years made it necessary for the BAA to increase its revenues and to broaden the sources thereof. However necessary, the BAA's aggressive efforts to turn the race into a money maker have proved something of an embarrassment. *See Boston Athletic Association v. International Marathons, Inc.*, 392 Mass. 356 (1981). Indeed, its original efforts to enforce the marks here in issue in the Courts of the Commonwealth foundered primarily on the laxity of its enforcement theretofore. *Boston Athletic Association v. Graphtex, Inc.*, Suffolk Superior Court No. 82365, slip op. at 3–4 (April 11, 1986) (Keady, J.), denial of preliminary injunction *aff'd* by the single justice of the Massachusetts Appeals Court, No. A.C.-86-0169-CV (April 18, 1986) (Fine, J.).

Even so, the names "Boston Marathon" and "BAA Marathon" are the BAA's most valuable and important asset. These names have been used by the BAA to refer to its race throughout this century. "Boston Marathon" is a service mark of the BAA registered July 2, 1985 on the principal register of the United States Patent and Trademark Office. "Boston Marathon," "BAA Marathon," and the BAA's logo have been registered since December 12, 1983 as service marks with the Secretary of the Commonwealth of Massachusetts under G.L. c. 110B, § 4. The principal revenues of the BAA are derived from granting to sponsors rights to associate their names with the race and the BAA's names "Boston Marathon" and "BAA Marathon."

In 1986 the BAA granted Image Impact an exclusive license, on a royalty basis, for the manufacture and sale of apparel, including T-shirts, hats, sweatshirts, tote bags and tennis and golf shirts under the names "Boston Marathon," "BAA Marathon" and the BAA unicorn logo. Image Impact has caused such apparel to be manufactured in New York State and has sold such apparel in Massachusetts and other states under those names since early 1986 to retailers and the public generally. Commencing in 1986, Image Impact and the BAA gave notice to imprinters, wholesalers, and retailers that Image Impact was the exclusive licensee of the BAA and that any unauthorized use on merchandise of the name "Boston Marathon," or a similar name or a colorable imitation thereof, would violate the exclusive rights of the BAA and its licensee.

In March 1986 there appeared on the market in the Greater Boston area a T-shirt imprinted "1986 Marathon," with three runners below those words and with the words "Hopkinton-Boston" under the three runners, marketed by the defendants herein, Mark Sullivan ("Sullivan") and Beau Tease, Inc. ("Beau Tease"). On April 2, 1986 the BAA and Image Impact commenced an action in the Suffolk Superior Court, Commonwealth of Massachusetts, against alleged infringes of its names, including as defendants herein, Sullivan and Beau Tease. *Boston Athletic Association v. Graphtex, Inc., supra.* That action was discontinued without prejudice, with the parties reserving their rights to assert their respective positions in any future proceeding.

The defendant Beau Tease subsequently designed and imprinted, and in March 1987 the defendant Mark Sullivan commenced to sell at the store "Good Life" in Hopkinton, T-shirts and other garments with the design "1987 Marathon," with three runners thereunder, and under the runners "Hopkinton Boston."

This action followed. On April 16, 1987 this Court preliminarily enjoined Beau Tease from selling T-shirts with the above described logo at the Boston runners expo, then set to commence on Saturday, April 18, 1987. Such a limited preliminary injunction fell far short of the BAA's claim of entitlement and in its motion for summary judgment it continues to press for considerably more sweeping relief. Upon careful reflection, however, this Court concludes that, with respect to the allegedly infringing logo here at issue, the BAA has obtained all the relief to which it is entitled.

True, the BAA is and was at all material times the owner of a properly registered federal trademark in the words "Boston Marathon" taken together. Further, this mark is, and was at all material times, valid and effective, and the BAA is the proper party to enforce its ownership rights in this mark. Further, the use of the name "Boston Marathon" in commercial products will cause the average Eastern Massachusetts observer to infer that there exists some sponsor standing behind, or in some way involved with, a product denominated by the mark "Boston Marathon."[1] What's more, the average individual member of the

---

[1] Despite the BAA's apparent opinion of its own notoriety and its own promotional activities, there remains a genuine issue of fact concerning whether the average member of the purchasing public appreciates that the BAA sponsors the race run on or about Patriot's Day commonly known as the Boston Marathon. As nothing turns on the Point, however, this factual issue is not "material."

It is clear beyond dispute, though, that for what it is worth, the wearability over time of the various T-shirts marketed in 1987 by the BAA's licensee, the plaintiff Image Impact, Inc. exceeds—in threads per square inch and in various sewing modalities—that of the T-shirts marketed by the defendants. They also cost more. Since the children who are the major market for T-shirts rapidly outgrow them or wear them out, an informed purchaser engaged in a strict cost benefit analysis could well choose the defendants' offering in view of the differential in price. Still, the plaintiffs' offering is the undisputed winner in wearability.

public who purchases a T-shirt bearing the logo "1987 Marathon" above three runners who are themselves above the words "Hopkinton-Boston" will appreciate that the writing and logo refers to and celebrates the race run on or about Patriot's Day from Hopkinton to Boston, commonly known in this area of New England and, indeed, worldwide, as the Boston Marathon.

Still, this Court concludes that the average individual member of the general buying public would not, when buying a T-shirt with the logo "1987 Marathon" above three runners above the words "Hopkinton-Boston," infer that the BAA somehow authorizes sponsors, or stands behind such a T-shirt, whether the shirt is purchased from a vendor on Washington street or from a store marketing such marathon memorabilia either in Boston, in Hopkinton, or anywhere along the route of the race. Nor would such an inference arise even among those people who appreciate that the BAA sponsors the race.[2]

In short, the defendants' offending logo celebrates and through a common sense, reasonable inference refers to an internationally acclaimed event. Neither the BAA's federal trademark or any common law rights can be construed so broadly as to prevent such reference, even in a commercial context. It is true that both the word "marathon" and the word "Boston"

---

[2] See footnote 1 supra. The Court recognizes that certain of the affidavits submitted by the Plaintiffs purport to raise a factual issue on this point. These portions of the affidavits, however, are hearsay and entitled to no evidentiary weight. There is, on this record, no evidence whatsoever that any disinterested individual purchased the defendants' offending T-shirt believing that he or she was buying a product sponsored or officially licensed by the BAA.

appear on the allegedly offending logo. But unlike the BAA approved T-shirts, where the word "Boston" is properly read to modify the word "marathon," here the adjective which modified the word "marathon" is the year 1987, and the phrase "Hopkinton to Boston" described the route. The BAA's trademark is the "Boston Marathon." It thus certainly has the legal right to exclude others from using the phrase "Boston Marathon" in connection with the BAA's own distinctive unicorn logo. Likewise, it would seem to have the legal right to exclude others from using the phrase "Boston Marathon" when that phrase is given such prominence as to give rise to any colorable confusion with the BAA's sponsorship of either the marathon or its authorization of memorabilia for the marathon. Beyond this, however, the legal rights of the BAA do not sweep. That is, even if used in a commercial context, references to the race run on or about Patriot's Day from Hopkinton to Boston are not denied to others simply because the BAA has a federal trademark in the phrase "Boston Marathon." More precisely, this Court rules that the specific T-shirt logo challenged in this action does not, as matter of law, give rise to any colorable confusion with products authorized by the BAA as part of its sponsorship of the particular road race in question [3]

---

[3] When this matter was before the Court for consideration of the issuance of the preliminary injunction, the Court reasoned that, as the BAA operates Runners' Expo on the weekend before the race, on the second floor of the Western Hotel, in which area a runner can file his or her official entry form and pick up his or her BAA race number, and in which area a variety of race memorabilia is marketed, individuals sufficiently interested in the race either to participate therein or to attend the Runners' Expo would understand that the BAA sponsors the race and that the memorabilia marketed at the Runners' Expo itself was BAA authorized. Ac-

Accordingly, in view of the foregoing, judgment must enter for the defendants in this particular case.

WILLIAM G. YOUNG
UNITED STATES DISTRICT JUDGE

---

cordingly, since the hearing on a preliminary injunction herein was, in point of fact, among the very first enforcement action taken by the BAA to protect its mark, and since the running of the race was imminent, this Court concluded that a preliminary injunction preventing Beau Tease from marketing the allegedly offending T-shirt at the Runners' Expo itself was warranted.

Since the BAA contracts with Conventures to put on the Runners' Expo and can restrict commercial access thereto in any way it desires, there is no longer a need for Judicial intervention by way of injunctive relief. Accordingly, upon the entry of Judgment herein, the preliminary injunction presently outstanding will he dissolved.

APPENDIX III, 5J—Opinion of U.S. Court of Appeals for the First Circuit in Boston Athletic Association v. Sullivan, *867 F.2d 22 (1989), Reversing District Court Judgment*

UNITED STATES COURT OF APPEALS
FOR THE FIRST CIRCUIT

No. 88-1352

BOSTON ATHLETIC ASSOCIATION, ET AL.,
Plaintiffs, Appellants,
v.
MARK SULLIVAN, ETC., ET AL.,
Defendants, Appellees

APPEAL FROM THE UNITED STATES DISTRICT COURT FOR THE DISTRICT OF MASSACHUSETTS
[Hon. William G. Young, *U.S. District Judge*]

Before
Campbell, *Chief Judge*,
Bownes and Selya, *Circuit Judges*

George C. Caner. Jr., with whom *John W. Van Lonkhuyzen* and *Ropes & Gray* were on brief for appellants.

Stephen M. Trattner, *Philip W. Tone*, *Jenner & Block*, *Lee N. Abrams*, and *Mayer, Brown & Platt* on brief for United States Golf Association, Amicus Curiae.

Glenn H. Shriberg with whom *Dana Ryan Turnbull* and *Shriberg & Sorbello* were on brief for appellees.

JANUARY 27, 1989

BOWES, *Circuit Judge*. In this service mark infringement case,[1] Boston Athletic Association (BAA) and Image Impact, Inc. (Image) appeal the denial of their motion for summary judgment and the concurrent granting of the defendants', Mark Sullivan d/b/a Good Life (Sullivan) and Beau Tease, Inc. (Beau Tease), motion for summary judgment. This case arises out of the sale by the defendants of T-shirts (hereinafter called shirts) and other wearing apparel with designs alleged to infringe on BAA's service marks "Boston Marathon," "'BAA Marathon" and its unicorn logo. We agree with the district court that there are no genuine issues of material fact, but disagree with the district court's determination of which side was entitled to summary judgment. We, therefore, reverse.

I. THE STARTING LINE

The standard for granting summary judgment in a trademark infringement case is as follows:

---

[1] Service marks and trademarks are similar yet distinct creatures. A trademark is used to distinguish one's goods from those made by others, while a service mark is used to distinguish one's services from those offered by others. In either case the marks are used to indicate the distinctive source of the goods or services, even if that source is unknown. *See Volkswagenwerk Aktiengesellschaft v. Wheeler*, 814 F.2d 812, 815 n.1 (1st Cir. 1987). For the purposes of this case, the distinction between the two types of marks is irrelevant; thus, cases discussing either apply. The services here are the operation and sponsorship of the Boston Marathon by BAA.

> Summary judgment is proper only "if the pleadings, depositions, answers to interrogatories, and admissions on file, together with the affidavits, if any, show that there is no genuine issue as to any material fact and that the moving party is entitled to a judgment as a matter of law." *Astra*, 718 F.2d at 1204; *Pignons*, 657 F.2d at 486; Fed.R.Civ.P. 56(c). A factual dispute is material if it "affects the outcome of the litigation," and genuine if manifested by "substantial" evidence "going beyond the allegations of the complaint." *Astra*, 718 F.2d at 1204 and *Pignons*, 657 F.2d at 486; *Looting Hahn v. Sargent*, 523 F.2d 461, 464 (1st Cir. 1975), *cert. denied*, 425 U.S. 904, 96 S.Ct. 1495, 47 L.Ed.2d 54 (1976).

Vokswagenwerk Aktiengesellschaft v. Wheeler, 814 F.2d 812, 815 (1st Cir. 1987); *see also Astra Pharmaceutical Products, Inc. v. Beckman Instruments Inc.*, 718 F.2d 1201, 1204 (1st Cir. 1983); *Pignons S.A. de Mecanique de Precision v. Polaroid Corp.*, 657 F.2d 482, 486 (1st Cir. 1981). "While infringement and unfair competition cases often present factual issues that render summary judgment inappropriate, this is not invariably so." *Kazmaier v. Wooten*, 761 F.2d 46, 48, 49 (1st Cir. 1985) (citations omitted). "In passing on a summary judgment motion, the court must view the record and draw inferences in the light most favorable to the opposing party." Id. (citations omitted). Because we believe summary judgment should have been entered for plaintiffs, we review the facts in the light most favorable to defendants.

Before we turn to the facts, however, me must deal with a preliminary matter. As discussed infra at 8, prior to the parties submitting cross-motions for summary judgment, the district court conducted an aborted trial at which the plaintiffs presented the majority of their case. The use of the trial record was urged by the parties in their cross-motions: the plaintiffs referred to the exhibits, while the defendants referred to both the testimony and the exhibits. Although the district judge did not explicitly address the point in his memorandum of decision, he did state that he had "[r]eviewed the entire file" in reaching his decision on the cross-motions for summary judgment. We assume that this review included the testimony and exhibits received in the aborted trial. Reference to prior trial testimony and exhibits is proper in summary judgment cases. *Advance Financial Corp. v. Isla Rica Sales, Inc.*, 747 F.2d 21, 27 (1st Cir. 1984). We have treated the trial record as part of the record before us.

II. THE START IN STATE COURT

We have taken the facts mainly from the district court opinions. BAA is a charitable organization whose principal activity has been conducting the Boston Marathon since it was first run in 1897. The race is run annually from Hopkinton to Boston on patriots' Day, the third Monday in April. In recent years, a day or two prior to the race an exposition has been put on by Conventures, Inc. under BAA's sponsorship. At the exposition, various businesses set up booths and sell shirts, running apparel, and sports items. The registered runners also pick up their numbers and official materials from the BAA booth.

Defendant Sullivan, a resident of Hopkinton, Massachusetts, retails wearing apparel under the name "Good Life" at a store in Hopkinton. Defendant Beau Tease, Inc. is a Massachusetts corporation doing business in Cambridge. It imprints and distributes merchandise, including shirts, to the trade.

In an effort to defray the costs of the race, BAA began an active campaign to market its name via licensing agreements. It registered the names "Boston Marathon" and "BAA Marathon" and its unicorn logo in Massachusetts in 1983 and "Boston Marathon" in the United States Patent and Trademark Office in 1985.

As early as 1978, the defendants were imprinting and selling shirts with the name "Boston Marathon" and various other terms including the year on them. In 1984, defendant Sullivan negotiated an agreement under which Beau Tease sold to BAA a large quantity of shirts which BAA gave away to the athletes and volunteers during the 1985 race. In 1986, Image, through its President, Mickey Lawrence, entered into an exclusive license with BAA for the use of BAA's service marks on wearing apparel including shirts. Starting in 1986, Image and BAA gave notice to imprinters, wholesalers, and retailers that Image was the exclusive licensee of the BAA and that any unauthorized use on merchandise of the name "Boston Marathon," or a similar name or a colorable imitation thereof, would violate the exclusive rights of BAA and its licensee.

By March of 1986, Beau Tease was imprinting and Sullivan was selling in the Boston area shirts imprinted as follows:

1986 Marathon
[Picture of runners]
Hopkinton–Boston

BAA brought suit in Massachusetts superior court against the current defendants, and others, alleging that the above design infringed upon its marks. The superior court denied its request for a preliminary injunction, *Boston Athletic Association v. Graphtex, Inc.*, Suffolk Superior Court No. 82365, slip op. (April 11, 1986); the denial was affirmed by a single justice of the Massachusetts Court of Appeals, No. A.C.-86-0169-CV (April 18, 1986) (Fine, J.). The action was discontinued without prejudice; the parties reserved their right to assert their positions in any future action.

In late 1986 and early 1987, Beau Tease began to imprint and Sullivan began to retail shirts and other apparel imprinted as follows:

1987 Marathon
[picture of runners]
Hopkinton–Boston

The 1987 shirts and the 1986 shirts were of poorer quality than plaintiffs' both as to manufacture and materials. The defendants were planning to sell their shirts and other items at the exposition.

III. THE CONTESTANTS REACH FEDERAL COURT

In 1987, the exposition was held on Saturday April 18 and the race on Monday April 20. On April 1, 1987, BAA and Image filed suit in the United States District Court for the District of Massachusetts alleging that defendants' 1986 and 1987 shirts, with the logos described above, infringed BAA's marks. The complaint alleged confusion in violation of the Lanham Act, 15 U.S.C. § 1114, and a similar provision in Massachusetts law, Mass. Gen. Laws Ann. ch. 110B, 511. The complaint also included additional state law counts for dilution, Mass. Gen. Laws Ann. ch. 110B, § 12, sale of counterfeits and imitations, Mass. Gen. Laws Ann. ch. 110B, 5 13, and unauthorized use of a name, Mass. Gen. Laws Ann. ch. 214, § 3A. Along with the complaint, plaintiffs filed a motion for a preliminary injunction, seeking to stop the manufacture and sale of any article bearing the name "Boston Marathon" or any similar name.

On April 8, 1987, the district court held a hearing at which it consolidated the preliminary injunction hearing with a trial on the merits; the defendants were deemed to have made a general denial. Prior to the trial, the parties agreed to certain facts including BAA's registration of its marks in 1933 and 1985. Also prior to trial, several affidavits were filed with the court.

Three days of trial were held on April 13, 14, and 15. During the trial, the plaintiffs presented most of their case. Lawrence, president of plaintiff Image, testified to instances in which people bought defendants' shirts at the 1986 exposition thinking they were plaintiffs'. This testimony was admitted over objection. On April 16, because the exposition was only two days away and the parties were concerned about whether the defendants could sell their shirts at the exposition, the district court received offers of proof as to the remaining witnesses and heard oral argument on the motion for a preliminary injunction.

In a bench opinion the court found that plaintiffs would probably succeed in showing that: 1. BAA's mark was valid and effective at all relevant times; 2. the name "Boston Marathon" when used on products would cause the average person to infer sponsorship by somebody, even if the average person did not realize that BAA was the sponsor; 3. defendants' designs referred to the Boston Marathon; 4. plaintiffs' shirts were of a higher quality than defendants'; and 5. people who attend the exposition, given their interest in running, would infer sponsorship by BAA of Beau Tease's shirts sold at the exposition. The court also found that sale of the same shirts in any other milieu, such as along the race course, would not cause an average person to infer sponsorship by BAA. Based on these findings, the court did not enjoin Sullivan in any way, but did preliminarily enjoin Beau Tease from selling shirts directly at the exposition or marketing to anyone who it knew would sell Beau Tease's 1987 shirts at the exposition.

On April 17, BAA appealed and moved for an injunction in this court. That same day, we denied the injunction because of a lack of irreparable harm. We noted that trademark infringement ordinarily causes intangible injuries which make injunctive relief appropriate. We felt, however, that such relief was not suitable in this case because of the annual and discrete nature of the harm, the availability of a damages remedy and the late date at which plaintiffs' instituted suit in federal court. On April 28, the appeal was dismissed on motion by the plaintiffs.

When the case returned to district court, the parties submitted cross-motions for summary judgment. The motions were bolstered by affidavits—some had been filed pretrial and some filed with the motions—and by references to the trial materials. Plaintiff Image's affidavit, executed by Lawrence, included instances of people buying defendants' 1987 shirts believing them to be plaintiffs'. Lawrence Newman, press liaison for BAA, submitted along with a second affidavit a series of newspaper articles and summaries of the articles, referring to the Boston Marathon and BAA for every tenth year from 1897 to 1967 and for every year from 1972 to l983 and for 1986 and 1987. On July 24, plaintiffs moved to amend their complaint to include a declaratory judgment claim with respect to their rights in the name "Boston Marathon." The motion also asked that their claim be broadened to include an injunction against defendants' design, already described, with any year on it. The district court allowed this motion on August 17, 1987.

On February 4, 1988, plaintiffs moved to amend their complaint further by including defendants' 1988 shirts and a design:

Boston
[picture of runner/s]
19xx

Plaintiffs also sought a preliminary injunction. On March 7, the district court rendered its decision. On March 11, the district court found the preliminary injunction request moot in light of its March 7 decision. It stated that it had considered the plaintiffs' motion relative to the 1988 shirts and that the March 7 opinion applied to those shirts as well.

The district court's March 7 decision found that BAA's marks were its most valuable asset and were at all relevant times valid and enforceable. It found that an average person would infer sponsorship by someone of a product carrying the logo "Boston Marathon," and that defendants' logos referred to the marathon. The court stated that there was a dispute whether the public would associate BAA with the Boston Marathon but that this dispute was not material. It held that the public would not infer that the defendants' logos were sponsored by BAA. The court explicitly disregarded Lawrence's affidavit evidence of confusion because it was hearsay and the court found no other evidence that any "disinterested" person was confused as to the source of defendants' shirts. The court also held that BAA's rights did not extend beyond the use of its exact service marks. The court ruled as a matter of law that there was no confusion between the defendants' and plaintiffs' shirts. The court concluded its opinion: "More precisely, this Court rules that the specific T-shirt logo challenged in this action does not, as a matter of law, give rise to any colorable confusion with products authorized by the BAA as part of its sponsorship of the particular road race in question." Judgment for the defendants was entered and the preliminary injunction was dissolved. This appeal followed.

IV. BAA'S RIGHT TO RUN

Defendants argue that they should prevail because BAA's marks are entitled to no protection for two reasons: 1. "Boston Marathon" has become a generic term inasmuch as it now refers to both the race and the services rendered by BAA; and 2. defendants' use of "Boston Marathon" on shirts from 1978 constitutes a prior usage.

With respect to genericness, defendants rely on *Anti-Monopoly, Inc. v. General Malls Fun Group*, 611 F.2d 296 (9th Cir. 1979), *appeal after remand*, 684 F.2d 1316 (1982), *cert. denied sub nom. CPG Products Corp. v. Anti-Monopoly, Inc.*, 459 U.S. 1227 (1983). In its first opinion, the Ninth Circuit concluded its summary of the law of genericness by stating that "when members of the consuming public use a game name to denote the game itself, and not its producer, the trademark is generic and, therefore, invalid." 611 F.2d at 304 (footnote Omitted). In its second opinion, the court relied heavily on a survey, which measured the motive of purchasers in selecting a "Monopoly" game, in deciding that "Monopoly" was a generic term. 684 F.2d at 1324–326. These holdings, however, were subsequently nullified by Congress. In 1984, Congress amended 5 14(c) of the Lanham Act, 15 U.S.C. § 1064(c), specifically because of the Ninth Circuit case. *See* S. Rep. No. 627, 98th Cong., 2d Sess., reprinted in 1984 U.S. Code Cong. & Admin. News 5718–5728. The amendment added the following to the section:

> A registered mark shall not be deemed to be the common descriptive name of goods or services [*i.e.* a generic] solely because such mark is also used as a name of or to identify a unique product or service. The primary significance of the registered mark to the relevant public rather than purchaser motivation shall be the test for determining whether the registered mark has become the common descriptive name of goods or services in connection with which it has been used[.]

The burden of proof is on the party seeking to have a registered mark declared a generic to show that it has become so under the above test. 3 R. Callman, The Law of Unfair Competition, Trademarks, and Monopolies § 18.25 at 231 (L. Altman 4th ed. 1983) thereinafter ___ Callman § ___). Here, the defendants have introduced no evidence on the issue of "primary significance" and thus, have failed to meet the burden of proof.

With respect to prior usage, it is axiomatic that "registration does not create the underlying right in a trademark. That right, which accrued from the use of a particular name or symbol, is essentially a common law property right . . . ." *Keebler Co. v. Rovira Biscuit Corp.*, 624 F.2d 366, 372 (1st Cir. 1980); *see also Volkswagenwerk*, 814 F.2d at 815–816 (quoting *Keebler).* Therefore, BAA's failure to register its marks until the mid-1980s is not dispositive. Furthermore, a mark provides protection not only for the product or service to which it is originally applied but also to related items or services. *See* 3 Callman § 19.23.

Here, the uncontradicted evidence, consisting mainly of media references[2] to the race, especially newspaper and magazine articles, shows that: 1. the race was originally called the Boston Athletic Association or Boston A.A. Marathon; 2. since 1917, the race has also been called the Boston Marathon; and 3. since at least 1977, a year before defendants' "prior usage," BAA used the names "B.A.A. Marathon" and "Boston Marathon" interchangeably.[3] This use by BAA undercuts defendants' prior use claim as to the words per se. As for the use of the words on shirts and other running apparel, such apparel is related to the service provided by BAA, the race, and BAA is entitled to enjoin use of its marks on such items. Cf. *Volkswagenwerk*, 814 F.2d 812 (holder of trademark for "Beetle" with respect to car sales entitled to enjoin defendant's use of the same name with respect to car repairs). We agree with the district court that BAA has

---

[2] The evidence also included videotapes of the race showing the names "BAA Marathon" and "Boston Marathon."

[3] *See, e.g.*, BAA 1977 Souvenir Booklet, part of ex. 68.

had valid and enforceable marks for the entire relevant time frame.

V. THE LONGEST STRETCH: LIKELIHOOD OF CONFUSION

Having held that BAA has enforceable rights in its marks, we turn to the central issue in this and most infringement cases: the likelihood of confusion. Claims for infringement of a registered trademark are governed by § 32(1) of the Lanham Act, 15 U.S.C. § 1114(1),[4] which provides, in pertinent part:

> Any person who shall, without the consent of the registrant—
>
> (a) use in commerce any reproduction, counterfeit, copy, or colorable imitation of a registered mark in connection with the sale, offering for sale, distribution, or advertising of any goods or services on or in connection with which such use is *likely to cause confusion or to cause mistake or to deceive*: . . . shall be liable in a civil action by the registrant for the remedies hereinafter provided.

(Emphasis added.)

---

[4] Likelihood of confusion is also an essential element under Mass. Gen. Laws Ann. ch. 110B, § 11, the state's trademark infringement statute. Because trademark infringement is defined in essentially the same terms under both the Lanham Act and state law, we will direct our discussion only to the former.

In order to determine whether defendants' shirts are "likely to cause confusion . . . ," we must first ask, "confusion as to what?" In the "typical" trademark infringement case, the "likelihood of confusion" inquiry centers on whether members of the purchasing public are likely to mistake defendants' products or services for plaintiffs' protected products or services within the same category. *See e.g., Pignons S.A. de Mecanique de Precision v. Polaroid Corp.*, 657 F.2d 482 (1st Cir. 1981) (cameras): *Keebler Co. v. Rovira Biscuit Corp.*, 624 F.2d 366 (1st Cir. 1980) (crackers); *President and Trustees of Colby College v. Colby College-New Hampshire*, 508 F.2d 804 (1st Cir. 1975) (colleges). One question before us is whether members of the purchasing public are likely to mistake defendants' T-shirts for those of plaintiffs. This was the main issue that was addressed and decided below.

There is, however, a distinct but inseparably related issue, not adverted to directly below, that is involved in this case. Defendants are using the Boston Marathon sponsored and operated by the BAA to promote the sale of goods which are adorned so as to capitalize on the race. This implicates what is called a "promotional goods" issue. *See generally*, 2 T.J. McCarthy, *Trademarks and Unfair Competition* § 24:3 (2d ed. 1984); Denicola, *Institutional Publicity Rights: An Analysis of the Merchandising of Famous Trade Symbols*, 62 N. Car. L. Rev. 603 (1984); Note, *Promotional Goods and the Functionality Doctrine: An Economic Model of Trademarks*, 63 Tex. L. Rev. 639 (1984). Under this issue, the "likelihood of confusion" inquiry focuses upon whether the purchasing public is likely to believe that the sponsor of the Boston Marathon produces, licenses, or otherwise endorses defendants' shirts.

We start with the matter decided below, "confusion of goods." Many of our findings and rulings also bear on the related issue of "promotional goods."[5]

A. CONFUSION OF GOODS

The First circuit has identified eight factors to be weighed in assessing likelihood of confusion.

> (1) the similarity of the marks; (2) the similarity of the goods; (3) the relationship between the parties' channels of trade; (4) the relationship between the parties' advertising; (5) the classes of prospective purchasers; (6) evidence of actual confusion; (7) the defendant's intent in adopting its mark; and (8) the strength of the plaintiff's mark. *Astra*, 718 F.2d at 1205; *Pignons*, 657 F.2d at 487. Examining the evidence favorable as it applies to [defendants], we must determine on the whole whether there is any genuine issue as to

[5] Chief Judge Campbell questions whether plaintiffs have made a sufficient showing to prevail on summary judgment on the basis of the "confusion of goods" approach, pages 17–26, infra. He believes that there remains a question of material fact, on this analysis, whether prospective purchasers would be likely to confuse defendants' T-shirts with plaintiffs'. He does not agree, therefore, with the full extent of the court's analysis on pages 17–26. Judge Campbell believes that the more appropriate approach is the "promotional goods" analysis set out on pages 27–36 of the court's opinion, in which he joins.

> likelihood of confusion. No one factor is necessarily determinative, but each must be considered. *Astra*, 718 F.2d at 1205; *Pignons*, 657 F.2d at 487–92.

Volkswagenwerk, 814 F.2d at 817; *see also Purolator, Inc. v. EFRA Distributors, Inc.*, 687 F.2d 554, 559 (1st Cir. 1982) (likelihood of confusion is "[t]he key element in any infringement action"); *Pignons*, 657 F.2d at 486–487 (likelihood of confusion is an element under both Massachusetts and federal law).

1. Similarity of the Marks

"'Similarity is determined on the basis of the total effect of the designation, rather than a comparison of the individual features.' *Pignons*, 657 F.2d at 487 (omitting citations)." *Volkswagenwerk*, 814 F.2d at 817. Meaning alone, without reference to appearance and sound, may be sufficiently close to constitute similarity. *See* 3A Callman § 20.18.[6]

It is evident that defendants' logos refer specifically to the "Boston Marathon." There is but one Boston marathon race; defendants' logos use the term "Marathon" and depicts runners. It is run annually; defendants' logos refer to a specific year implying an annual event. The race begins at Hopkinton

---

[6] One of plaintiffs' shirts, ex. 25, has imprinted on it an artistic representation of the race course from Hopkinton to Boston, is entitled "The Boston Marathon" in large yellow letters, and contains depictions of runners along the course. Though not identical, plaintiffs' and defendants' shirts carry a similar message.

and ends in Boston; defendants' logos include these cities. Despite this, defendants have introduced no evidence showing that they have taken steps to turn their similarly marked products into dissimilar ones by clearly distinguishing their products, and their lack of BAA sponsorship, from those sold by plaintiffs. When one uses a mark similar to one already in use, there is generally an affirmative duty to avoid the likelihood of confusion. *Volkswagenwerk*, 814 F.2d at 817–818; see *Astra*, 718 F.2d at 1205 (even where defendant clearly marked its product with its company name, similarity might be found); *Pignons*, 657 F.2d at 487 (use of manufacturer's name and distinctive packaging undercut similarity claim); cf. *Leathersmith of London, Ltd. v. Alleyn*, 695 F.2d 27, 29–30 (1st Cir. 1982) (similar term was used only in conjunction with the defendant's company name and then, only descriptively), *cert. denied*, 459 U.S. 1209 (1983); *President and Trustees of Colby College v. Colby College-N.H.*, 508 F.2d 804 (infringement found despite defendant's use of state name to eliminate confusion).

The district court's holding that plaintiffs' rights did not sweep any further than their actual marks is not a correct application of trademark law. Such a rule would eviscerate trademark law because "few would be stupid enough to make exact copies of another's mark or symbol. It has been well said that the most successful form of copying is to employ enough points of similarity to confuse the public with enough points of difference to confuse the courts." *Baker v. Master Printers Union of New Jersey*, 34 F.Supp. 808, 811 (D.N.J. 1940).

Here, the meaning of the two marks is more than similar, it is identical. This overcomes any difference in appearance between them.

2. Similarity of the Goods

The parties offer virtually the same goods: shirts and other wearing apparel. Thus, "[u]nder this factor, there is a strong likelihood of confusion." *Volkswagenwerk*, 818 F.2d at 813; *compare id.* (both parties were in the business of automobile sales and service) *with Astra*, 718 F.2d at 1205–1206 (plaintiff sold a local anesthetic while defendant sold a blood analyzer) *and Pignons*, 657 F.2d at 487, 488 (plaintiff sold an expensive, high quality camera while defendant sold a relatively inexpensive instant camera).

3. Relationship Between the Parties' Channel of Trade

4. Relationship Between the Parties' Advertising

5. Classes of Prospective Purchasers

As in some of our previous cases, we treat these three factors simultaneously. *See Volkswagenwerk*, 814 F.2d at 818.

The parties sell their shirts predominantly in Boston area retail shops, at the exposition, and along the race course. Sales are largely seasonal, centering on the race date. The parties use the same general method of advertising: displays in store windows, in booths at the exposition, and along the race course. Prospective purchasers are drawn from the public at large. The shirts involved here retailed for about $7–10 and were sometimes sold under hectic conditions.

Inexpensive items, bought by the casual purchaser, are not likely to be bought with great care. "Courts have found less likelihood of confusion where goods are expensive and purchased after careful consideration." Pignons, 657 F.2d at 489; *see also* 3A Callman § 20.10 at 60.

The virtual identity between the parties' sales outlets and advertising methods, as well as the purchasing public's lack of opportunity to exercise discrimination in making such purchases, all point toward a likelihood of confusion.

Before we move to the sixth factor, we must first address the district court's initial division of the purchasing public into two classes. In fashioning its preliminary injunction, the court split the purchasing public into a class of those interested enough in racing to attend the exposition and all others. It found that only the former were likely to connect BAA with the Boston Marathon, and thus, were the only ones likely to infer sponsorship of defendants' products by BAA. In its summary judgment decision, the court stated that there was a genuine issue as to the public's knowledge of BAA's sponsorship of the Marathon but that this issue was not material because resolution of the issue would not alter the outcome.

Distinctions based on expertise can be useful in analyzing likelihood of confusion, see, e.g., *Astra*, 718 F.2d at 1206–1207; *Pignons*, 657 F.2d at 489, but we find no reason for such a distinction here. Unlike the sophisticated hospital personnel involved in *Astra* or the expert camera buffs in *Pignons*, it is the general public that is the market for shirts commemorating the Boston Marathon. In making its distinction, the court appears to have reasoned as follows: defendants' logos mean "Boston Marathon"; Boston Marathon shirts imply sponsorship by someone; the public (as opposed to those who attend the exposition) does not know that BAA sponsors the Marathon; therefore, the public cannot infer that BAA sponsors defendants' shirts[7]. The key step in this reasoning—the public's lack of knowledge of BAA's sponsorship of the race—is not supported in the record. Indeed, the evidence is to the contrary. Plaintiffs submitted voluminous, uncontradicted evidence, in the form of numerous newspaper and magazine articles dating back to 1897, videotapes of television broadcasts, and encyclopedia entries, all showing that the public was continually exposed to the fact of BAA's sponsorship of the Boston Marathon. Defendants argue that the plaintiffs' evidence is not sufficient to show the public's knowledge because a public poll was not conducted. The lack of survey data, however, does not fatally undercut plaintiffs' claims. The defendants offered no evidence tending to

---

[7] To the extent that the court's distinction was based on the purchasing public's lack of knowledge that the source of the shirts was Image, through its license, such knowledge is irrelevant. See 3A Callman § 21.07 at 25 (indeed, the purchasing public does not normally know the source of the article. It suffices that the public normally assumes that articles bearing the same mark are from the same source.") In this case, the district court found, and we agree, that the public will infer sponsorship by some organization when it sees a Boston Marathon shirt. Thus, the public's lack of knowledge as to the exact identity of that source is irrelevant on this issue.

contradict plaintiffs' assertions. Plaintiffs were not bound to a particular form of evidence. A poll might have been more accurate, but the lack of one does not nullify the evidence plaintiffs did introduce.

We find that no genuine issue of fact exists as to the public's general awareness of BAA's sponsorship of the Boston Marathon; there was, therefore, no reason to divide the purchasing public into two classes.

6. Evidence of Actual Confusion

Mickey Lawrence, president of Image Impact, reported in her affidavit that she had encountered a shopper at the Filene's department store who expressed surprise when Lawrence told her that defendants' shirt, which the shopper was wearing, was not an "official" Boston Marathon shirt. The district court refused to consider this account, holding that it was inadmissible hearsay. We think that the account was not hearsay, however, because it was not "offered in evidence to prove the truth of the matter asserted." Fed. R. Evid. 801(c). The statement was made not to prove that the defendants' shirts were in fact officially authorized, but rather to show that the declarant, a member of the public, *believed* that they were officially authorized.

Lawrence described two other instances where members of the public had bought defendants' shirts believing them to be officially sponsored shirts; one incident involved a 1986 shirt bought at the exposition, the other a 1987 shirt bought at the race.[8] She also described events occurring at her booth during the 1986 exposition:

> People would come over after they had been shopping. They would get to our booth and they would say, oh, I think I like that T-shirt better. Can I exchange this one? And they would take out a [1986] . . . shirt [sold by defendants].
>
> . . . .
>
> And I would tell them or one of the salespeople would say, that isn't one of our shirts. You will have to return it where you bought it. And then there would be indignation of, well, it's a Boston Marathon shirt. Why can't I return it at the Boston Marathon booth? This happened many times to many of the people who were selling, all of the people that we had hired to do it. And it happened throughout the course of the race—of the expo.

While not as accurate as a survey might have been,[9] this evidence shows that some people were actually confused as to who

---

[8] The fact that one of these incidents involved a client of Lawrence's does not make it less relevant; rather, it explains why the person went directly to Lawrence when he had a complaint about the shirt he bought.

[9] Defendants make a similar argument regarding the lack of survey data with respect to actual confusion. For essentially the same reasons as already set forth in connection with the lack of a poll, we find it unpersuasive. We do not mean to imply that surveys are not a valuable method of showing actual confusion or sponsorship; we merely decline to require them as the only way of proving these factors.

sponsored defendants' shirts. This factor, then, weighs in favor of a likelihood of confusion.

7. Defendants' Intent in Adopting Their Marks

The facts can only be interpreted to mean that defendants sought to profit from BAA's sponsorship of the Boston Marathon. The defendants chose designs that obviously referred to the Marathon, put those designs on the same types of clothing sold by the plaintiffs, sold those-shirts at the same time and in the same manner as the plaintiffs to the same general purchasing public. Defendants' actions clearly show their intent to trade on BAA's sponsorship and management of the Boston Marathon.

8. Strength of BAA's Mark

"The distinctiveness and reknown [sic] of a trademark determine its relative strength or weakness, which, in turn, defines the scope of protection to be accorded the mark against others which are confusingly similar." 3A Callman 5 20.43 at 345 (footnote omitted). We have found the following factors useful in determining a trademark's relative strength: the length of time a mark has been used and the plaintiff's relative renown in its field, *Pignons*, 657 F.2d at 491; the strength of the mark in plaintiff's field of business, especially by looking at the number of similar registered marks, *Astra*, 718 F.2d at 1209; and the plaintiff's actions in promoting its mark, *Volkswagenwerk*, 814 at 819.

Here, although BAA has only relatively recently registered its marks, it used them for a long period of time before registration. The Boston Marathon is one of the oldest and most prestigious marathons in this country. BAA, as a charitable organization, does not have the same impetus to advertise that a for-profit company would have. Nonetheless, its broad media exposure serves a similar purpose; it makes known to the public the BAA's sponsorship of the Boston Marathon. Finally, no evidence was introduced that others have obtained, or have not been able to obtain, registration of similar marks in the United states Patent and Trademark Office or its Massachusetts counterpart. *Compare Astra*, 718 F.2d at 1209 (plaintiff or its parent company held all five federal trademarks using "ASTRA" in the health products field, and thus, had "a certain degree of strength").

The "strength" factors militate in favor of a finding that the mark held by BAA in "Boston Marathon" is a strong one. *Therefore*, broad protection of the mark is warranted.

Based on the undisputed facts and the pertinent law, plaintiffs have proved that the purchasing public are likely to confuse defendants' shirts with those of plaintiffs.

B. THE PROMOTIONAL GOODS ISSUE

The question here is whether the purchasing public is likely to believe that the sponsor of the Boston Marathon, produces, licenses or endorses defendants' shirts. Whether or not purchasers happen to know that the sponsor of the Boston

Marathon is an organization called the "Boston Athletic Associations" is irrelevant to this "likelihood of confusion" analysis. *See* 15 U.S.C. § 1127, as amended (defining "service mark" as a mark "indicat[ing] the source of the services, even if that source is unknown"). Cf. 1 J.T. McCarthy, *Trademarks and Unfair Competition* § 15:2, at 663–64 (2d ed. 1984). In order to establish infringement in a promotional goods case, it has traditionally been the plaintiff's burden to show that prospective purchasers are in fact likely to be confused or misled into thinking that the defendant's product was produced, licensed, or otherwise sponsored by the plaintiff. See e.g., *Supreme Assembly v. J.H. Ray Jewelry Co.*, 676 F.2d 1079, 1082 (5th Cir. 1982); *International Order of Job's Daughters v. Lindeburg & Co.*, 633 F.2d 912, 919 (9th Cir. 1980), *cert. denied*, 452 U.S. 941 (1981); *University of Pittsburgh v. Champion Products, Inc.*, 566 F.Supp. 711 (W.D. Pa. 1984); *NFL Football Properties, Inc. v. Wichita Falls Sportswear, Inc.*, 532 F.Supp. 651 (W.D. Wash. 1982).

The facts bearing on this type of confusion have been, to a great extent, already set forth in our "confusion of goods" analysis. We therefore only summarize them here. The applicable law is, however, discussed *in extenso.*

There can be no doubt that the language and design on defendant's shirts intentionally calls attention to an event that has long been sponsored and supported by the BAA—an event that is, in fact, the subject of its registered mark. Defendants' shirts are clearly designed to take advantage of the Boston

Marathon and to benefit from the good will associated with its promotion by plaintiffs. Defendants thus obtain a "free ride" at plaintiffs' expense. In the oft quoted words of the Supreme Court in *International News Service v. Associated Press*, 248 U.S. 215 (1918), because the Boston Marathon has achieved its renown as a result of BAA's "expenditure of labor, skill, and money," such unlicensed use of BAA's mark would permit defendants to "reap where [they have] not sown." Id at 239. Like Rosie Ruiz, a notorious impostor in the 1980 Boston Marathon, defendants would be given a medal without having run the course.

Under these facts, the plaintiffs have to prove, of course, that the defendants are trading on plaintiffs' mark and good will. We do not think, however, that plaintiffs also have to prove that members of the public will actually conclude that defendants' product was *officially* sponsored by the Marathon's sponsor (whoever that sponsor may be). One difficulty with presenting such proof is that few people, other than legal specialists, could venture an informed opinion on whether someone using the logo of the sponsor of a sporting event is required to have the permission of the event's sponsor. Lacking such knowledge, the question of approval is pure guesswork, To ask a factfinder to determine whether the public would think that defendants' shirts were "authorized" or "official" shirts is to ask it to resolve a confusing and, in many contexts, virtually meaningless question. Asking a factfinder to make such a determination also raises a problem of circularity:

> If consumers think that most uses of a trademark require authorization, then in fact they will require authorization because the owner can enjoin consumer confusion caused by unpermitted uses or charge for licenses. And if owners can sue to stop unauthorized uses, then only authorized uses will be seen by consumers creating or reinforcing the perception that authorization is necessary. This is a "chicken and the egg" conundrum.

2 J.T. McCarthy, *Trademarks and Unfair Competition* § 24:3, at 170 (2d ed. 1984).

The pertinent case law recognizes the difficulty of asking factfinders to decide whether particular uses are "authorized". The Fifth Circuit has held that a factual showing of confusion about source or sponsorship need not be made in order to enjoin a manufacturer of cloth emblems from the unlicensed sale of National Hockey League team emblems. The court held:

> The confusion or deceit requirement [of 15 U.S.C. § 1114] is met by the fact that the defendant duplicated the protected trademarks and sold them to the public knowing that the public would identify them as being the teams' trademarks. The certain knowledge of the buyer that the source and origin of the *trademark symbols* were in plaintiffs satisfies the requirement of the act.

Boston Professional Hockey Ass'n, Inc. v. Dallas Cap & Emblem Mfg., Inc., 510 F.2d 1004, 1012 (5th Cir.) (emphasis added), *cert. denied*, 423 U.S. 868 (1975).[10] More recently, the Eleventh Circuit affirmed an injunction against the sale of "Battlin' Bulldog Beer," with cans emblazoned with the University of Georgia's canine mascot, in part on the ground that "'confusion' may relate to the public's knowledge that the *trademark*, which is 'the triggering mechanism' for the sale of the products, originates with the plaintiff." *University of Georgia Athletic Ass'n v. Laite*, 756 F.2d 1535, 1546 (11th Cir. 1985) (citing *Boston Professional Hockey Ass'n*, 510 F.2d at 1012) (emphasis in original).

Other examples of such increased concern with a mark holder's rights can be found in decisions by both the Second and Seventh Circuits to enjoin toy manufacturers from the unlicensed manufacture and sale of toy cars. *Warner Bros. v. Gay Toys, Inc.*, 658 F.2d 76 (2d Cir. 1991), *decision on appeal after remand*, 724 F.2d 327 (2d Cir. 1983); *Processed Plastic Co. v. Warner Communications. Inc.*, 675 F.2d 852 (7th Cir. l9B2). In each case plaintiff's evidence showed that children bought defendant's toy car (or prevailed on their parents to buy it for theme because they identified it with the "General Lee" car on plaintiff's "Dukes of Hazzard" television show. There was no

---

[10] We note, however, that since *Boston Professional Hockey*, the Fifth Circuit has reaffirmed the traditional view that the Lanham Act requires a showing of confusion as to source or sponsorship. *Supreme Assembly v. J.H. Ray Jewelry Co.*, 676 F.2d 1079, 1082 (5th Cir. 1982); *Kentucky Fried Chicken Corp. v. Diversified Packaging Corp.*, 549 F.2d 368, 388 (5th Cir. 1977).

probative evidence showing that the children or their parents were likely to believe that the television show's producers had authorized or licensed the toy. Nevertheless, the courts held that the evidence that purchasers recognized defendant's toy as plaintiff's "General Lee" car was sufficient to provide the required "likelihood of confusion."[11]

In *Gay Toys*, the Second Circuit moved quickly from the evidence of the purchasers' recognition of the car as the "General Lee" car to the inference that "many of the consumers did confuse the 'Dixie Racer' [defendant's toy car] with the 'General Lee' and assumed that the car was sponsored by Warner Bros." 658 F.2d at 79. As the district court noted on remand, the Second Circuit's opinion seemed to "creat[e] a conclusive presumption that if children are reminded of the 'General Lee' by seeing a facsimile thereof, they will assume distribution of the facsimile to have been 'sponsored' by plaintiff." *Warner Bros. v. Gay Toys, Inc.*, 553 F.Supp. 1018, 1021 (S.D.N.Y.), *aff'd*, 724 F.2d 327 (2d Cir. 1983). In *Processed Plastic*, the Seventh Circuit, in its opinion affirming an injunction against the toy manufacturer, emphasized the defendant's admission that it had "*deliberately* copied the 'General Lee' car to capitalize on the popularity of the TV show." *Processed Plastic Co.*, 675 F.2d at 857 (emphasis added). The court noted that in cases of

---

[11] Because Warner had no registered trademark on its "General Lee" car, the *Gay Toys* and *Processed Plastic* cases were decided under § 43 of the Lanham Act, 15 U.S.C. § 1125 (1982) (forbidding false designations of origin), rather than § 32 of the Lanham Act, 15 U.S.C., § 1114 (1982), which refers only to registered marks. The opinions are equally relevant to § 32 cases, however.

intentional copying, the second comer is generally "presumed to have intended a confusing similarity of appearance and to have succeeded in doing so." Id. (citation omitted). Following this line of cases, the court held that the toymaker "did not introduce evidence to rebut the inference that its intentional copying of the 'General Lee' car effectively created confusion on the part of the consuming public." *Id.* at 858.

In the present case, we adopt a similar presumption. Given the undisputed facts that (1) defendants intentionally referred to the Boston Marathon on its shirts, and (2) purchasers were likely to buy the shirts precisely because of that reference, we think it fair to presume that purchasers are likely to be confused about the shirt's source or sponsorship. We presume that, at the least, a sufficient number of purchasers would be likely to assume—mistakenly—that defendants' shirts had some connection with the official sponsors of the Boston Marathon. In the absence of any evidence that effectively rebuts this presumption of a "likelihood of confusion," we hold that plaintiffs are entitled to enjoin the manufacture and sale of defendants' shirts.

Our holding that there is a rebuttable presumption in BAA's favor is consistent with the holdings of other courts in analogous cases of intentional copying. For example, the Second Circuit has held that when there is intentional copying of a product's trade dress, "the second comer will be presumed to have intended to create a confusing similarity of appearance and will be presumed to have succeeded." *Perfect Fit Indus., Inc. v. Acme Quilting Co.*, 618 F.2d 950, 954 (2d Cir. 1980) (citations omitted). *See also Universal City Studios Inc. v. Montgomery Ward & Co.*, 207 U.S.P.Q. 852, 857 (A.D.Ill. 1980) (defendant's use of plaintiff's mark "Jaws" on a trash compactor, "with an intent to capitalize on the plaintiff['s] mark permits the court to draw the strong inference of likelihood of confusion"). But *see Toho Co. v. Sears, Roebuck & Co.*, 645 F.2d 788, 791 n.2 (9th Cir. 1981) (stating, in contrast to *Universal City studios*, that "in order to raise the inference of a likelihood of confusion, a plaintiff must show that the defendant intended to profit by *confusing consumers*") (emphasis in original).

In the present case, the facts clearly show that defendants intentionally referred to the Boston Marathon on their shirt in order to create an identification with the event and, thus, to sell their shirts. This evidence is itself sufficient to raise the inference of a likelihood of confusion. Given this presumption in favor of plaintiffs and the fact that defendants offered no evidence that would rebut the presumption, there is no genuine issue of material fact about the "likelihood of confusion."

We acknowledge that a trademark, unlike a copyright or patent, is not a "right in gross" that enables a holder to enjoin all reproductions. *See University of Notre Dame du Lac v. J.C. Gourmet Food Imports Co.*, 703 F.2d 1372, 1374 (Fed. Cir. 1983). In Justice Holmes's words, "When the mark is used in such a way that does not deceive the public we see no such sanctity in the word as to prevent it being used to tell the truth. It is not taboo." *Prestonettes Inc. v. Coty*, 264 U.S. 359 (1924). But when a manufacturer intentionally uses another's mark as a means of establishing a link in consumers' minds with the other's enterprise, and directly profits from that link, there is an unmistakable aura of deception. Such a use is, by its very nature, "likely to cause confusion, or to cause mistake, or to deceive." 15 U.S.C. § 1114(1). Unless the defendant can show that there is in fact no likelihood of such confusion or deception about the product's connection to the trademark holder, such a use can be enjoined.

VI. THE FINISH

Applying the pertinent law to the facts as considered in the light most favorable to defendants, we hold as follows:

(l) There is no genuine issue of fact with respect to the likelihood of confusion of goods. Nor is there any genuine issue of fact that the purchasing public will likely believe that the sponsor of the Boston Marathon produces, licenses or otherwise endorses defendants' shirts and other goods with logos referring to the Boston Marathon. These two findings stem from the same set of facts,

(2) The plaintiff, BAA, owns the name "Boston Marathon," and the defendants' shirts imprinted with logos suggesting that event constitute an infringement of BAA's mark. This includes the design "Boston; [runner/s]; l9xx," which was the subject of plaintiffs' amended complaint submitted on February 4, 1988.

(3) The judgment of the district court is reversed. Judgment shall issue for the plaintiffs,[12] which shall include the following permanent injunction:

> The defendants, Mark Sullivan d/b/a/ Good Life and Beau Tease, Inc., and all persons and entities acting in concert or in participation with them, are hereby enjoined from manufacturing or selling goods displaying the name "Boston Marathon" or any other design which is confusingly similar to or a colorable imitation of "Boston Marathon," including goods which are imprinted with "19xx Marathon; [runners]; Hopkinton–Boston," or with "Boston; [runner/s]; 1988."

Costs awarded to appellants.

---

[12] In their motion for summary judgment the plaintiffs stated that their claim was confined to injunctive relief only. Thus there is no issue of damages.

Endnotes

1. "[T]he man known to two generations of courtroom imposters as Ivan the Terrible." Richard Smith, "Charles Wyzanski, a Harvard and a Renaissance Man," *Boston Globe*, 21 September 1986.

2. *See* Ron Chernow, *The Warburgs* (New York: Random House, 1993), 251: "Charles [Wyzanski], thirty-seven, was an overseer of the Harvard Corporation who had already argued nine cases before the Supreme Court. Max [Wolf] was thrilled to have this *Wunderkind* son-in-law. Charles ended up suffering from manic-depression, confronting Gisi [Warburg] with a problem already too prevalent in her own family."

3. *United States v. Vera Green and Albert Green*, Criminal Nos. 58-39-W and 58-40-W (D.Mass. 1958).

4. *United States v. Green*, Criminal Nos. 58-39-W and 58-40-W (D.Mass. 1958), Stipulation of Facts. See also Memorandum for Defendant of attorney Bruno Schachner.

5. Although it is hard to believe today, there was at the time case dicta (statements in an opinion not necessary to the

decision) implying that embezzled properties were not "income" as the word was used in the Internal Revenue Code.

6. After conceding the embezzlement, Green's attorney argued absence of criminal intent to cause an evasion of the corporate taxes: "The indictment concerned with the corporate returns is more simply dealt with. Solely as a matter of common sense, intent to steal seems inconsistent with intent to confer upon the victim a tax benefit." Memorandum for Defendant, n.4, p. 8. However, the entry by the defendants of fictional expenses was a given, and the defendants would have to know and intend that the reduction of net income by these expenses would confer on the corporation a tax benefit illegitimately reducing Botwinik's taxable income. The violation of federal law was concurrent with, and not inconsistent with, the violation of state law.

7. *United States v. Thomas H. Worcester*, Criminal Nos. 57-62-W and 57-63-W (D.Mass. 1957), charge to the jury (Sept. 4, 1960), p. 38. Quoting from the Supreme Court's opinion in *Tank Truck Rentals v. Commissioner of Internal Revenue*, 356 U.S. 30, 33–34 (1958), decided one year before trial in the *Green* case and two years before trial in the *Worcester* case, Judge Wyzanski charged his *Worcester* jury:

> Equally well-established is the rule that deductibility . . . is limited to expenses that are both ordinary and necessary to carrying on the taxpayer's business. . . . A

> finding of "necessity" cannot be made, however, if allowance of the deduction would frustrate sharply defined national or state policies proscribing particular types of conduct, evidenced by some governmental declaration thereof.

The *Truck Rentals* case reiterated a passage from *Commissioner of Internal Revenue v. Heininger*, 320 U.S. 467, 473 (1943): "Where a taxpayer has violated a federal or a state statute and incurred a fine or penalty he has not been permitted a tax deduction for its payment." 356 U.S. at 34.

8. "Whoever . . . with intent to steal or embezzle converts . . . the property of another . . . shall be guilty of larceny." Mass. G.L. c. 266, § 30.

9. *United States v. Andrews*, 342 F.Supp. 1261 (April 5, 1972).

10. Federal law authorizes an appeal by the United States from an order of a district court dismissing an indictment prior to commencement of trial. 18 U.S.C. § 3731.

11. *United States v. Andrews*, 462 F.2d 914, 918 (1st Cir. May 19, 1972).

12. Eric Pace, "Charles E. Wyzanski, 80, Is Dead," *New York Times*, 5 September 1986, col. 1, p. 20.

---

13. *Los Angeles Times*, 6 September 1986, p. 7.

14. *Cape Cod Food Prods. v. National Cranberry Ass'n*, 119 F.Supp. 242, 243 (D.Mass. 1954).

15. Fearless Fosdick, a takeoff on Dick Tracy, was Li'l Abner's hero.

16. *See Boston Athletic Ass'n v. United States District Court*, Petition for Writ of Mandamus against Judge William G. Young, No. 88-1178 Orig. (1st Cir. 1988), reproduced in Appendix III, 5H.

17. *United States v. Hon. Charles E. Wyzanski, Jr.*, Petition for Writ of Mandamus, No. 5755 Orig. (1st Cir. 1960), App. III, 1B, ¶ 11 (references to transcript omitted in quote).

18. *United States v. Wyzanski, J.*, Order of November 3, 1960, No. 5755 Orig. (1st Cir. 1960).

19. *In re United States*, 286 F.2d 556, 565 (1st Cir. February 2, 1961), also reproduced as Appendix III, 1C.

20. Charles E. Wyzanski, "The Essential Qualities of a Judge," a chapter in Wyzanski, *The New Meaning of Justice* (Boston: Little, Brown, 1956), reprinted in *Handbook for Judges*, Winters, ed. (Chicago: The American Judicature Society, 1975), p. 92.

21. *United States v. Worcester*, 190 F.Supp. 548, 560 (D.Mass. January 3, 1961) (opinion denying Callahan motions to quash witness subpoena). The quoted passage was quite irrelevant to the *Worcester probation* proceeding before the court. It is likely that Judge Wyzanski anticipated the First Circuit's decision, which would be rendered the next month on the mandamus petition against him, and had decided he would prefer that his misbehavior in the *Standard Coil* trial be thought due to some temporary aberration, rather than to ignorance. A higher court could correct him, but it could not educate him.

22. *Fong Foo v. United States*, 369 U.S. 141, 143 (1962). Fong Foo was an individual defendant in the criminal case, *United States v. Standard Coil Products Co.*, Criminal No. 60-6-W (D.Mass. 1960), and an intervenor in *In re United States*, 286 F.2d 556, 565 (1st Cir. 1961).

23. *Fong Foo v. United States*, 369 U.S. at 145.

24. Will McDonough, "A Change of Course: BAA Marathon Ready to Go Commercial," *Boston Globe*, 26 February 1982, p. 27.

25. Tom Derderian, *Boston Marathon: The History of the World's Premier Running Event* (Champaign, Ill.: Human Kinetics Publishers, 1994), p. xix. Other U.S. winners in the 1896 Olympics, all from the Boston area, were James B. Connolly (hop-step-jump), Ellery H. Clark (high jump and broad jump),

W. W. Hoyt (pole vault), T. P. Curtis (high hurdles), Sumner Paine (revolver shoot), and John Paine (rifle shoot). Arthur Blake was second in the 1,500 meters and ran the marathon without training to provide an American presence.

26. A BAA track meet had just finished at the Irvington Oval when the marathon runners began to arrive—to the applause of the meet competitors as well as the spectators.

27. *Boston Morning Journal*, 20 April 1897, p. 1.

28. *In re Boston Athletic Association*, No. 57474 (Bankr. D.Mass. 1935), Petition of William F. Garcelon.

29. *Stoneman v. Fox Film Corp.*, 295 Mass. 419, 425 (1936). Because New York law governed, the court quoted from and cited New York cases. But the background statutes and law of the Commonwealth were the same.

30. The BAA had been set up in 1978 as an organization to which charitable donations could be made under section 501(c)(3) of the Internal Revenue Code. The 1978 bylaws provided that upon any winding up of its affairs, in the absence of a section 501(c)(3) successor, the BAA's assets should be distributed "for such similar public charitable purposes as the Supreme Judicial Court of the Commonwealth shall determine." ¶ 14.2. The BAA was ruled a "charitable corporation" in the course of the 1983 hearings within the attorney general's office over the determination of the Division of Public Charities

director that the agreement with Medoff violated the 15 percent fee solicitation limit of Mass. G.L. c. 68. *Attorney General v. International Marathons, Inc.*, 392 Mass. 370, 372 (1984).

31. *Milton Frank Allen Pub. v. Georgia Ass'n of Pet. Ret.*, 224 Ga. 518, 162 S.E.2d 724 (1968).

32. *Id.*, 162 S.E.2d at 729.

33. *Boston Athletic Ass'n v. International Marathons, Inc.*, C.A. No. 57376 (Mass. Suffolk Super. Ct. 1982), Rulings, Order and Memorandum of Decision on the Plaintiff Boston Athletic Association's Request for Interlocutory Relief (September 28, 1982).

34. The court itself questioned the theory: "Although the Attorney General's Public Charities' Division's characterization of the Agreement as involving activities by professional fund solicitors pursuant to an agreement between a charitable corporation and the solicitor is open to question and may ultimately be ruled to involve a legitimate licensing scheme . . . the action here by the Attorney General is entitled to presumptive validity." *Id.* at 2. We considered this theory our weakest ground, and it would ultimately be rejected by the Supreme Judicial Court. *Attorney General v. International Marathons, Inc.*, 392 Mass. 370, 372 (1984).

35. *Boston Athletic Ass'n v. International Marathons, Inc.*, 392 Mass. 356 (1984).

---

36. *Id.* at 366–67.

37. *Id.* at 366.

38. *Id.* at 367.

39. *Attorney General v. International Marathons, Inc.*, 392 Mass. 370, 374 (1984).

40. *Boston Athletic Ass'n v. International Marathons, Inc.*, C.A. No. 57376 (Mass. Suffolk Super. Ct. 1982), Findings, Rulings and Orders (March 12, 1986).

41. *Id.*, Finding 13, p. 15.

42. The story you are about to read is true, but people names have been fictionalized.

43. See Mass. G.L. c. 49, § 42 (Ter. ed. 1932). The statute was repealed over 30 years ago. The original enactment was Chapter XCVIII of the General Laws of 1825.

44. "N.Y. to Show Film on Bridgewater," *Boston Herald Traveler*, 29 September 1967, p. 3.

45. *Boston Herald Traveler*, 2 October 1997, p. 16.

46. *Grove Press, Inc. v. Gerstein*, 378 U.S. 577 (1964) (*Tropic of Cancer*); *Memoirs v. Massachusetts*, 383 U.S. 413 (1966) (*Fanny Hill*); *Grove Press, Inc. v. Christenberry*, 276 F.2d

433 (2d Cir. 1960) (*Lady Chatterley's Lover*); and *Attorney General v. Naked Lunch*, 351 Mass. 298 (1966).

47. Edith Lederer, "'*Titicut Follies*' Opens in N.Y.: Bridgewater Film 'Nauseating,'" *Boston Herald Traveler*, 4 October 1967, p. 10.

48. Thomas C. Gallagher, "Furor Sure Over 'Follies,'" *Boston Herald Traveler*, 4 October 1967, p. 34.

49. *Commonwealth of Massachusetts, Charles W. Gaughan as Superintendent of MCI Bridgewater and Guardian of James C. Bulcock, and John A. Gavin, Commissioner of Correction v. Frederick Wiseman and Bridgewater Film Company, Inc.*, Eq. No. 87538 (Mass. Suffolk Super. Ct. 1967), referred to hereafter as *Commonwealth v. Wiseman.*

50. Contrast Mass. G.L. c. 272, § 33: "Whoever exhibits for hire . . . a minor or mentally ill person who is deformed . . . shall be punished. . . . "

51. Contrast the Hippocratic Oath passage: "Whatsoever things I see or hear . . . in my attendance on the sick . . . which ought not to be noised abroad, I will keep silence thereon, counting such things to be sacred secrets."

52. See Peter Lucas, "What Are Rights of Insane," *Boston Herald Traveler*, 16 October 1967, p. 15.

---

53. Wiseman's answer to the Commonwealth's lawsuit declared that "the film *Titicut Follies* has been widely recognized and acclaimed as a powerful and artistic documentary film." Answer of the Respondents Wiseman and Bridgewater Film Company to the Substitute Bill in Equity (hereafter "Answer"), ¶ 20. *Titicut Follies* did win awards at the 1967 Florence Festivale de Popoli. See Thomas W. Benson and Carolyn Anderson, *Reality Fictions: The Films of Frederick Wiseman* (Carbondale, Ill.: Southern Illinois University Press, 1969), p. 90. When the awards were brought to the attention of Judge Kalus at the trial, he ruled them irrelevant, remarking that they might, however, "be very interesting as a commentary on our times and on those who make literary judgments as to artistic value." *Commonwealth v. Wiseman*, Eq. No. 87538 (Mass. Suffolk Super. Ct. 1967), Trial Transcript (hereafter "Tr."), vol. IV, pp. 18–37.

54. Tim Taylor, "'Crass Commercialism' of '*Titicut Follies*' Angers Legislators," *Boston Herald Traveler*, 18 October 1967, p. 22.

55. James Southwood, "The Story Behind the Titicut Follies Row," *Boston Herald Traveler*, 8 October 1967, p. 56.

56. Thomas C. Gallagher, "Movie 'Outrageous'—Knowles," *Boston Herald Traveler*, 24 October 1967, p. 26.

57. Peter Lucas, "Wiseman Denies Rights Violated," *Boston Herald Traveler*, 26 October 1967, pp. 1, 4.

58. Peter Lucas, "Follies 'Double Cross' Charged," *Boston Herald Traveler*, 12 October 1967, p. 1.

59. Grove Press persuaded a panel of the Court of Appeals for the Second Circuit, in a 2-1 decision, to vacate a jury verdict that *I Am Curious-Yellow* was obscene. This result was reached notwithstanding "a number of scenes which show the young girl and her lover nude. Several scenes depict sexual intercourse under varying circumstances, some of them quite unusual. There are scenes of oral-genital activity." *United States v. A Motion Picture Film*, 404 F.2d 196, 198 (2d Cir. 1968). The First Circuit agreed with the Second Circuit majority. Writing for a three-judge First Circuit panel, which also divided 2-1, Judge Aldrich granted an injunction against prosecution of exhibitors of the film. *Karalexis v. Byrne*, 306 F.Supp. 1363 (1st Cir. 1969).

State court judges were less tolerant. In *Wagonheim v. Maryland State Bd. of Censors*, 258 A.2d 240, 244 (Md. 1969) the Maryland Court of Appeals, one judge dissenting, held that the film "taken as a whole, appeals to a prurient interest in sex and is patently offensive." The Supreme Court of Georgia ruled against the film, observing that "if the film does not go substantially beyond the customary limits of candor in representing sexual matters, then there are no limits of candor in this country." *Evans Theater Corp. v. Slaton*, 180 S.E.2d 712, 714 (Ga. 1971). The Supreme Court of Arizona also found the film

---

obscene. *NGC Theatre Corp. v. Mummert*, 489 P.2d 823 (Ariz. 1971).

The U.S. Supreme Court granted a Grove Press petition for certiorari to review the Maryland ban and also took on review of the Massachusetts injunction against prosecution of the exhibitor of the film, two decisions directly in conflict. By the time the case was heard in the Supreme Court, however, Justice Douglas, who had voted for certiorari, had recused himself. (He was publishing his latest book, *Points of Rebellion*, in the Grove Press magazine, *Evergreen Review*.) The judgment of the Maryland court against the film was affirmed by an equally divided Supreme Court. *Grove Press, Inc. v. Maryland State Bd. of Censors*, 401 U.S. 480 (1971) (per curiam decision, without opinion). The injunction of the Massachusetts federal court against prosecution of the exhibitor was vacated, but on the newly developed independent ground of *Younger v. Harris*, 401 U.S. 37 (1971), restricting federal courts from enjoining state prosecutions. *Karalexis v. Byrne*, 401 U.S. 216 (1971).

60. Edward De Grazia and Roger K. Newman, *Banned Films: Movies, Censors and the First Amendment* (New York: R. R. Bowker Co., 1982), p. 125.

61. N.Y. Civil Rights Law § 50 (McKinney).

62. *Time, Inc. v. Hill*, 385 U.S. 374 (January 9, 1967). Time was by then publisher of *Life* magazine.

63. *Cullen v. Grove Press, Inc.*, 276 F.Supp. 727, 729 (S.D.N.Y. 1967).

64. *Id.* at 728–29.

65. *Id.* at 731.

66. Answer, ¶ 7.

67. Answer, ¶ 7.

68. Answer, ¶ 16.

69. Answer, ¶ 18.

70. Answer, ¶ 20.

71. Answer, ¶ 21.

72. Answer, ¶ 46.

73. *Commonwealth v. Wiseman*, Eq. No. 87538 (Mass. Suffolk Super. Ct. 1967), Findings, Rulings and Order for Decree (January 4, 1968), reproduced in Appendix III, 4C, referred to hereafter as "Finding(s)."

74. See Mass. G.L. c. 127, §§ 23–29, 36–37.

75. Transcript of trial testimony of Commissioner Gavin (hereafter "*witness name*, Tr.") 3-7; *Gaughan*, Tr. 4-26 to 27.

---

76. *Gavin*, Tr. 3-10.

77. *Gavin*, Tr. 3-8 to 9.

78. The letter was trial exhibit (referred to hereafter as "Ex.") 1, reproduced in Appendix III, 4A; the statement that accompanied the letter was Ex. 1A.

79. Finding 6.

80. Ex. 8; *Gavin*, Tr. 3-65.

81. Ex. 2.

82. Ex. 3.

83. *Richardson*, Tr. 12-108 to 110.

84. *Gavin*, Tr. 3-20 to 23, 88 to 90, 96; *Gaughan*, Tr. 4-30 to 34, 146 to 155; Finding 1.

85. Ex. 4.

86. Ex. 5A, reproduced in Appendix III, 4B. Also Ex. 8.

87. *Gaughan*, Tr. 4-35 to 36.

88. *Wiseman*, Tr. 14-104 to 105.

89. *Gaughan*, Tr. 4-36 to 37.

90. *Wiseman*, Tr. 14-104 to 106.

91. *Eames*, Tr. 6-110.

92. Ex. 8; *Eames*, Tr. 6-108 to 110.

93. *Gaughan*, Tr. 4-40 to 41, 179 to 181; *Moran*, Tr. 6-73 to 76; *Sullivan*, Tr. 9-90 to 92; *Pierce*, Tr. 9-132 to 134; *Hutchings*, Tr. 9-149 to 150; *Pacheco*, Tr. 10-26 to 27.

94. *Eames*, Tr. 7-55.

95. Ex. 43.

96. *Pacheco*, Tr. 10-27.

97. *Gaughan*, Tr. 4-182 to 183; Pacheco, Tr. 10-27 to 28.

98. *E.g.*, *Provinzano*, Tr. 10-109 to 112; *Cullen*, Tr. 10-171 to 173; *Gadry*, Tr. 9-161 to 163, 164 to 166; *Sullivan*, Tr. 9-92 to 93. Finding 3: "Twelve security guards . . . testified that, upon objection by each of them to Wiseman on diverse and separate occasions during the filming of sequences involving nudity and obscenity . . . Wiseman assured the security guards that they had 'nothing to worry about,' that the officials of the department had the right to approve and edit the film after it was completed and before it was shown."

99. Findings 4 and 21.

100. *Gaughan*, Tr. 4-49 to 50; *Wiseman*, Tr. 13-172.

101. *Gaughan* Tr. 4-52; Finding 10.

102. *Wiseman*, Tr. 14-156.

103. *Gaughan*, Tr. 4-51 to 54; Finding 10.

104. *Richardson*, Tr. 12-113 to 115; *Gaughan*, Tr. 4-56 to 58; *Greenman*, Tr. 11-150 to 152.

105. *Greenman*, Tr. 12-31 to 32.

106. Ex. 15.

107. *Greenman*, Tr. 12-4 to 5, 22, 61; Findings 9, 11.

108. Finding 9 n.

109. *Greenman*, Tr. 12-17 to 23; *Gavin*, Tr. 3-34 to 39, 41 to 43; *Gaughan*, Tr. 4-72 to 76; *Richardson*, Tr. 12-115 to 121; Finding 13.

110. *Gavin*, Tr. 3-43; Ex. 7A; Finding 13.

111. See nn. 89–92.

112. *Wiseman*, Tr. 13-122 to 123.

113. Answer, ¶ 16.

114. Finding 14; *Wiseman*, Tr. 13-134.

115. *Eames*, Tr. 7-39; Finding 14.

116. Finding 14.

117. Stipulation, Tr. 7-20 to 29.

118. Ex. 58; Finding 11.

119. *Tartakoff*, Tr. 8-20 to 21, 34, 38 to 39, 42 to 43, 45, 49, 50, 52 to 54, 56; *Allen*, Tr. 10-200 to 201, 204, 11-6 to 7, 8 to 9, 11, 16 to 17, 23, 26, 29. Dr. Allen was Director of Clinical Psychiatry and Acting Medical Director at Bridgewater State Hospital. Dr. Tartakoff was a visiting psychiatrist.

120. Dr. Leon Shapiro, a psychiatrist called by Wiseman on use of the film in the teaching of medical students, testified on cross-examination that patients shown in the film from their behavior appeared to be insane. *Shapiro*, Tr. 16-185. Film critic Richard Shickel, called by Wiseman as an expert on artistic film value, testified on cross that he saw people in the film who were "mad." *Shickel*, Tr. 16-59.

121. Wiseman testified on direct examination that an inmate who is shown in the film "looking into the camera and waving his hand with a kind of greeting" had thereby nodded

assent to his filming. *Wiseman*, Tr. 14-131 to 132. This patient was described in his medical record as "an imbecile with spastic paralysis" (September 9, 1958) and as a "mute retardate. . . . A breathing mass of nothingness who has long since ceased to lead a mental life" (February 11, 1958). Ex. 33.

122. Letter, Wiseman to Fifth Moscow International Film Festival, April 26, 1967, Ex. 44; also Ex. 46 and Finding 7.

123. *Wiseman*, Tr. 14-81 to 83.

124. *Wiseman*, Tr. 14-83 to 87. In *Reality Fictions: The Films of Frederick Wiseman* (Carbondale, Ill.: Southern Illinois University Press, 1969), which contains a lengthy discussion of *Titicut Follies*, authors Thomas W. Benson and Carolyn Anderson claim that Wiseman's cross-examination "answers were usually direct, often extremely detailed" (p. 77).

125. *Cullen v. Grove Press, Inc.*, 276 F.Supp. 727, 729–30 (S.D.N.Y. 1967).

126. See Joseph Harvey, "Titicut Follies Survives 5M Suit," *Boston Globe*, 2 March 1972, p. 10.

127. Ex. 8, *Gavin*, Tr. 3-65.

128. *Gavin*, Tr. 3-91.

129. Ex. 15.

130. August 11, 1965, meeting: *Gavin*, Tr. 3-10; *Gaughan*, Tr. 4-27 to 28. January 28, 1966 meeting: *Gavin*, Tr. 3-20 to 23, 88 to 90, 96; *Gaughan*, Tr. 4-30 to 34, 146 to 155.

131. *Gaughan*, Tr. 4-40 to 41, 179 to 181; also *Moran*, Tr. 6-73 to 76; *Sullivan*, Tr. 9-90 to 92; *Pierce*, Tr. 9-132 to 134; *Hutchings*, Tr. 9-149 to 150; *Pacheco*, Tr. 10-26 to 27.

132. *E.g.*, *Provinzano*, Tr. 10-109 to 112; *Cullen*, Tr. 10-171 to 173; *Gadry*, Tr. 9-161 to 163, 164 to 166; *Sullivan*, Tr. 9-92 to 93. Finding 3: "Twelve security guards . . . testified that, upon objection by each of them to Wiseman on diverse and separate occasions during the filming of sequences involving nudity and obscenity . . . Wiseman assured the security guards that they had 'nothing to worry about,' that the officials of the department had the right to approve and edit the film after it was completed and before it was shown."

133. *Gaughan*, Tr. 4-49 to 50; Finding 10.

134. *Greenman*, Tr. 12-31 to 32.

135. Exs. 23, 24.

136. Samuel D. Warren and Louis D. Brandeis, "The Right to Privacy," 4 *Harv. L. Rev.* 193 (1890).

---

137. *Roberson v. Rochester Folding Box Co.*, 64 N.E. 442 (N.Y. 1902).

138. *Id.* at 450.

139. *Themo v. New England Newspaper Publ'g Co.*, 306 Mass. 54 (1940); *Frick v. Boyd*, 350 Mass. 259 (1966).

140. *Frick v. Boyd*, 350 Mass. at 264 (1966).

141. *Restatement (Second)* of *Torts* § 652D(b) (Tent. Draft No. 13, 1967).

142. *Id.*

143. *Commonwealth v. Wiseman*, Eq. No. 87538 (Mass. Suffolk Super. Ct. 1967), Findings, Rulings and Order for Decree (January 4, 1968), reproduced in Appendix III, 4C, referred to hereafter as "Finding(s)." The 25 paragraphs of the findings summarize the facts found by the court and give the court's conclusions of law. The findings were later adopted, with minor amendments, as the court's Report of Material Facts to the Supreme Judicial Court.

144. Answer, ¶ 20.

145. Civil Liberties Union of Massachusetts (CLUM) Press Release of October 28, 1967, published in "Titicut Follies Movie Case Presents Complicated Issues," *Civil Liberties in the*

Bay State (Winter 1968): 5, and Thomas W. Benson and Carolyn Anderson, *Reality Fictions: The Films of Frederick Wiseman* (Carbondale, Ill.: Southern Illinois University Press, 1969), p. 68–69.

146. Brief of Civil Liberties Union of Massachusetts (hereafter "CLUM Brief"), p. 10.

147. CLUM Brief, p. 11.

148. CLUM Brief, p. 11 n.6.

149. CLUM Brief, p. 15. The CLUM Brief relied on the *Time v. Hill* footnote passage:

> This limitation to newsworthy persons and events does not, of course, foreclose an interpretation of the statute to allow damages where 'Revelations may be so intimate and so unwarranted in view of the victim's position as to outrage the community's notions of decency.' . . . This case presents no question whether truthful publication of such matter could be constitutionally proscribed.

Time, Inc. v. Hill, 385 U.S. 374, 383 n.7 (1967).

150. CLUM Brief, p. 22.

---

151. *Commonwealth v. Wiseman*, 356 Mass. 252, 257 (1969). See the reported opinion for verification of quotations.

152. "Focusing Again on Titicut; Frederick Wiseman Replies [to Elliot Richardson]," *Civil Liberties Review* (Summer 1974): 149; republished in *Frederick Wiseman*, Thomas R. Atkins, ed. (New York: Monarch Press, 1976), p. 69.

153. Wiseman, as quoted in Alan Westin, "'You Start Off With a Bromide': Conversation with Filmmaker Fred Wiseman," *Civil Liberties Review* 1 (Winter/Spring 1974): 67.

154. See n. 149.

155. *Wiseman v. Commonwealth* (Supreme Court No. 621, Oct. Term, 1969), Petition for a Writ of Certiorari to the Supreme Judicial Court of Massachusetts, p. 5.

156. *Wiseman v. Commonwealth*, Petition for a Writ of Certiorari, p. 28.

157. *Milk Wagon Drivers Union v. Meadowmoor Dairies*, 312 U.S. 287, 301–02 (1941) (dissent).

158. *Konigsberg v. State Bar of Cal.*, 366 U.S. 36, 65 (1961) (dissent).

159. *New York Times Co. v. United States*, 403 U.S. 713, 717 (1971).

---

160. *Id.* at 719.

161. *Amalgamated Food Employees Union v. Logan Valley Plaza*, 391 U.S. 308, 337 (1968).

162. *Wiseman v. Massachusetts*, 398 U.S. 960 (1970).

163. *Wiseman v. Commonwealth* (Supreme Court No. 621, October Term, 1969), Petition for Rehearing, p. 2.

164. *Wiseman v. Massachusetts*, 400 U.S. 860 (1970).

165. Edward DeGrazia and Roger K. Newman, *Banned Films: Movies, Censors and the First Amendment* (New York: R. R. Bowker Co., 1982), p. 128.

166. The vote of the seven participating judges divided 4-3 for certiorari. Although Justice Douglas a year later, sitting alone in a circuit justice capacity, stated that "three out of seven are enough to grant a petition for certiorari" (*Pryor v. United States*, 404 U.S. 1242, 1243 (1971)), the Supreme Court has never adopted any such rule or practice, and it adhered to the rule of four in the *Wiseman* case.

167. *Wiseman v. Massachusetts*, 400 U.S. 954 (1970).

168. *Commonwealth v. Wiseman*, Eq. No. 87538 (Mass. Suffolk Super. Ct. 1967), Statement of the Case and Order (September 22, 1989).

169. *Id.*, Memorandum of Decision (August 1, 1991).

170. *Boston Athletic Ass'n v. Sullivan*, C.A. No. 87-0802-Y (D.Mass.), Memorandum of Decision (March 7, 1988), p. 3.

171. Senate Report No. 98-526 gives this reason for the Trademark Counterfeit Act of 1984 provision authorizing seizure orders: "As counterfeiters have built larger and more professional enterprises, they have become increasingly callous towards the judicial process. In particular, once given warning that a trademark owner has discovered their illegal operation, many counterfeiters will simply destroy or conceal their illegal merchandise before any court can examine it." *1984 U.S. Code Cong. & Ad. News*, 3627–28.

172. A party can acquire an interest in land by "adverse possession"—open and notorious use without interruption for twenty years. Mass. G.L. c. 187, § 2.

173. *National Ass'n of Blue Shield Plans v. United Bankers Life Ins. Co.*, 362 F.2d 374, 377 (5th Cir. 1966).

174. A mark may be infringed by words that are different from, but that have the same meaning as, the mark. In *Louisiana World Exposition, Inc. v. Logue*, 221 U.S.P.Q. (BNA) 589 (E.D. La. 1983), *aff'd*, 746 F.2d 1033 (5th Cir. 1984), the name "Louisiana World Exposition," referring to an event held

at New Orleans in 1984, was infringed by the defendant's use of the name "1984 New Orleans World Fair." In *Hancock v. American Steel & Wire Co. of New Jersey*, 203 F.2d 737, 740 (C.C.P.A. 1953), the mark "Cyclone" infringed "Tornado." In *Masterpiece of Pennsylvania, Inc. v. Consolidated Novelty Co.*, 180 U.S.P.Q. (BNA) 785 (S.D. N.Y. 1973), the plaintiff's trademark "Mountain King" was infringed by "Alpine King" because, the court said, "the use of different words with similar meanings may also tend to confuse."

A picture can infringe a word mark. In the case *In re Rolf Nilsson AB*, 230 U.S.P.Q. (BNA) 141, 143 (T.T.A.B. 1986), a silhouette of a lion with the letter "L" infringed the owner's mark "Lion." In *Izod, Ltd. v. Zip Hosiery Co.*, 405 F.2d 575, 577 (C.C.P.A. 1969), a tiger head configuration infringed the mark "Tiger Head." In *Beer Nuts Inc. v. King Nut Co.*, 477 F.2d 326, 329 (6th Cir. 1983), the mark "Beer Nuts" was infringed by the combination of "King's Snack Nuts" and a picture of a stein of beer.

Additional cases holding that the plaintiff's mark was infringed by the defendant's somewhat different but similar mark were *LaTouraine Coffee Co. v. Lorraine Coffee Co.*, 157 F.2d 115 (2d Cir. 1946) ("Lorraine" confusingly similar to "LaTouraine"); *S. C. Johnson & Son, Inc. v. Drop Dead Co.*, 210 F.Supp. 816 (S.D. Cal. 1962) ("pledge" infringed "promise"); *General Foods Corp. v. General Mills, Inc.*, 167 U.S.P.Q. (BNA) 638, 639 (T.T.A.B. 1970) ("Arise" confusingly similar to the opposer's mark "Awake"; "they are synonyms which may be

---

used interchangeably"); *Specialty Brands, Inc. v. Coffee Bean Distributors, Inc.*, 748 F.2d 669 (Fed. Cir. 1984) ("Spice Island" likely as a matter of law to be confused with registered mark "Spice Valley"); *Playboy Enterprises, Inc. v. Chuckleberry Publishing, Inc.*, 486 F.Supp. 414 (S.D.N.Y. 1980) ("Playmen" infringed "Playboy"); *George W. Luft Co. v. Zande Cosmetic Co.*, 142 F.2d 536 (2d Cir. 1944) ("Zande" infringed "Tangee"); *Giant Food, Inc. v. Nation's Foodservice, Inc.*, 710 F.2d 1565 (Fed. Cir. 1983) ("Giant Hamburgers" held to infringe the plaintiff's mark "Giant"); *Miss Universe Inc. v. Flesher*, 605 F.2d 1130 (9th Cir. 1979) ("Miss USA" infringed by "Miss Nude USA"); *Palisades Pageants, Inc. v. Miss America Pageant*, 442 F.2d 1385 (C.C.P.A. 1971) ("Little Miss America" infringed "Miss America"); *In re National Novice Hockey League, Inc.*, 222 U.S.P.Q. (BNA) 638 (T.T.A.B. 1984) (insertion of "Novice" did not vitiate confusion with NHL).

Contrast Judge Young's Memorandum of Decision (*Boston Athletic Ass'n v. Sullivan*, C.A. No. 87-0802-Y (D.Mass. March 7, 1987), p. 8 (see Appendix III, 5I): "[The BAA] certainly has the legal right to exclude others from using the phrase 'Boston Marathon' in connection with the BAA's own distinctive unicorn logo. Likewise, it would seem to have the legal right to exclude others from using the phrase 'Boston Marathon' when that phrase is given such prominence as to give rise to any colorable confusion with the BAA's sponsorship of either the marathon or its authorization of memorabilia for the marathon. Beyond this, however, the legal rights of the BAA do not sweep." But see the response of the court of appeals that the do-not-sweep ruling "is not a correct application of trademark law." *Boston Athletic Ass'n v. Sullivan*, 867 F.2d 22, 30 (1st Cir. 1989).

175. Lanham Act, 15 U.S.C. § 1114, and Mass. G.L. c. 110B, § 11.

176. *Boston Athletic Ass'n v. Graphtex, Inc.*, C.A. No. 82365 (Mass. Suffolk Super. Ct. 1986), Decision on Plaintiff's Request for a Preliminary Injunction (April 11, 1986), p. 4.

177. *Boston Athletic Ass'n v. Discoveries, Ltd.*, No. A.C.-86-0169-CV (Mass.App.Ct.), Memorandum and Order (April 18, 1986). Discoveries and Graphtex (see n. 176) were codefendants in the same case.

178. *Sarrouf v. New England Patriots Football Club, Inc.*, No. 121012 (Mass. Norfolk Super. Ct.), Memorandum of Decision (April 24, 1985), p. 12, n.5.

179. "All that is necessary to establish a secondary meaning is that the ordinary buyer associates the mark with a single source, regardless of whether the buyer knows who that source is." 1 J. T. McCarthy, *Trademarks & Unfair Competition,* § 15.2, pp. 663–64 (2d ed. 1984). See also Lanham Act, 15 U.S.C. § 1127, as amended ("service mark" is a mark identifying "the services of one person, including a unique service, from

the services of others" and indicates source "even if that source is unknown").

180. Court of Appeals for the First Circuit, No. 87-1317 (April 17, 1987). Frank Swift, a lawyer, was president of the BAA.

181. Reported at 128 U.S. 514, 523–24 (1888).

182. *Boston Athletic Ass'n v. International Marathons, Inc.*, 392 Mass. 356, 364 (1984).

183. *Union Carbide Corp. v. Ever-Ready, Inc.*, 531 F.2d 366, 381 (7th Cir. 1976).

184. Lawrence Newman, a BAA member and marathon runner, collected a plethora of newspaper articles on the Boston Athletic Association Marathon, covering a 100-year period. These were reduced to representative groups and summarized, yielding 32 exhibits of articles reporting on a BAA-Boston Marathon connection in the years 1897, 1986, and 1987, and in every tenth year after 1897:

Ex. No.	*Item*	*Ex. No.*	*Item*
47	1897 articles	64	1973 summary
48	1897 summary	65	1973 summary
49	1907 articles	66	1975 summary
50	1907 summary	67	1976 summary
51	1917 articles	68	1977 articles

52	1917 summary	69	1977 summary
53	1927 articles	70	1978 summary
54	1927 summary	71	1979 summary
55	1937 articles	72	1980 summary
56	1937 summary	73	1981 summary
58	1947 summary	74	1982 summary
59	1957 articles	75	1983 summary
60	1967 summary	76	1986 articles
61	1967 articles	77	1986 summary
62	1967 summary	78	1987 articles
63	1972 summary	79	1987 summary

The exhibits with an authenticating affidavit were submitted in support of the summary judgment motion. Sample articles and summaries are reproduced in Appendix III, 5C and 5D.

185. "The defendants . . . move this Court enter summary judgment for the defendants based upon . . . the testimony taken in the uncompleted trial; and the exhibits admitted into evidence . . . ." Defendants Motion for Summary Judgment, C.A. No. 87-0802-Y (July 22, 1987).

186. *Boston Athletic Ass'n v. Sullivan,* No. 88-1352 (1st Cir. 1987), I Record Appendix, p. 281.

187. Canon 3(A)(5) in both codes.

---

188. Fed.R.Civ.P. 79(a).

189. *E.g.*, Rule 45(b)(1) of the Federal Rules of Appellate Procedure ("The circuit clerk must maintain a docket and . . . must record all papers filed with the clerk."); Rule 79(a) of the Massachusetts Rules of Civil Procedure (same as federal rule); Rule 31(b) of the Massachusetts Rules of Appellate Procedure ("The clerk shall keep a book known as the docket. . . . All papers filed with the clerk . . . shall be entered chronologically in the docket.").

190. *Boston Athletic Ass'n v. United States District Court*, Petition for Writ of Mandamus to Young, J., No. 88-1178 Orig. (1st Cir. 1988), p. 9.

191. Plaintiffs' Memorandum on Its Entitlement to a Preliminary Injunction (April 1, 1987), 13 pages; Plaintiffs' Trial Brief (April 13, 1987), 33 pages; Plaintiffs' Supplementary Trial Brief (April 16, 1987), 12 pages; Memorandum of BAA in Support of Its Motion for Summary Judgment (July 13, 1987), 15 pages; Plaintiffs' Memorandum in Support of Its [1988] Motion for Preliminary Injunction (February 4, 1988), 4 pages. See cases cited n. 174.

192. The BAA was not the only party skewered by Judge Young's decision; until it would be set aside or otherwise judicially disapproved, it announced the law within the First Circuit. When the United States Golf Association brought the U.S.

Open to The Country Club, Brookline, Massachusetts, in June 1988, it was confronted with sale of competing golf hats and shirts imprinted "1988 Open," with pictures of golf balls and references to Brookline. Judge Walter Skinner, a colleague of Judge Young, at first denied the USGA a restraining order, relying in part on the Young decision. *United States Golf Ass'n v. John Doe*, C.A. No. 88-1413-S (D.Mass. 1988). The USGA then went out and collected affidavits from purchasers who said that they assumed the marks on the counterfeit goods referred to the USGA's "U.S. Open," and that if they had known the goods were not authorized by the USGA, they would not have purchased them. Although Judge Skinner then issued an injunction, USGA marketing, in the interval, had lost sales and momentum. The USGA's *amicus* brief argued that the USGA should not have been required to present evidence of actual confusion, that the natural inference of U.S. Open sponsorship from defendants' use of marks similar to "U.S. Open" made likelihood of confusion inevitable.

Bibliography

Books

Atkins, Thomas R., ed. *Frederick Wiseman*. New York: Monarch Press, 1976.

Benson, Thomas W., and Carolyn Anderson. *Reality Fictions: The Films of Frederick Wiseman*. Carbondale, Ill.: Southern Illinois University Press, 1969.

Chernow, Ron. *The Warburgs*. New York: Random House, 1993.

De Grazia, Edward, and Roger K. Newman. *Banned Films: Movies, Censors and the First Amendment*. New York: R. R. Bowker Co., 1982.

Derderian, Tom. *Boston Marathon: The History of the World's Premier Running Event*. Champaign, Ill.: Human Kinetics Publishers, 1994.

Restatement (Second) of Torts, § 652D(b) (Tent. Draft No. 13, 1967).

Winters, ed. *Handbook for Judges*. Chicago: American Judicature Society, 1975. Reprint of "The Essential Qualities of a Judge," a chapter in Wyzanski, Charles E., *The New Meaning of Justice*. Boston: Little, Brown & Co., 1956.

Wyzanski, Charles E. *The New Meaning of Justice*. Boston: Little, Brown & Co., 1956.

Articles

Gallagher, Thomas C. "Furor Sure Over 'Follies,'" *Boston Herald Traveler*, 4 October 1967, p. 34.

"Movie 'Outrageous'—Knowles," *Boston Herald Traveler*, 24 October 1967, p. 26.

Harvey, Joseph. "Titicut Follies Survives 5M Suit," *Boston Globe*, 2 March 1972, p. 10.

Lederer, Edith. "'*Titicut Follies'* Opens in N.Y.: Bridgewater Film 'Nauseating,'" *Boston Herald Traveler*, 4 October 1967, p. 10.

Lucas, Peter. "Follies 'Double Cross' Charged," *Boston Herald Traveler*, 12 October 1967, p. 1.

"What Are Rights of Insane," *Boston Herald Traveler*, 16 October 1967, p. 15.

"Wiseman Denies Rights Violated," *Boston Herald Traveler*, 26 October 1967, pp. 1, 4.

McDonough, Will. "A Change of Course: BAA Marathon Ready to Go Commercial," *Boston Globe*, 26 February 1982, p. 27.

"N.Y. to Show Film on Bridgewater," *Boston Herald Traveler*, 29 September 1967, p. 3.

Pace, Eric. "Charles E. Wyzanski, 80, Is Dead," *New York Times*, 5 September 1986, col. 1, p. 20.

Smith, Richard. "Charles Wyzanski, a Harvard and a Renaissance Man," *Boston Globe*, 21 September 1986.

Southwood, James. "The Story Behind the Titicut Follies Row," *Boston Herald Traveler*, 8 October 1967, p. 56.

Taylor, Tim. "'Crass Commercialism' of '*Titicut Follies*' Angers Legislators," *Boston Herald Traveler*, 18 October 1967, p. 22.

"Titicut Follies Movie Case Presents Complicated Issues," *Civil Liberties in the Bay State* (Winter 1968): 5.

Warren, Samuel D., and Louis D. Brandeis. "The Right to Privacy," 4 *Harv. L. Rev.* 193 (1890).

Westin, Alan. "'You Start Off With a Bromide': Conversation with Filmmaker Fred Wiseman," *Civil Liberties Review* 1 (Winter/Spring 1974): 67.

Wiseman, Frederick. Letters: "Focusing Again on Titicut," *Civil Liberties Review* 1 (1974): 148.

Index

(Appendix texts and Endnotes not indexed.)